797,885 Books
are available to read at

Forgotten Books

www.ForgottenBooks.com

Forgotten Books' App
Available for mobile, tablet & eReader

ISBN 978-1-330-91686-5
PIBN 10121130

This book is a reproduction of an important historical work. Forgotten Books uses state-of-the-art technology to digitally reconstruct the work, preserving the original format whilst repairing imperfections present in the aged copy. In rare cases, an imperfection in the original, such as a blemish or missing page, may be replicated in our edition. We do, however, repair the vast majority of imperfections successfully; any imperfections that remain are intentionally left to preserve the state of such historical works.

Forgotten Books is a registered trademark of FB &c Ltd.
Copyright © 2015 FB &c Ltd.
FB &c Ltd, Dalton House, 60 Windsor Avenue, London, SW19 2RR.
Company number 08720141. Registered in England and Wales.

For support please visit www.forgottenbooks.com

1 MONTH OF FREE READING

at

www.ForgottenBooks.com

By purchasing this book you are eligible for one month membership to ForgottenBooks.com, giving you unlimited access to our entire collection of over 700,000 titles via our web site and mobile apps.

To claim your free month visit:

www.forgottenbooks.com/free121130

* Offer is valid for 45 days from date of purchase. Terms and conditions apply.

English
Français
Deutsche
Italiano
Español
Português

www.forgottenbooks.com

Mythology Photography **Fiction** Fishing Christianity **Art** Cooking Essays Buddhism Freemasonry Medicine **Biology** Music **Ancient Egypt** Evolution Carpentry Physics Dance Geology **Mathematics** Fitness Shakespeare **Folklore** Yoga Marketing **Confidence** Immortality Biographies Poetry **Psychology** Witchcraft Electronics Chemistry History **Law** Accounting **Philosophy** Anthropology Alchemy Drama Quantum Mechanics Atheism Sexual Health **Ancient History** **Entrepreneurship** Languages Sport Paleontology Needlework Islam **Metaphysics** Investment Archaeology Parenting Statistics Criminology **Motivational**

THE FAROES AND ICELAND:

STUDIES IN ISLAND LIFE

BY

NELSON ANNANDALE

DEPUTY SUPERINTENDENT OF THE INDIAN MUSEUM
PART AUTHOR OF 'FASCICULI MALAYENSES'

WITH 24 ILLUSTRATIONS

AND AN APPENDIX ON THE CELTIC PONY

BY

F. H. A. MARSHALL, D.Sc.

OXFORD
AT THE CLARENDON PRESS
1905

313
A6

HENRY FROWDE, M.A.
PUBLISHER TO THE UNIVERSITY OF OXFORD
LONDON, EDINBURGH
NEW YORK AND TORONTO

TO
PROFESSOR EDWARD B. TYLOR,
D.C.L., LL.D., F.R.S.

IN ACKNOWLEDGEMENT OF WHAT I OWE TO BOTH
HIS WRITTEN AND HIS SPOKEN WORD.

PREFACE

THE present work is the result of a series of summer and autumn holidays spent, between the years 1896 and 1903, in the Faroes and Iceland. Several of the studies of which it is composed have appeared in a form more or less different elsewhere; but in each case new facts have been added or theories elaborated, while purely technical details have been omitted or relegated to appendices throughout.

Professor E. B. Tylor, assisted by Mrs. Tylor, has most kindly read the manuscript and suggested not a few valuable emendations. Among other friends I am specially indebted for advice and criticism, references to literature, or the use of illustrations to Mr. Henry Balfour, of the Pitt-Rivers Museum, Mr. W. Eagle Clarke, of the Royal Scottish Museum, Professor J. Cossar Ewart, Mr. Eustace Gurney, and Dr. F. H. A. Marshall. My acknowledgements are also due to the proprietors of *Blackwood's Magazine* and *The Scotsman*, who have permitted me to make use of matter already published in their pages.

INDIAN MUSEUM, CALCUTTA:
February, 1905.

CONTENTS

CHAPTER I

THE PEOPLE OF THE FAROES 1–30

    Position and extent of the islands—Government—Police abolished—Education—Physical characters of the people—Dress—Origin of the Faroemen—Historical legends—The 'Scottish Princess'—Effects of in-breeding—The 'Westmen'—Bretons—French pirates—Ethnology of the Faroemen—The Farish dialect—Moral character of the islanders—Newspapers—Folklore—Trolls—Mermaids—The seals and Pharaoh's host—Churches—The Farish bishops—Religion—The Clergy—Culture of the people.

CHAPTER II

LIFE IN THE FAROES 31–66

    Population—Thorshavn—Travelling in the islands—Absence of roads—Regulations for hiring boats—A Farish village—Evening work—The uses of whales' bones—Children's games—Interior of the houses—The old hall at Kirkeboe—Farmhouses—Whales—A whale-hunt—Whaling stations—Superstitions about whales—Seals—A seal-hunt—Hares—Rats and mice—The Farish house-mouse—The Farish wren—The Farish raven—Sea birds—The puffin—Puffin-catching—The Fulmar petrel and its migrations—The gannet—Albatrosses in the Faroes—Fowling rights—Rope-making—Fisheries—Halibut-fishing—Amusements—The Farish Dance—Ballads—Marriage ceremonies.

CONTENTS

CHAPTER III

THE ALGERIANS IN ICELAND 67-92

A Westman legend—Icelandic accounts of the raid of 1627—Reputed origin of the raid—The fate of its instigator—Two expeditions start from Barbary—A ship from 'Kyle' reaches Iceland and raids the south coast—Relations between British fishermen and the pirates—Mishap at Bessastad—Return to Africa—Reception at 'Kyle'—The Algerian expedition—It raids the west coast for eight days—Cruelty of the renegades—The pirates reach the Westman Isles—Mutual suspicion of the Danes and the Icelanders—The pirates land on Heimey—The death of Jón the Martyr—The traitor Thorstein—The legend of Herjolf's gold—The voyage to Algiers—Fate of the captives—The adventures of Einar Loptsson—The travels of Olaf Eigilsson—Jón Jónsson's letter—Return of the survivors—No African blood in the modern Icelanders.

CHAPTER IV

THE BIRD-CLIFFS OF THE WESTMAN ISLES . . 93-129

The people of the Westman Isles—Infantile mortality—Origin of the islanders—The bird-cliffs—Tenure of fowling rights—Sulnasker—Bird laws—The Eider-duck—Collection and preparation of eiderdown—The puffin—Puffin-catching—Albino puffins—The Fulmar petrel—Its food—Whale-parasites—Swarms of small crustaceans—Fulmar-catching—Uses of the fulmar—Fuel—The legend of Sulnasker—Gannets—A visit to Sulnasker—Shearwaters—Stormy and Fork-tailed petrels—The Little auk and the Halcyon—Fat in human diet—Leprosy.

CHAPTER V

MODERN ICELAND 130-165

Civilization in ancient Iceland—Scenery—Character of the modern Icelander—The horse in Icelandic life—Reykjavik—The village on Heimey—Farm-houses—Decoration—The common dormitory—Icelandic art—Patterns—Embroidery—The social system—Personal names—Farm life—Winter occupations—The effects of education—Drink—Absence of religion—Clergy—Physical characters of the Icelanders—The people of European slums—Differences between the Icelanders and the Faroemen—The 'Icelandic type'—Its probable origin—Population at different dates—Emigration to America.

CONTENTS vii

CHAPTER VI

DOMESTIC ANIMALS IN ICELAND AND THE FAROES . 166-198
Poultry—Cats—The Icelandic dog—'Liver-plague'—The dogs of the Faroes—Different breeds—Prepotency—The horse—Its history in Iceland and the Faroes—The 'Celtic' pony—Survival of different races of horses—Trade in Icelandic ponies—Horse-furniture—Horse-fighting—Carnivorous horses and cows—Icelandic and Farish cattle—Sheep—Different breeds in the Faroes—Life of the sheep in the islands—Dried mutton—Wool—Its preparation—Spinning-wheels and spindles—Sheepskin—The use of tormentil—Its preparation—The survival of primitive implements.

CHAPTER VII

AGRICULTURE IN THE ISLANDS, WITH NOTES ON INSECT LIFE 199-217
Climate—Corn formerly grown in Iceland—Wild oats—Barley in the Faroes—The preparation of cornfields—Primitive spades—Reaping—Grain-houses—Artificial ripening of grain—Threshing and winnowing—Only women allowed to take part—Mills—Baskets for holding and measuring grain—An Icelandic basket—Brooms of birds' wings—Hand-querns—Hay in the Faroes—Tenure of land—Two kinds of hay in Iceland—Fruit and vegetables—Crossbills—Insects—Main differences between sub-arctic and tropical insects—Flies—Moths and butterflies—Wingless insects—Beetles—Scale-insects—The Ghost moth.

CONCLUSIONS 218-220

APPENDIX. THE CELTIC PONY. BY F. H. A. MARSHALL 221-229

LIST OF AUTHORITIES 230

INDEX 235-238

LIST OF ILLUSTRATIONS

THORSHAVN, FAROES	*Frontispiece*
THORSHAVN, FAROES	*To face p.* 32
PEAT-HOUSES, DWELLING-HOUSE, AND BOAT-HOUSE, NAALSOE, FAROES	,, 36
BOAT PROPPED UP WITH A PILOT WHALE'S SKULL, FAROES	,, 38
IRON LAMP FROM NAALSOE, FAROES (EDINBURGH MUSEUM)	,, 41
SPINNING-APPARATUS FOR MAKING AND WINDING HORSEHAIR STRING, FAROES	,, 57
APPARATUS WITH SINGLE AND TRIPLE CRANKS FOR TWISTING HORSEHAIR STRING INTO 3-PLY ROPE, MYGGENAES, FAROES	,, 58
HEIMARKLETTEN FROM HELGAFELL, WESTMAN ISLANDS	,, 80
PINNACLE ROCKS ON NORTH SIDE, WESTMAN ISLANDS	,, 81
BEE-HIVE HUT, FORMERLY USED FOR DRYING STOCK-FISH, ICELAND	,, 83
CLIFFS ON SOUTH SIDE OF HEIMEY, WESTMAN ISLANDS	,, 96
THE FOWLING-NET, HEIMEY, WESTMAN ISLANDS .	,, 104
PUFFIN-CATCHING, ON CLIFFS ABOVE THRAELA-EYDI, HEIMEY, WESTMAN ISLANDS; SHOWING ISTHMUS CONNECTING TWO PARTS OF THE ISLAND, WITH CIRCULAR SHEEP-FOLD UPON IT	,, 105
YOUNG FULMAR ON THE DEFENSIVE . . .	,, 115
BRASS LAMP, WESTMAN ISLANDS	,, 116
HOME FROM SULNASKER, WESTMAN ISLANDS . .	,, 117
LID OF CARVED BOX, DATED 1767, BELONGING TO A WOMAN, A— L—'S DAUGHTER (DÓTTIR), ICELAND	,, 145
MODERN ICELANDIC HORN SPOON, WITH INITIALS OF A MAN, G— S—'S SON	,, 146
ICELANDIC TAPESTRY (EDINBURGH MUSEUM), THE UPPER STRIP WAS MADE SHORTLY AFTER THE REFORMATION, THE LOWER STRIP EARLIER . .	,, 147
CARDING WOOL, NAALSOE, FAROES . . .	,, 193
LIVING-ROOM IN OLD-FASHIONED FAROE FARM-HOUSE, AT SAXEN, STROMOE, SHOWING SPINNING-WHEELS	,, 194
ICELANDIC PONY IN WINTER COAT. (From Ewart's *Multiple Origin, &c.* Photo by G. A. Ewart.)	,, 222
ICELANDIC PONY, SHOWING TAIL-LOCK IN MID-WINTER. (From Ewart's *Multiple Origin, &c.* Photo by G. A. Ewart.)	,, 224
FAROE PONY, THORSHAVN	,, 226

CHAPTER I

THE PEOPLE OF THE FAROES

ALTHOUGH the Faroes have not the glaciers and the forests of Norway, nor the geysers and volcanoes of Iceland, they are full of a beauty quite their own, with their towering sea-cliffs and scattered, half-transparent mists. Far from being mere arctic rocks in the ocean, they have a climate warmer than that of parts of Scotland, though they do lie nearly 200 miles north-west of Shetland, while their vegetation, if rarely more than a few inches high, is as luxuriant as the shallowness of the soil and the winter storms will allow. The buttercups seem larger than those on the mainland, and the bushes appear of a brighter green.

. . . .

Seventeen of the islands are now inhabited, supporting a population of over 15,000, and one of them—Stromoe or Stream Isle—is twenty-seven miles in length. Thorshavn, the capital town, is on the east coast of this island, opposite Naalsoe or Needle Isle; but the richest and most modern village is said to be Thrangisvaag on Suderoe (South Isle).

The islands have been incorporated with the kingdom of Denmark for many years, and send two members to the Danish Parliament; but the islanders retain a certain independence, rendered necessary by their remote position. Local affairs are managed by an assembly called Lagthing which sits at Thorshavn, and exemption from conscription and from many import and export duties is enjoyed. The Lagthing is under the presidency of an amtmand appointed for life by the Danish king, but its members are elected by ballot every three years from the resident population, each one having a deputy elected to succeed him in the event of his death or retirement, without the trouble of a by-election. For the two months in summer, during which the House is sitting, the members are paid from the proceeds of a poll-tax levied on all voters, that is to say, on all men over twenty-five years of age who have never been in prison.

This tax may only be paid in cash, but there are others which may be paid in kind—so many pounds of butter from each cow that is kept, so much wool from each sheep that is slaughtered, and one-thirtieth part of all the pilot whales that are killed. The taxes are collected by sheriffs, who are always native Faroemen. They visit each village in their several districts at least four times in the year, and preside at the distribution of the whales after a successful whale-hunt has taken place.

Legal matters are very simply managed. Except in Thorshavn there are no lawyers. Important cases, civil and criminal, are tried, without a jury, by the judge at Thorshavn; he is nominated by the king for a term of years, and has always been a Dane. Petty thefts and such matters are brought before the sheriffs on their quarterly visits, and obedience to sanitary by-laws is supposed to be enforced by the headman in each village. The final appeal in all cases is to the Danish Parliament.

There were until lately twenty-four policemen; but their ordinary duties did not extend beyond Thorshavn, where only two of them were on duty in uniform at a time. Outside the town they acted as crew of the amtmand's official boat, for which they received extra pay; and if a crime was reported from the country, one of them was sent to bring the criminal to the capital. This, however, was a rare event, not only because crimes are seldom committed, but also because the Faroeman is by nature peaceable and prefers that scandals should not go beyond his own village. The policemen have now been abolished, and it is every citizen's duty to see that the law is maintained and that no rioting occurs, especially when a crew of drunken foreigners is on shore. The old fort at Thorshavn, built by the naval hero Magnus Hugnessen in 1588 and strengthened to repel a threatened English invasion in the time of Nelson's wars, was until recently the only prison in all Faroe. At least one other has been built within recent years, chiefly, the natives declare, for the benefit of Shetland fishermen, who do not, however, visit Thorshavn so frequently as once they did. As the law only permits a prisoner to be given bread and water, and as this is hardly a generous diet in a northern climate, an arrangement is generally made whereby a man who is detained for more than a few days serves his term in periods of three days, enjoying three days' freedom between each, so that his punishment is spread out over twice the estimated period. Under ordinary circumstances there is no danger of his escape during the periods of respite, and, should a ship come in while he is free, he can easily be clapped in gaol until it sails. Long sentences are served in Denmark.

In Thorshavn and in a few of the country villages schools have been built where elementary education is carried on in Danish, and in the capital there is now a small teachers' college. Most of the people, who have, as it were, local option in educational matters, prefer to teach their children at home. If they elect to have a school in their village, not only must they send the children to it, but they must also grant the teacher (whose salary is paid by the Government) pasturage for a cow and other rights which they appear to consider extravagant. As a rule, the results of home education are excellent, and even the simplest peasants often have a wide knowledge of history and geography.

Danish is the language of the church services and the Lagthing, as well as of the schools, and most of the people understand it well; but there is no sign that the local dialect, which will be mentioned in more detail later, is becoming even obsolescent.

. . . .

They may be described as a finely built and handsome race, though the women seem to be very delicate and to age young. Both sexes have an air of refinement and dignity often seen among true peasants, and the men are unusually handsome. They are not tall, indeed their mean stature is well below that of many European races, but they are well proportioned, with broad shoulders and magnificently developed legs. Their costume, moreover, shows them off to advantage, for it consists (with the exception of a loose coat, which is not always worn) of tight-fitting garments which do not conceal their physique. This only refers to the men, for the women have quite ceased, even in the remoter districts, to wear their distinctive dress. Except in Thorshavn, however, they still have the wisdom to avoid hats and bonnets, covering their heads with a folded shawl or kerchief when out of doors. The men's costume consists of either a knitted jersey, generally of a soft brown shade, or a short, tight-fitting jacket of cloth adorned with metal buttons in front, black knee-breeches, with more buttons at the knees, and felt-like grey stockings. On their heads they wear caps somewhat resembling those of the Neapolitan fishermen in shape, but rather broader in proportion to their height and made of specially woven woollen stuff, which is usually ornamented in very narrow stripes either of red and dark blue, red and black, or dark blue and black. Their foot-gear consists of rather high-heeled shoes, with a metal buckle in front, or, more commonly, of rough hide or sheepskin shoes, which are fastened round the ankle by means of white woollen strings. The women wear similar shoes, but with blue or red strings instead of white; the sheepskin *skegvar* are only for house or village wear, and wooden clogs, with toe-caps of dressed leather, are worn over them out of doors.

If a Faroeman is asked his nationality, he will reply, 'I am a Faroeman!' If reminded that Faroe is a part of Denmark, he will say, 'Yes, but our ancestors came from Norway, and the only Dane who came to these parts at the settling was killed in Iceland.' This anti-Danish feeling is not, however, so strong as it is in Iceland, where many of the people desire a republic. Indeed, it is little more than sentimental, being chiefly kept alive by the contemptuous behaviour of the Danes of Thorshavn. It is perhaps based on the sense of injustice felt when the Danes, who had stepped into Norwegian possessions by the conquest of Norway, retained these possessions, through an oversight on the part of those who drew up the treaty, on the secession of Norway from the Danish kingdom in the first half of the nineteenth century. With very few exceptions, all the chief officials have been Danes, and when in 1897 a native was appointed amtmand for the first time in history, his reception among the Danish residents was by no means cordial, though he had taken a brilliant degree at the University of Copenhagen and had had a distinguished career in the Danish Civil Service, and even claimed descent from the kings of Scotland.

The ancestors of the Faroemen were, as they assert, of Norwegian extraction, though it is probable that their blood was by no means pure. It is certain that the Norwegians who established themselves in the Hebrides and Ireland intermarried with the native population, and, from what we know of the colonization of Iceland, it is practically certain that the majority of the first settlers in the Faroes came not direct from Scandinavia but from the British Isles, where some of them had been in residence for two generations. That the blood of the original settlers has remained pure is rendered unlikely both by the local traditions and by the physical character of the people.

Of the legends dealing with the introduction of foreign blood the following has an interest quite apart from the historical doubts to which it may give rise. History gives it no justification, but its details are as romantic as those invented by any novelist and, without being true as to its main contentions, it may well be founded on a real event.

In the little valley of Kongsdaal, in the island of Naalsoe, the foundations of a few small huts or cottages can still be traced among the hayfields and potato-patches of the village of Eide. One of these ruins, which is rather larger than the rest, though its size does not exceed that of a small bedroom in a modern house, is known among the people as the 'Princess's House.' They say that in it, long ago, a Scottish princess dwelt. She was a daughter of Jacobus, King of Scotland, and she married in secret a page named Eric, who came to her father's Court from abroad. At length discovery was imminent, and she sailed away with her husband and many followers in a ship, which came at last to the Faroes. Here the Black Death had lately raged, and had slain the inhabitants of Naalsoe. So she caused her servants to build her a house in Kongsdaal, where she soon gave birth to a son. Even to the Faroes her father followed her. The first object that met his gaze as he landed on Naalsoe was his little grandson, who chanced to be playing on the shore. The boy was like his mother, and the king knew that he was his grandson at a glance. The boy's beauty and manly look paved the way for forgiveness, and King Jacobus relented towards the princess and her husband and begged them to return to Scotland with him. This they declined to do, and her father sailed away to Scotland without them again. The boy, who had reconciled father and daughter by his birth, was destined to cause trouble with another monarch by his death.

When the king had returned to Scotland, his grandson played again on the beach, where, falling on his knife by accident, he killed himself; and then King Christian of Denmark, who disliked the princess because she was a Roman Catholic, confiscated from her half her island, giving half of what he took to a noble of his Court and keeping half for himself. About one-third of Naalsoe is still crown land, and the British consul at Thorshavn tells me that half of the island was, as an historical fact, taken from its former owner as a punishment for 'popery.' Who this owner really was I cannot say, but the people of the island firmly believe her to have been the daughter of King James II of Scotland, in whose time it is just possible that she reached the Faroes, though she was not a king's daughter, and though the persecution of Romanists must have taken place generations later.

For all this, certain families, who claim descent from the 'princess,' remain exclusive in their marriages until the present day. Do not they claim to be the offspring of the Scottish kings? For this reason the people of this tiny island, whose population hardly numbers more than two hundred, are said to have been indignant until quite lately if any of their sons chose a bride from without its boundaries. One woman, by no means old, stated to me that she had been practically boycotted on Naalsoe when first her husband, a Naalsoe man, brought her home, because she herself was of Stromoe birth.

It is said that the in-breeding resulting from this exclusiveness produced many deaf and imbecile children, but, so far as I have been able to discover from recent inquiries, the statistics available are too restricted to permit any dogmatic assertion on the point. At the present day there are two imbeciles on the island, but though this would give an average of nearly one per cent., it is quite within the range of probability that so small a number, whatever percentage it may represent, is no more than coincidental, and that it would have been practically the same whether two thousand or twenty people had formed the population. Taking matters in the rough, it is more than probable that the whole population of all the islands is, in a sense, inbred, but I can find no proof that it is therefore morally, mentally, or physically degenerate, except that in-breeding may very possibly have produced a certain diminution in stature, though even this feature, granted its existence, may be explained on other grounds.

It is said by some that the 'Scottish princess's' followers did not remain on Naalsoe, which was entirely peopled by her children, but that some of them at any rate migrated thence to Suderoe. It has been noted by several observers that the people of the latter island are, on an average, shorter and darker than those of the rest of the group, and recent investigations of a scientific nature have fully confirmed these remarks.

Moreover, the people themselves claim to have had a different origin from other Faroemen and speak a slightly peculiar dialect, though the difference is rather in pronunciation than in the structure of the language. The Suderoe folk often say that they are of Irish, or rather 'Westman' origin; and the 'men of the West' in old Norse history included both the inhabitants of Ireland and those of the outer Hebrides. They generally appear as prisoners of war, and it seems that the Norse vikings frequently took wives from among them. They gave a name to the Westman or Vestmann Isles off the south coast of Iceland, where a party of them, who had slain their Norse master, took refuge for a while at the end of the ninth century, being soon exterminated by the murdered man's avengers. The isthmus on which they landed is still called Thraela-eydi or Slaves' Isthmus. They also gave a name to Westmannhavn on the north-west coast of Stromoe—a place which their ships are said to have frequently visited. Some believe that they actually formed a pre-Scandinavian population in Suderoe and were there slaughtered by the vikings, sufficient of their blood remaining to influence the physical characters of their conquerors. A certain amount of evidence is given for this view by the fact that a breed of sheep appears to have existed in the Faroes, and especially on the little islands near Suderoe, before the Norse settlement, and, indeed, to have given a name to the group (*fær*= sheep, *ey*= island). It is impossible that these sheep could have originated in little islands separated by nearly two hundred miles of sea from any other land; it is unlikely that they are so ancient as any former land connexion which may have existed with this country, or that they could have been introduced by other than human agency, though they may conceivably have been brought by a drifting wreck, as the brown rat is said to have been brought to Faroe in the eighteenth century. Against the view that Suderoe was inhabited at the time when the Norsemen first reached it must be placed the silence of the *Færeyinga Saga* or 'Tale of Thrond of Gate,' which was translated into English some years ago by Professor York Powell. It is true that this saga was written in Iceland, probably as late as the thirteenth century, while the events it records took place in the tenth; but it must have been compiled from native, probably from contemporary, origins, and it seems improbable that there should be no reference in it to the aborigines of the country with which it deals, had any aborigines existed within a century of the happenings which it describes. In my opinion, at any rate, the introduction of Westman blood took place at a later date, though the question whether these so-called men of the West may not have been really identical with the little 'Finmen' who are known to have visited Orkney and Shetland in skin canoes, is at present a moot one.

The following story, which was told me in Thorshavn by an old man, explained the Westman strain in the people of Suderoe to its narrator's complete satisfaction, and although the fatuous pedantry which gives it point, as it was told me, is merely ridiculous, it records an event which may well have occurred more than once.

'A long time ago a small foreign vessel anchored off Suderoe. On board there was a woman, the captain's wife. Now the Faroemen were very rude in those days, and the chief man on the island, who lacked a wife at the time, went out to the ship with many boats full of his followers, seized the woman, and took her ashore. The crew of the ship was small, the islanders were many; and the captain was forced to leave his wife to her fate and to set sail with all speed. As he departed his cry was heard on shore: "*Ma femme! Ma femme!*" To this day there is a village on Suderoe called after her, Famöyen, for she was forthwith married to her captor, and the people thought that her name was Fam. And this proves that the people of Suderoe are Irish, for I have heard that *femme* is the Irish for wife!'

It is known that French pirates did visit the islands, and that in the sixteenth century their visits were frequent.

The Danes of Thorshavn are fond of asserting that the dark complexions of the Suderoe folk are due to intercourse with these pirates, with Brittany fishermen and with the Barbary corsairs, and the story narrated, absurd as it is in its philology, might give a certain weight to supposition of the kind. But I can find no confirmatory evidence as regards the Bretons, while the belief that the Algerians are responsible for any physical change in the people of the Faroes is at least as unconfirmed as the view that the dark hair and skin so common in parts of Shetland are due to shipwrecked mariners from the Spanish Armada. On this point see Chapter III.

During the last six or seven centuries there has probably been very little introduction of foreign blood into the Faroes; indeed, during the last three and a half centuries, very little intercourse with foreigners at all, though a recent ancestress of one prominent family in Stromoe is known to have been a Czech or other Eastern European, who met a Faroeman on the Continent and married him. In the sixteenth century the King of Denmark established a crown trading monopoly which persisted until 1856, and this naturally restricted commerce with the outside world, smuggling being the only method by which unauthorized merchants could introduce their goods. Undoubtedly smuggling existed on a large scale, and, judging from articles of furniture occasionally seen in the houses and from tradition, considerable dealings took place with the Dutch. It is said, moreover, that a Scottish ship was in the habit of visiting Saxen in the north of Stromoe clandestinely every spring, but that the extraordinary natural harbour which formerly existed at this point became silted up during the course of a single winter storm, and that when the smuggler came in spring she ran aground on the new-formed sands and remained there as a wreck. Certain pebbles found upon the shore are said to be her ballast, and what purported to be her anchor was removed only a year or two ago by a blacksmith from Thorshavn. Whether she was ever opposed I do not know, but a stone cannon-ball was dug up at Saxen within the last ten years. Smuggling, however, is not a form of intercourse likely to lead to frequent intermarriage, and there is no reason to believe that it has had an effect on the physical characters of the people of the Faroes.

These characters have recently formed the subject of an elaborate memoir by Dr. F. Jørgensen, who was resident as a medical man in Suderoe for several years, and the present author has added his mite as regards the men of Thorshavn. From our investigations it appears that two very distinct types persist among the Faroemen—one fair-haired, with grey or blue eyes, a ruddy complexion and a moderate stature, usually accompanied by delicate features and a round or moderately short head; the other short, dark, with rather coarser features and a decidedly long head. The latter type is far more prevalent in Suderoe than in the northern isles. There is every reason to associate it with the tribes which, for want of a better name, are commonly known to ethnologists as 'Iberians'; while the fair type represents that of the Norse vikings, though somewhat modified as regards cranial type. The so-called Iberian tribes have got their name because they are said to have resembled a certain Spanish people called *Iberi* by classical authors, but it would be a mere assumption to assert dogmatically that they ever had any connexion with Spain themselves; they included (probably) the Picts, some of the ancient Britons, especially in Wales, and possibly—this is little but a guess —the aboriginal population of Scandinavia. The name 'Iberian' as applied to this dark strain in the islands of north-west Europe is particularly unfortunate, seeing that it is liable to perpetuate the belief that many of the dark individuals now existing in what were once Scandinavian settlements are the lineal descendants of the crew of the Spanish Armada. It is well recognized by all who have studied Norse antiquities that just such a strain existed in the viking age, though it appears, as it were, to have become concentrated and intensified in certain districts, whether owing to a fresh introduction of 'Iberian' blood or owing merely to environmental factors it is impossible to be quite sure. I should not be sorry, as far as physical anthropology is concerned, to lay stress upon factors of the kind in the production of the races of mankind; but evidence on matters of the kind is at present very scanty.

By combining tradition with anthropometry it is possible to say with some confidence that the Faroeman, while mainly of Norse descent, is partly the offspring of the small, dark, long-headed and very primitive tribes which ethnologists call 'Iberian,' and further, that the 'Iberian' element, as the measurements show very clearly, is more in evidence at the present day in Suderoe than in the northern isles, or at any rate than in Stromoe, Waagoe, and Naalsoe. The introduction of foreign blood into the last of these islands, if it is more than a myth, need not have been foreign in a wide sense at all; for it is worthy of note that the hero of the tale has a very characteristic Scandinavian name, and much of Scotland was, of course, at one time largely peopled by the so-called 'Danish' hordes.

The Farish dialect, universally spoken by the natives of the islands, is interesting as showing their isolation. It differs from modern Icelandic widely in pronunciation, and to a less degree in structure, having undergone a completely different course of development from that of Shetland (which has lately become quite obsolete), though the two had a common origin in the classical Norse of the ninth and tenth centuries. It is only some fifty or sixty years since Farish began to be written, and its orthography is still unsettled. Hitherto it had been growing up for centuries as a spoken dialect, until two friends, one at home in Faroe and one at college in Copenhagen, began to correspond in it. Within the last half-century several collections of the old ballads, which have been handed down verbally for many generations in the islands, have been published in Denmark, and quite recently the printing-press at Thorshavn has issued translations into Farish of English, French, and even Icelandic works, including the *Færeyinga Saga*. The ballads, the age of which varies greatly, deal with subjects as widely separated as bird-catching in the islands and the 'Charlemagne epic.' Comparatively few of the people can read or write their native dialect, however well they may read and write

Danish; but newspapers, generally weekly or fortnightly, are constantly being started at Thorshavn, the bulk of the matter appearing, as a rule, in Danish, but poems and sketches in Farish being often included. They rarely enjoy more than a very modest length of life. Farish is generally written like Icelandic, with the two characters, representing *dh* and *th*, which have dropped out of modern English.

. . . .

In spite of (or perhaps rather because of) their mixed origin, the Faroemen have retained many of the virtues of their Norse forbears far more completely than the majority of their distinguished kin have done. Norway is rapidly being corrupted by the tourist and by 'modernism'— perhaps the more baneful of the two influences; the Danes are more than half Germanized; the Icelanders are becoming demoralized by drink and slavish self-complaisance; but the Faroeman has escaped or recovered from these disasters, and by his combined hospitality, courtesy to strangers, honesty, sane gaiety, and cleanliness of person and home, resembles what was best among the heroes of the ancient sagas; while centuries of peaceful living have destroyed in him the tendency towards the characteristic viking vices of cruelty and bloodthirstiness, and (to some extent) the overweening attraction of the wassail-bowl. His chief faults in the modern world appear, put briefly, to consist of a lack of originality, a want of superfluous energy, and a fondness for gossip and scandal; unless, indeed, we are to include among faults a harmless superstition, which, in the twentieth century, still ventures to believe in trolls and mermaids.

Norse hospitality, courtesy and honesty need no comment; but there are in the Faroes two customs connected with hospitality which are worthy of note. Even when payment for board and lodging is accepted from a stranger—and the persistence with which, in remote villages, it is often refused is one of the traveller's embarrassments—it is usual to offer him on his departure some little gift, such as a pair of native shoes, some local delicacy, or any trifle in which he may have displayed an interest. The second custom is strongly reminiscent of the 'butter in a lordly dish' which Jael, the wife of Heber the Kenite, presented to Sisera, and may once have had a very practical significance. It is rarely met with nowadays, though occasionally revived for the benefit of a stranger interested in such matters. Formerly, if a stranger came to a village where he had no friends, the chief man in the village came out to meet him, invited him into the house, and set before him a great bowl of curdled sour milk, which he and his host's family partook of together, each dipping his or her spoon into the common supply, and often seasoning the meal with angelica preserve—still a favourite condiment in the islands.

It is a common belief that no Scandinavian people is really cheerful, and that all are oppressed by a singular and morbid gloom, derived from the dark winters and frequent fogs of their native lands. The notion is probably founded on the lack of gaiety in modern Norwegian literature, and is well borne out by the psychology of the modern Icelander, who is very often what would certainly be called a morbid person in the healthy sections of English society. Doubtless this gloomy nature has a physical basis, for physicians and surgeons who have had experience of Icelandic patients in foreign hospitals sometimes talk of the *morbus Islandicus*, meaning thereby the curious lack of energy which often causes their patients, when all else appears to be going well, to die of sheer determination not to live. How far this *morbus Islandicus* is identical with the acute nostalgia which killed so many of the labourers exported from the South Sea Isles in less compassionate times, is a question that cannot be answered without more detailed investigation. At any rate, an eminent surgeon assures me that while it is common among both Icelanders and natives of Shetland, and even Scottish Highlanders, it is quite unknown among Faroemen.

Any one who has travelled in a boat rowed by Faroemen can testify that they are naturally a gay and a humorous people; every rock of peculiar form is the subject of some jest, at which all are convulsed with laughter, every sheep on the slopes above the water affords by its antics, as it runs away from the noise, an excuse for further jokes. The Faroeman, however, is reserved and proud, and very shy when in company which he suspects of scornful wonder at himself. Therefore he treats the ordinary British tourist with a somewhat glum silence, especially when the foreigner insists on poking about his cottage without permission; and he is intensely afraid of being laughed at. Even the fact that an Englishman has brought a tent with him to the islands is against him in the opinion of the islanders, for why cannot he be content with their fare and their lodging, which is clean and good if very simple?

When the time comes for me to describe a whale-hunt some delicate humanitarians may object to my stating that the Faroemen are not bloodthirsty. But although there is more blood shed in killing a whale than in killing a sheep, we have no proof that pain is felt in proportion to bulk. Except at whale-hunts, there appears to be an innate peacefulness in the Faroeman, which may be physiologically akin to the *morbus Islandicus*, though its manifestation is so different. 'When Shetland folk get drunk,' a Faroeman once said to an English artist, 'they fight. We love our brothers, and when we're drunk we love them all the more.' Instead of fighting, as a matter of observed fact, they dance and sing with others in a like condition to themselves.

Let it not be thought, however, that they are habitual drunkards; few of them are that. Their ordinary drink is coffee, and only on rare occasions, such as the feast after a successful whale-hunt or sometimes on St. Olaf's day, their annual festival, do they drink too much strong drink. Their sense of propriety, moreover, as regards women, is said to be so excessive that if a woman says as much as 'Good morning' to a man to whom she is not related, she loses her reputation. In photographing Faroe girls I have been much embarrassed by the necessity that everything said to them had first to be translated to my guide, and then passed on through an old woman who was present. My guide understood exactly what was wanted; but the old woman was very stupid, and it was not considered correct for him to attempt to pose them. The man absolutely refused to speak to them direct. However, this extreme modesty is probably an exaggeration of the true state of affairs, though it cannot be doubted that the morality of the islanders is of a higher order than that prevalent in most Scandinavian peasant districts, in many of which it is unusual for a woman to marry until she has either had a child or is expecting one very shortly. This is certainly the case in some parts of Iceland, and it usually means no more than what may be described as anticipating the wedding ceremony.

For the Faroeman's lack of originality and want of

energy two main reasons may be given—the climate of the islands and the conservatism of those whose practical outlook is naturally limited to a very small portion of the world's surface. The climate of the Faroes is by no means ideal even in summer, for although the air may then be warm, and at the same time exhilarating for the stranger, rain is commoner than sunshine, and fog commoner than either. The winter is not very cold, and frost and snow rarely last for very long; but the frequent intervals of thaw are largely occupied by hurricanes of wind, not uncommonly accompanied by thunderstorms, which do not occur in summer. This is not weather to encourage energy, especially when there is no ordinary work which can be done during a great part of the year, and no market for extraordinary labour; for there are neither tourists to buy trinkets and curios nor internal wealth to be expended on the luxuries of life.

The conservatism of the Faroes would appear to many business men even worse than their climate. They build their houses with wood, they roof them with birch-bark, they paint them with tar—because their ancestors in Norway did so a thousand years ago. Wood, birch-bark, and tar are all perishable, all come from abroad, and are all, therefore, expensive, but they put up with these and many other disadvantages rather than break away from tradition, and the only materials of native production which enter into the construction of their dwellings are the rough stones of which the cellars and foundations are built and the turf with which the roofs are covered, over the birch-bark. However, this particular proof of the Faroeman's dislike of change has at least the merit of making their villages most picturesque, and there are many others (some of which will be mentioned in subsequent chapters) even more astonishing in the present century of mechanical progress, pointing back almost to prehistoric times. Here I may mention the use of the *wooden* weighing-beam with fixed weights—a characteristic Scandinavian implement, which reappears in a slightly different form, after a gap of much intervening territory, in regions so remote as India and Siam. The weight it records is usually so inaccurate that its employment in commercial transactions has long been forbidden by Danish law, but in the Farish villages most of the households still use it, for their own satisfaction, in preference to any more elaborate type of steelyard or other weighing-machine.

I have met at least one native reformer in the islands, besides those more or less Danified people who live in Thorshavn; but even he is in many respects a staunch conservative. Born over seventy years ago, in his youth he travelled much, and was now a cabinetmaker in Copenhagen, now assistant to a blacksmith in New South Wales, and now a marine—during the Schleswig-Holstein war—in the Danish navy. Then, ere he grew old, he returned to Stromoe, his native isle, with a little money saved, bought land, and settled down to his old life. In spite of his wanderings, the old Adam often appears upon the surface. He has roofed his little house with slates—an example which his neighbours, in spite of his advice, have refused to follow—he has taught his fellow islanders to boil their fish-oil out of doors; he has never ceased to warn them, quite in vain, of the danger of throwing fish offal and the like into the stream and then drinking the water below. Yet, when he first heard that ladies commonly rode bicycles in England, he was so astonished that he exclaimed that the world would not last long. London to him was so big, so black, and so full of rogues, that he

hardly ventured out of his lodgings when he spent a few
days there on his way home from Australia; but his
feelings towards Englishmen are so kindly that the priest
of his village has laughingly named him 'English consul.'
Indeed, it often appears that the Faroemen and their
ancestors have been so long out of the world that when
they enter it now they pass through it unchanged.

Taking their general honesty into account, the way in
which they frequently libel their neighbours can only be
excused on the ground of lack of conversation in a limited
environment, and even this is no excuse for the manner in
which they sometimes talk of those whom they call their
friends. It seems to be correct to modify all eulogisms
with some exception, frequently an accusation of being a
drunkard; but it must be indeed difficult to find anything
to talk about in a little group of islands, many of them
isolated even from one another, and continued laudation of
one's neighbours would probably grow wearisome to most
of us under the circumstances.

In a copy of one of the local newspapers in my possession
seven and three-quarter columns are devoted to the affairs
of the islands, while all the foreign news is compressed
into a quarter of a column. The wildest rumours are
constantly arising, and are carried from village to village
by the milkmaids, who act as the purveyors of gossip,
meeting their friends from the next community as they
search for wandering cows on the hills in the evening, and
so hearing and telling all that people say. Several times
when travelling in the islands I have been asked whether
it is a fact that the British Government is about to seize
Stromoe, in order to get a harbour for the British fleet at
Westmannhavn, where there is a curious natural haven
entirely surrounded by land except for a very narrow but

rather deep channel at one end. When such stories occur a little private scandal is not wonderful.

Farish superstitions, however, are of a very harmless nature, dealing mostly with trolls, mermaids, and water-spirits. Although the word troll is often translated witch—and rightly so when dealing with old Norse or modern Scandinavian folklore—it does not appear to convey to the modern Faroeman any idea of human depravity. The trolls are rather the 'little people,' who live inside the fairy mount, from which they issue at night or in solitary places, to dance, or to play mischievous tricks on human beings, or sometimes to steal a child. In days of old they were stronger and more powerful than now—witness the legend of the Needle's Eye, a natural archway which pierces the cliff at the south-east corner of Naalsoe.

It is as follows: Once upon a time there lived in the Faroes a troll who wished to have an island of a certain size as an estate, and finding none of the correct size, determined to tie two of the smaller islets together. To accomplish this he bored a hole through the end of Naalsoe and another through the end of Sandoe opposite, and then fastened the two islands together with his hair, which he twisted into a rope without cutting it off. Then he went down into the sea and began to swim out towards the west, dragging Naalsoe and Sandoe behind him; but his neck proved unequal to the strain, and his head came off and was turned into the rock still called Trolhoved or Troll's Head. Trolhoved is now a valuable bird-cliff, but at one time it was said to be haunted by a terrible bullock, which prevented any man from landing on it. The bullock belonged in some mysterious way to the troll, and may have been his ghost.

Another legend about a troll tells how a woman serving in a farm gave birth to a son, whom she concealed in the mountains, feeding him on milk which she stole from her master's cows. The boy grew up strong and bold, and one day met a troll. The troll challenged him to a wrestling-bout, promising to fulfil three wishes if overcome. After a long struggle the youth threw the troll, who asked what his three wishes were, saying at the same time that they could only be fulfilled if no one laughed. The youth wished, firstly, that gannets should come and breed in the Faroes; secondly, that a tree-trunk should be brought by the sea every spring; and thirdly, that a particular kind of whale, described as having only one eye in the centre of its head, should strand itself every summer. This was on Naalsoe. The gannets came, but the people of the island laughed at their huge beaks, and they flew away to the little islet of Myggenaes, which is still their only breeding-place in the Faroes. The tree-trunk came, but the people laughed at something peculiar in its roots, and it floated away to Kolter, where the people said that they did not want it, as their church was blown down every winter and they did not wish to be obliged to repair it again. They would have the material to do so and no excuse for not doing so, if the tree-trunk came every spring. So it came no more. The whales stranded themselves; but the people laughed at their one eye, and they swam away to Suderoe, where it is said that a school still strands itself every summer.

The trolls are no longer so powerful as of yore. A disease to which cattle are liable is still ascribed to them, being called 'troll-riding.' It is probably due to the animal eating some poisonous herb, and causes it to be much puffed up and to lie on one side. Landt, writing a century ago, describes how the men of his day cured it, or rather professed to do so, by sweeping a broom over its back or moving a candle over it, believing that the sickness was caused by a troll riding on the animal's back.

The most definite way, however, in which the little people still show their activity is that of kidnapping [1] little girls. It is firmly believed that they still do so, and a story is even told of an English lady whom they snatched away as she was sketching by the shore, having landed from a yacht. When a child hears the trolls calling her, she rushes along towards their hill with supernatural swiftness. A man once told me that his father was out fishing on the west coast of Stromoe in a bay which is about five miles round but only about a mile across. He saw a little girl running round the bay exceedingly fast, and rowed ashore to see what was the matter. He found that she had run from one point to the other in twenty minutes. There is an old woman named Rachel who still comes into Thorshavn every day with milk from the farm of Kirkeboe. She has done so for many years, and in the course of her work has walked so far that she is often called 'the woman who has walked three times round the world.' Old Rachel appears to be half-witted, and her loss of sense is believed, by herself as well as by others, to be due to the fact that when a little girl she was stolen by the trolls and spent ten days inside the fairy mount. After ten days' absence from home she was found lying on the top of an almost inaccessible cliff, so hungry that she had gnawed her own fingers.

The mermaids are not quite so malicious, but content themselves with entangling the fishermen's lines and

---

[1] Many similar stories were known to Debes in the Seventeenth century. He also gives another version of the legend of the troll's three promises, talking of the troll as a giant. He regarded all such beings as manifestations of Satan.

snapping off their hooks. It is said that they frequently do this, and if more than three hooks are lost in rapid succession without apparent cause it is certain to be attributed for a fault to them, and the fisherman goes home. It is only very rarely that they rise to the surface and let themselves be seen, but stories are told of fisherman who caught a mermaid in their nets, and were so terrified by its moans that they threw it back into the sea. Regarding mermaids Debes says: 'So in the year 1670, there was seen at the West of Feroe, before *Tualboe plaine*, a mairmade close by the land, during two hours and a half; by many men not only of Tualboe, but also of other places of Suderoe, she stood upright above the water, having long hair on her head spread on water round about, holding a Fish in her hand with the head downwards.' In the same context he refers to 'other monsters (which) have appeared in Feroe in the Figure of Boats.' He says that time will teach whether the appearance of such monsters portends misfortune. It is possible that the real mermaids are skates and hagfishes; for the former have exceedingly powerful teeth and the Danish fishermen say that they can transform themselves into huge suckers by pressing their fins down on the bottom, so that it is practically impossible to draw them up when once they feel the hook; while the hagfish entangles the lines with its own slime, crawling among them as it feeds on the other fish already caught.

A curious belief, also found in other Scandinavian countries, links the seals, which formerly abounded in the caves of several of the islands, with the soldiers of Pharaoh who were lost in the Red Sea. According to the Faroemen they were not drowned but turned into seals, which swam away to the north. There is a conical hill on Naalsoe which the seals were said to climb once a month, throwing off their skins and dancing in human form for a night. Men are reported to have gained wives of great beauty by surprising these offspring of the Egyptians and burning or concealing the skins they had discarded. If once the women discovered the stolen robe, however, they returned to the sea, never to come ashore again. I have even heard this story quoted in the Faroes as an etymological explanation of the name of the group—though there is far less similarity of sound between the words 'Faroe' and 'Pharaoh,' or rather their Norse equivalents, in the mouth of a native than in that of an Englishman.

In some villages the fishermen still believe, as they did a century ago, that the left leg of the heron—an occasional visitor to the Faroes—will protect them against disaster and ensure them luck if they wear it on their persons.

Naturally many legends current in these little islands are connected with the sea. The first church upon them, according to some, came floating of its own accord from Norway, where a pious queen had made a vow, in return for recovery from illness, to set up a church in some land where no church had formerly been. To fulfil her vow she caused a church of wood to be built and placed in the sea, praying that it might float to some suitable shore. It was stranded at Thrangisvaag in Suderoe. According to others, it was not a church that came in this way but the old hall, built of solid pine-trunks, which still exists as part of the farmhouse (once of the bishop's palace) at Kirkeboe in Stromoe. Three days after the hall itself arrived, a priest, who was walking by the sea, picked up the round piece of wood used as a cover, in wet weather or at night, for the hole in the roof through which the smoke of the fire, set in the middle of the floor, escaped. It is said, however, that fishermen in danger at sea still make a vow to pay an offering to the modern church at Thrangisvaag in memory of its predecessor's origin.

A better authenticated tradition ascribes the first church in the Faroes to Sigmund, one of the heroes with whom the *Fœreyinga Saga* deals. The ruins of an ancient wall, now known as *Leighuus* or dead-house, are reputed to be the remains of his building. They stand at Kirkeboe, in the south-west of Stromoe, where the remains of buildings belonging to several different periods still exist.

Kirkeboe was the seat of a bishop until the Reformation reached the islands, and although it is stated that this great religious movement caused but little stir in the Faroes, local traditions point in another direction. The story goes that the last Roman Catholic bishop of the Faroes, who lived at the time of the acceptance of the Reformation in Denmark, determined to finish the building of a monastery left half built by a certain Bishop Hilarius, or at any rate to complete the chapel, which only lacked a roof to make it perfect. He sent out missioners throughout his diocese to requisition money for the purpose. The southern people were willing enough; the northerners came down in a body to Kirkeboe. The bishop, who was a notorious glutton, was just about to dine in the old wooden hall when they came. He begged to be allowed to eat his dinner before they slew him; they replied that they could wait. But he had a secret passage from the cellar beneath the hall to the roofless chapel of Hilarius. Along this he made his way, appearing to the assembled northerners on the top of the wall and claiming sanctuary. They said again that they could wait, and after three days' vigil he fell from the wall and was killed. As he fell outwards the sanctuary was not defiled[1]. Though the

[1] No such event is recorded by Debes in his account of the bishops

staircase by which the bishop climbed to the top of the chapel wall can still be traced, the secret passage cannot now be found.

From that day to this the building has remained without a roof, carefully repaired when injured by a storm but otherwise untouched. It is a small but massive structure, with narrow pointed windows along the sides and a high rounded arch for a doorway at the west end. On the north side a small side chapel opens from the main building, having an extremely asymmetrical, but approximately circular window high up in its east wall. There are several curiously carved supports for the roof-beams which were never laid, one of them said to be a portrait bust of Bishop Hilarius; but the most curious, and probably the most interesting feature of the ruin is a representation of the Crucifixion carved on a block of stone let into the east wall on its outer surface. The carving is placed high above the ground, and is much worn, but the figures appear to be far more archaic than those inside the chapel. There has been an inscription on the upper part of the panel, but it is now quite illegible.

Tradition has it that this carved slab was sent to the Faroes by King Canute, and that it marks the hiding-place of a golden treasure. The lower part of it is broken, and it is said that a servant in the farm at Kirkeboe broke it in searching for this treasure not so very long ago, but that remorse came upon him, with horror of his sacrilege, before he completed his search. It is quite probable that this slab is older than the rest of the ruins, and possibly it may have been removed to its present position from some more ancient building.

of Faroe. Possibly the popular legend is really founded upon the troubles of the first and only Protestant bishop, who was harassed by French pirates at Kirkeboe and finally fled to Norway.

The Faroemen now are Lutherans. Every village has its church, even when it contains but a few houses. The older churches are generally built of wood and thatched with turf; often they are only to be distinguished from the dwelling-houses by their greater comparative length and by a little white belfry, which is perched on the west end of the roof. At present there are only six priests in the islands, of whom half chance to be Danes and half natives; but, if the priest is absent in another part of his parish, service is read in each church every Sunday by a layman. At christenings, weddings, and funerals the lay reader, who is appointed in each village by the priest, has the right of standing next the priest with an open prayer-book in his hand. On this a small fee is placed by the relatives of the baby, bride, or dead person. The senior priest in the islands has the title of provost or dean. Lately a number of persons have left the Lutheran community to ally themselves with some Baptist 'missionaries,' who came from Shetland, causing great dissension by their preaching.

The people in the country villages appear to be naturally devout, and it is curious to notice, as many besides myself have done, that the number of men who go to church is usually greater than that of women. Their obedience to the fourth commandment, if not puritanical, is consistent, and charity appears to be part of their moral as well as their social code.

The priests, as a rule, are well-educated men, and several of them (including Landt in the eighteenth and Debes in the seventeenth century) have in past times contributed largely to our knowledge of the islands. The very peasants, too, although comparatively few of them can read or write Farish, are, in very many cases, exceedingly well informed, often surprising the traveller by their knowledge of history, geography, and even foreign literature. Some years ago, at Kollefjord in Stromoe, I met a man [1] who had never left the islands, but could speak excellent English and Danish, and could read German, French, and Icelandic. He had learnt them in the winter evenings, in order that he might have something to read; and, what was even more extraordinary, he knew how to apply what he had learnt. From some vegetable seeds which he had procured from Scotland a plant of the common ragwort had come up. Struck by the beauty of the yellow flower, and considering it a rarity, he was even more pleased with it than if it had been the cabbage he expected. On my telling him its English name he gave me, in a very modest way, a little discourse on the etymology of the word 'wort.' He told me that his great ambition was to see a real diamond, and he seemed quite at a loss to understand what a country could be like where all the fields were level.

Such men are by no means rare in the Faroes.

[1] In anthropological investigations instances of high culture of this kind among primitive peoples often need a very careful investigation, and the inquirer must be prepared to find real traces of foreign influence in unexpected quarters. A friend of mine in the Faroes is an old sailor who now keeps the 'hotel' in Thorshavn. I have frequently noticed that in reckoning up the number of persons who will need a meal he refers to them as so many 'piece.' Had I not known that he had been several voyages to China, the analogy with the 'pidgin' *piece* would probably have struck me as an instance of independent evolution.

CHAPTER II

LIFE IN THE FAROES

IN the former chapter I have dealt with the origin, character, beliefs, and education of the Faroemen; I now propose to sketch their daily life, their homes, their occupations, and, to some extent, the birds and animals which are of importance to them.

Out of a population of well over 15,000, between 5,000 and 6,000 live in Thorshavn, the capital. The homes of the rest are scattered round the coasts of the various islands, generally in villages of from a dozen to fifty or sixty households. There are a few solitary farmsteads, but these are the exception, not the rule. The conditions of life in the capital differ considerably from those in the villages; for Thorshavn, being a port, has become in its manners a little like the rest of the world. Being in fairly regular communication with Denmark and Scotland, and being on the direct route to Iceland, it is subject, during the summer, to short invasions of British tourists, who do not, save on rare occasions, penetrate further into the country.

The people of Thorshavn have learnt that money is valuable, and, in a few instances, that courtesy to strangers is unnecessary. It is only in Thorshavn, and perhaps in Thrangisvaag, that beggars are experienced. Here men have seen the comparative luxury in which the Danes and a few rich native merchants can afford to live. Many of the people here are store-keepers or shop assistants; they are divided among themselves by distinct differences in rank and occupation; they have many virtues and many amiable qualities, but they lack something of the primitive freshness of their country cousins.

Their town has changed less than they, though within the last seven years considerable alterations have been apparent. When I first knew Thorshavn, eight years ago, many of the boathouses by the landing-place were still secured by wooden 'tumbler' locks, with wooden or iron keys; but now these have almost entirely disappeared in favour of modern padlocks purchased from abroad. Still, even the Lagthinghuus is built of wood, bearing on its roof a luxurious crop of grass; only the amtmand's official residence, the big school, and a few other buildings, most of which are quite recent, in their solid stone ugliness mar the picturesque appearance of the irregular streets and stairways, bordered by houses on whose walls the tar has faded to many a rich shade of brown and grey, shaded from the fitful gleams of misty sunshine by the overhanging greenery of the house-tops, which contrasts finely with the whitewash on the walls of the cellars below.

In winter time oil lamps are set at intervals in the streets; but they are removed in summer, and in autumn so Stygian a gloom broods on the town at midnight that its steep flights of steps, narrow passages, and precipitous openings on to the sea make it a very labyrinth full of pitfalls for the unhappy wanderer. Worse still are the cesspools, approached by passages which are often wider than the streets themselves. It is a story commonly told to tourists, but repudiated with much scorn by the inhabitants of Thorshavn, that the oil lamps are removed because the Faroemen are so fond of oil that they would climb the posts and drink it. Of course this is not the

THORSHAVN, FAROES

[*To face p. 32*

case; the lamps are merely removed from motives of economy.

Far more interesting than Thorshavn, with its half-ordinary life, is the real Faroe, where the latest improvement in machinery is the *skotsrok*, a very rude form of spinning-wheel introduced from Scotland in the seventeenth century. Here the women may still be seen grinding the corn in a hand-quern and pounding tormentil roots with a waterworn stone.

To see this region the traveller must visit a village in the country at some little distance from Thorshavn.

To reach any such village in the Faroes means a journey. Distances, even in the same island, are far greater than their measurement in miles would indicate; for the only road in the islands is one of about a mile and a half long, and ends in a sea of mud abruptly, half-way up a steep hill between Thorshavn and Kirkeboe. Cairns of stones, set up at regular intervals of about sixty yards along the ridges of the hills, show where the other tracks should be; but as there is no means of distinguishing between one set of cairns and another (or, indeed, between cairns proper and village boundary stones), and as the routes to different places frequently cross one another, it would be hard to find one's way by their help alone, even when the whole country is not buried in a fog so thick that a sheep is indistinguishable from a cairn at a few yards' distance. In a fog even the natives frequently lose themselves, and fatal accidents from falls over precipices occasionally happen. There are a certain number of ponies running wild upon the hills, but until within the last few years little attempt was made to train them, and they were only used for bringing down peat from the hills or, occasionally, for exportation to Scotland and Denmark.

The sea is the Faroeman's highway, which leads, when practically all dwellings are on the coast, equally from village to village and from island to island. So well recognized is this that a householder is appointed in every village, whose duty is to provide for the journey of any traveller as far as the next village at any time on a week-day or after noon on a Sunday. This man, who is called *skütskaffer*, is appointed by the amtmand; he receives no pay beyond a commission on the boats and boatmen he provides, and the office is generally regarded as thankless. A man to whom it is offered cannot refuse acceptance, but he is usually relieved after a short tenure. The skütskaffer is bound to procure a boat and eight oarsmen, who receive a fixed rate of pay per mile, the owner of the boat getting the pay of one man as hire. The cost works out to something like threepence a man per mile, not including the boat.

Some years ago the Government built and subsidized a small steamer, which should visit the different villages and collect passengers and goods for Thorshavn at regular but somewhat lengthy intervals. At first it was a great success; when the novelty wore off people began to grumble at the fares, though the Sunday excursions from the capital still remained popular; 'which was very foolish,' as the reformer who has been mentioned remarked to me. 'The fare on the "Smyril" from Thorshavn to my village is two krone; but if a man walks he wears out a pair of oxhide shoes—which also cost two krone—and has all the trouble of walking as well.'

The difficulty and expense of travelling in the islands largely explain why the life led by the villagers is so remote from that of the present day; and perhaps the best idea of their life is to be gained from a description of a typical village. Kvivig, the village chosen here, is distant by land some fourteen to eighteen miles from Thorshavn. (The exact distance no one knew until the recent survey of the islands was completed, for time and space are things of which it is hard to obtain a definite statement in the Faroes. Indeed, clock time and sun time are often at variance, and I have known the former to differ by two hours in villages only three miles apart.)

Built in a break in the high basalt cliffs, the village of Kvivig lies scattered on both banks of a stream, which rushes from the hill-top close behind. Close in on three sides there are hills; and then, across the sound, more hills on the island of Waagoe. A few miles to the south, Mount Skelling, one of the highest hills in the Faroes, towers from the sea to the height of nearly 3,000 feet, and, yet further on, the islet of Kolter, with its single cone-shaped hill, floats green on the waters.

Perhaps the time when the strange northern beauty of the scene strikes the foreigner most is when he sees it from the hills above late on an August evening, after a day's wandering in the fog. The time of sunset is drawing nigh, and still all things lie hidden below in a dense white cloud of mist. In an instant the whiteness thins, reveals the landscape with all its colours intensified and its outlines blurred, and then rolls off completely, leaving fragments of itself, here wreathing the stony crown of Skelling, there floating along the surface of the sea, over the hills of Waagoe, and over the base of Kolter. Above, the sky is grey; but away in the distance the dying sunlight sparkles on islands and on water, tingeing the mist-fragments with a deepening pink and lightening the green summit of many a rocky headland. The hills re-echo with the cries of whimbrels and plovers, and the terns, fearing for their half-fledged young on the rocks, screech as they wheel low in the air. Sloping down towards the village on either side of the stream are the crofts of the villagers, surrounded by a common wall and drained and divided by little trenches, in which the foliage of the marsh marigold is now luxuriant. Six weeks earlier the trenches are a blaze of gold with the flowers—a gorgeous contrast to the fields, which are all ablow with ragged robin. The pink and the gold together make a show of colour which the tropics can rarely emulate. Now, on all sides, patches of yellowing barley contrast finely, if less magnificently, with green potato-tops and new-mown hay; while here and there there is a plot where the bloom on the uncut grass shines through the moisture with a glow of purple-pink that seems peculiar to the Faroes.

Beneath lies the village, its gloom only brightened by the green grass on its house-tops and by a solitary patch of colour—the pastor's garden, in which a border of yellow flag-flowers, a rare exotic in the Faroes, are now in their prime. Close by the shore of broken rocks nestle the long, low boat-sheds of rough stones and turf; then comes the church, with its little white steeple rising conspicuous from the grass which covers its roof; and then a mass of some fifty small, black and white, two-storeyed cottages, each with its wall covered with rows of drying fish, floats for the nets, and strips of dried whale-meat, and each with at least one 'dry-house' (in which mutton and whale-meat are preserved) standing beside it like a skeleton of itself, the sides being formed of laths of wood set a few inches apart from one another so that the air has a free entry. Further up still, where the stream becomes a series of small cascades, stand several of the old-fashioned 'Norse' water-

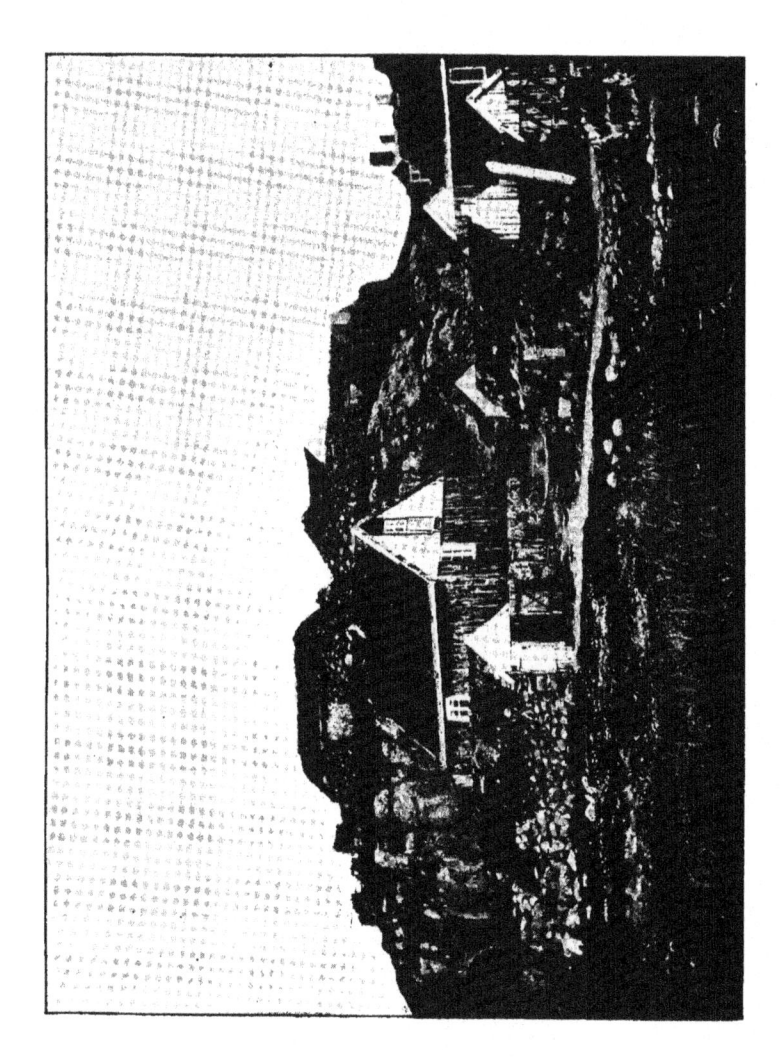

PEAT-HOUSES, DWELLING-HOUSE, AND BOAT-HOUSE, NAALSOE, FAROES

[*To face p. 36*

mills, in which the wheel revolves in a horizontal plane and turns the stone direct.

The serious work of the day—the fishing and haymaking—is over, but still much remains to be done. Beside the stream many women are busy stacking the fish in the course of salting, and covering them in for the night. Down the slopes come the milkmaids. They are almost the only barefooted people in the islands, and even they wear stockings from which the lower parts have been omitted; they trace the cows, which wander loose on the hills, by testing the heat of the droppings with their toes. Their full wooden pails are slung on their backs by woollen cords, and they knit and sing as they return from the higher pastures. In those households where the practice still survives of only preparing one day's meal at a time, the corn for the morrow has all been ground; but the last load of hay has not yet come in. Men, who look like moving haystacks, are carrying it down to the village piled up in wooden creels upon their backs, or storing it away in the houses built for its reception. Here and there an old man sits at his cottage door mending a hay-rake or fitting the short, straight blade of his scythe to its handle, that all may be in readiness for the morrow's work. The village carpenter has just finished his day's work on the boat that he is building, and is carrying in what remains of the wood and of the wool, with which he caulks the seams. Perhaps another man may be seen in some corner chopping up a hard black mass with an axe. The stuff is dried whale-meat, and he intends to boil it down as a meal for his cow[1]; for he has been too busy all day in the

---

[1] A few people in the Faroes stall their cows at night throughout the year, but the majority do not do so in summer (see Chapter VI).

hayfield or at sea to take her out beyond the wall to pasture, and hay must not be wasted in summer time lest there should be 'hay need' in the dark days of winter. Behind little walls, built half of rough stones and half of pilot whales' skulls, huge black cauldrons of saithe-liver oil are simmering over fires of peat or of fresh whales' bones, each presided over by a woman or a child. On the shore some men and boys, who have been out saithe-catching in the bay or shooting puffins for their evening meal, are dragging up their narrow boat, raised in front and behind like the viking ship, over rollers of whale rib.

The children are romping round the houses, or, where they dare, in the steep hayfields. The younger amongst them drag about the bones from the back of the pilot whale like toy carts, though carts are things they have never seen. Others produce a buzzing noise by rapidly twirling one of the little disks of bone from near the end of the whale's tail on a loop of woollen yarn. The older boys are playing at a game called 'sheep dogs' on the hillside. One of them stands above and rolls down a small hoop, made by fitting several rams' horns into one another; another boy stands below, provided with a piece of driftwood or a small plank borrowed from the carpenter, and strives to hit the hoop uphill, the others chase it when he misses and bring it back to the bowler. Most of the children chew pieces of dried saithe or stalks of angelica as they play, the latter not crystallized as we see it on cakes at home but plucked fresh from the plant. Angelica reaches its finest growth wild upon the crags of the islands of the north, but at Kvivig it also flourishes in an enclosure, built no one knows by whom, behind one of the two village shops—shops in which many things, Scotch and Danish, can be bought, but nothing of native workmanship, except

BOAT PROPPED UP WITH A PILOT WHALE'S SKULL, FAROES

[*To face p. 38*

a few woollen jerseys, too rough for natives to wear, which may be sold to some chance fisherman from Shetland or Iceland.

A village so built and ordered may be insanitary; for the headman probably neglects his duty, and the people have not a good water-supply like that recently introduced at Thorshavn. All of its many odours are not sweet. Fish offal floats in the stream and encumbers the narrow spaces between the houses; but fresh air and lack of apprehension work wonders, and the ducks and poultry act as scavengers, and so become fat and tasty. Nor, except in rare cases, does the filth penetrate within the houses. There things are clean, if neither tidy nor ornamental. Men and women take off their wooden clogs outside the house and leave them on a little mat at the kitchen door—the real entrance to the house, though there is generally another for the use of distinguished visitors. The housewife's chief objection to an English lodger is that he will insist on wearing nails in his boots, which mark her carefully scrubbed deal floors.

In Iceland, vermin of all kinds often abound even in houses which have an outward look of comfort; but in the Faroes I have never experienced anything worse than fleas. A hundred years ago Landt remarked that the bed bug did not occur naturally in the Faroes, and that even when accidentally introduced in furniture brought from abroad it soon died out. This is the case to-day, or at any rate the noxious brute is very rare. The fact is difficult of explanation, for *Cimex lectuarius* is almost world-wide in its distribution, and despite the general cleanness of the Faroe houses they are often badly in want of ventilation. The use of box beds in the walls of the living rooms is not altogether obsolete, though the heavy curtains with which it was formerly considered fitting that the bed of the householder and his wife should be enshrouded are now almost a thing of the past. Usually, however, there is a complete lack of mural decoration in those rooms which are in everyday use, though that in which visitors are received is often papered and provided with pictures. The plain deal walls, as a rule unpainted, provide scanty lodging for unpleasant insects, and the housewife's scrubbing-brush leaves few corners unexplored.

I have already described the houses of the Faroemen as far as their external appearance goes. Inside there are no passages, and each room opens out of another. Nowadays, the rooms are seldom large, but formerly every wealthy householder had a hall of handsome proportions, occasionally of great size, attached to his dwelling. So far as I am aware, only one such hall now exists. It is the hall—to which reference has already been made—at Kirkeboe. The logs of which it is built are of considerable girth, not smoothed on the outside or cut into planks. The roof is high and near its centre there is a circular hole through which the smoke of the fire, lit on the floor beneath it, at one time escaped. An American cooking-stove has now replaced the fire, and the hole is glazed and serves as a window—a luxury which was originally represented by a few interstices in the walls. In rainy weather, when a shutter was put on the smoke-hole, the hall must have been almost dark. The floor along the side in which the door opens to the exterior is raised so as to form a kind of dais, which is occupied by a long wooden bench. The ends of the bench are elaborately carved in a characteristic Scandinavian pattern of entwined dragons; but probably they are not ancient. The walls are decorated with trophies of whale-spears and fowling implements; and several of

IRON LAMP FROM NAALSOE, FAROES (EDINBURGH MUSEUM)

[To face p.

the old-fashioned fish-oil lamps, now almost obsolete in the islands, are suspended from them.

These lamps differ considerably from the 'crusie' of Scotland and Iceland. They are of iron; square, rather flat, and with an open spout (for the reception of a rush wick) at each corner. Another vessel, of exactly the same shape as the lamp but rather smaller, is hung to it by means of a couple of hooks, which are bent over its edge at either side. This is to catch the drippings of oil. The whole is suspended by means of a hoop of metal, which arches over the upper vessel, having a hole bored in its centre through which a cord or hook may pass. The great difference between the Faroe *kaala*, as it is called, and the Scotch crusie lies in the fact that the former is made for suspension from above, while the latter, which is rarely square in shape, is made so that it may be hung up on to a nail behind.

Such halls are now obsolete, but the larger houses still have a room, either the kitchen or one adjoining it, in which the servants take their meals together. This room is usually at one end of the house and has a door opening to the exterior. In old-fashioned buildings the walls are partly occupied with box beds, which can be closed by a sliding panel; but between these there are generally several spinning-wheels, which are fixed on to the wall. Wooden benches run round the room, and a smaller bench, which usually stands in the centre, has the important function of supporting a large wooden trencher, in which the meals are contained. Very often there is only one plate and one knife, the former being passed round from man to man after the meat has been cut up with the knife. In eating they make use of the knife which every Faroeman wears at his belt.

In a Faroe village, wealth and poverty, rank and difference of trade, have no place. There is land enough for everybody, nearly everybody has land either of his own or held on such a tenure that it is practically his; any man, by a few seasons' fishing off the coast of Iceland, can make sufficient to buy the three essentials for marriage and housekeeping —a cow, a boat, and the materials for a house. The seas all round the islands swarm with a life sufficient to afford sustenance, if not wealth, to any one who is willing to work; but the land is too poor to produce a fortune for even the most industrious or the most cunning. Consequently, the people have remained true peasants, but without a lord beneath the king, until the present day. Indeed, their practical equality is one of the first things to strike a visitor. In Thorshavn and in Thrangisvaag there are rich men and poor men, but elsewhere in the Faroes there are, to all intents and purposes, neither. It is true that the *kongsbondin* or crown tenant, whose land has probably been in his family for generations, is richer than the young man who has just returned from the fishing off Iceland; but neither is exactly a boor, though one may have been educated in Europe and the other may never have entered a school in his life. It is true also that every village has its carpenter and its smith; but every man can build his house and put together the wooden furniture it contains, can forge his knife and whale-spear and fishing-hooks, and is a fisherman, a whaler, and agriculturist, a shepherd, a tanner, a shoemaker, and, if he lives near a 'bird mountain,' a bird-catcher too. The one man who is not quite of the same class as his neighbours is the store-keeper, who is often a Dane or a Dane's agent, and sometimes acts as a petty tyrant, ruling the people through their financial indebtedness to him.

Nor is it only the men who are thus versatile. As in the household of the early Indo-Europeans, the daughters are the milkmaids; but every matron can spin, can knit, can weave on the hand-loom, knows how to cure stockfish, to dye wool, whether with aniline dyes—'horrible poisons from Europe,' as the old folk call them—or with home-made decoctions of lichens, seaweed, geranium, clover, or other native plants, though these preparations are now almost obsolete. A more arduous operation is the preparation of tormentil root, with the powder made from which sheepskin leather is dressed. It is out of this leather that the thin village shoes are made by women, who knit their woollen strings; but the hide shoes worn on the hills or at sea are made by men, the hide being mostly imported from abroad.

. . . .

Already the word 'whale' has occurred again and again, but not more often than is its due; for the whale not only supplies the Faroeman, his dog, and even his cow, with a large proportion of their winter food, but it also provides him with fuel, with oil for his lamp, with floats for his nets, with toys for his children, with string (the sinews), and with many other useful articles. More than this, whaling is the national sport of the islands.

The whale which is pursued, however, is not any of the great whalebone whales, but a comparatively small toothed species, which seldom reaches more than twenty feet in length—the *Globicephalus melas* of science, known in English as the pilot whale, and called 'ca'in' whale in Shetland. The former name is derived from its habit of swimming in large schools, each of which appears to follow a chosen leader or 'pilot.' The Faroemen call it *grind* or gate whale, because the old Scandinavians were in the habit of chasing it into a kind of trap, which was provided with gates that could be shut behind the school, thus preventing their escape.

When the *grind* whales are sighted in the Faroes great excitement prevails and quickly spreads throughout the islands. Every village sends as many men as can go. Sometimes, when the men are away and busy, women take their place in the boats, which are launched as soon as the rumour arrives. All the little boys go about shouting at the pitch of their voices, and boats immediately assemble from every direction. When the school is approached a consultation is held and some suitable bay is decided on for the kill. Then the boats, getting in between the whales and the open sea, commence to drive them gradually ashore. In every boat, which usually has eight oarsmen, one man stands upright, holding a lance with which to prick the whale's back. All the oarsmen help to terrify the beasts by shouting; stones are flung at them and guns fired.

As the destined bay is neared, the prey is pressed harder and harder. All along the beach women and children watch in silence, for even a dog's bark may cause the whales to turn and break through the lessening semi-circle of their pursuers. Then, at last, the pilot of the school, mad with terror and pain, dashes towards the shore. Soon he is stranded and cannot get back. The rest of the whales follow him to destruction. The lancers step out of the boats on to their backs, and deal their death-blow by severing the spinal column at the neck and destroying the brain with a large pointed knife made for the purpose.

Meanwhile the sheriff has arrived. He commences the work of distribution by measuring the whales, which have been dragged beyond the reach of the tide by means of ropes and iron hooks, which are thrown into their flesh. One-tenth of the total length of the school is then put aside. Of this one-third is the sheriff's fee, a third is claimed as a tax, and a third goes to the Church. Of the nine-tenths which remain he divides a certain proportion among the people of the district where the kill has taken place; men, women, and children all get their share, a yearly census being taken in each village for the purpose. The rest of the school is distributed equally among all the boatmen from other districts who have arrived before the last whale was dead. It is illegal to use harpoons with movable heads in hunting this kind of whale, doubtless for fear of selfish appropriation.

The bodies of the whales are quickly hacked in pieces. The blubber is removed, to be subsequently boiled down into oil. The flesh is either salted and preserved in casks, or, more frequently, it is merely washed in brine, cut up into strips, and hung to dry on the walls of dwellings or in the 'dry-houses.' It becomes black and hard, and is rather despised even by the natives in this condition, though they are fond of fresh or salted whale-meat. After a bad hay-harvest, however, it forms an important item in the food of the cows, which eat it readily when it has been boiled until it is quite soft.

Formerly larger whales, such as the rorquals and, occasionally, the great cachalot or sperm whale, were only procured when they happened to be stranded or to lose their way in the narrow channels between the islands. The one-eyed whale which, according to the legend, strands itself every year at Suderoe is probably the true bottle-nose; but I have not been able to obtain accurate information on this point. Debes and Landt tell a curious tale as to how the people of the northern island catch a whale called *dogtingen* or 'dogling.' They row up to it and scratch its back with an oar. This causes it to lie still, and they then stop up its blow-hole with wool. The beast, it is stated, will not dive down under such conditions. A hole is bored in its blubber (or, according to Debes, its eyelid) as it lies still on the surface, and it is dragged to the shore. It is even asserted that the boring of the hole causes a pleasant sensation to the whale. When it has been got ashore, however, it becomes very violent, and beats about with its tail. The whole story sounds apocryphal, especially as Landt does not appear to have had much personal knowledge of Suderoe, though his information regarding Stromoe is extremely accurate. It is possible, however, that certain whales really do like being scratched, perhaps to free them from the so-called 'whale-lice,' which cling so firmly to their hides. In Oriental seas a shark, which the Malays call the 'stupid' shark, is captured by a process somewhat analogous to 'tickling' trout on a large scale, and, though a shark is a fish and a whale is not, it often happens that animals which live in similar environments have similar habits.

Some years ago a Norwegian lighthouse-keeper in the Faroes started a small whaling station, with a steamer and apparatus for shooting and preserving 'finners' and other of the whalebone whales, which had hitherto been considered practically worthless in the islands. Indeed, they had been regarded rather as a menace to boats, as accidents had occurred owing to their rising to the surface suddenly. On one occasion, as I was crossing from Myggenaes to Waagoe, five of them came near the boat, spouting all round us, and the boatmen were seriously alarmed. The Norwegian's experiment, however, was a very great success, and he was soon copied by several others, both Norwegians and natives. There are at least four stations now in the Faroes, and several have been lately set up in Shetland. They have existed for many years in Iceland, where the fishermen have actively opposed them, as has also been the case in Norway. It is asserted by some that they are beneficial to the fisheries, while others believe that they ruin them. In Norway special legislation regarding whaling steamers has proved a political necessity, and in the Faroes, where the bulk of the people have no direct interest in them, they are said to have scared away the pilot whales, comparatively few schools of which have been taken recently. It is, on the whole, still a moot question whether the chase of whales with a steamer and a harpoon gun can have any direct or indirect influence on the migration of fish, even supposing that a considerable number of whales are killed every year. The whalers do not interfere with the pilot whales of set purpose, but supposing that they keep the fish from coming near shore, either directly or because the whales no longer pursue the fish, it is clear that they must prevent the pilot whales, which feed on fish, from coming too.

Before leaving whales, I may mention that a species of *Tipula* or daddy-longlegs, known in Farish as *grindalók*, or guide of the pilot whale, is believed to be the forerunner of the school, and that when it is plentiful people say that the whales will soon come. I may also mention that the appearance of a beluga or white whale is regarded as a very lucky omen. Several came down from the Arctic regions in the summer of 1903.

At one time the common seal and the Greenland seal were both abundant in the Faroes, where they bred in caves. Now the indigenous individuals of both species have been quite exterminated, though a few come south from Iceland in winter. Some years ago, at a time when the islanders were particularly anxious to attract English tourists, a law was passed which put a price on the heads of the seals, in order that the trout-fishing in the lakes and streams might be improved. The seals were thus exterminated, and the skins used in making wallets and the like are now mostly imported from Iceland.

A century ago seal-hunting was an important matter, and I propose to quote Landt on the subject at some length, as his account is extremely vivid and cannot now be superseded:—

'Of the two kinds of seals commonly found here,' he says, 'one is *Phoca vitulina* and the other *Phoca hispida*. The first are either shot, or when they lie asleep on the shore the natives steal upon them and knock them on the head with clubs; the other kind are caught in the following manner. At the time when the young ones are pretty large and fat, the natives repair to these holes (which he has previously described as proceeding from the sea under rocks, and as being so large that a boat can enter them) with two boats, one of which enters the cavern, while the other remains at the mouth. Between the boats there is a rope eighty fathoms in length, in order that if the boat in the inside should be filled with water, the people in the outer one may be able to pull it out. . . . (The boats) are furnished with lights; but they must be concealed in the boat as much as possible, lest the seals, perceiving the glare of them too soon, should make their escape. These lights are large candles formed of old linen, twisted together and dipped in tallow. When the boatmen have got so far in that they can reach the dry bottom, the first man springs from the boat with his club, the second man then jumps out, bearing a light in each hand, which must be held well up, that they may not be extinguished by the water, and he is soon followed by a third, having his club ready prepared also. As soon as the seals, which are lying in the dry bottom, perceive the men and the lights, they rush towards the water; but the men endeavour to give them a well-aimed blow on the head or snout, by which they are stunned, and they then dispatch them by cutting their throats. It sometimes happens that the large males, when they find that they cannot escape, become furious and make an obstinate resistance. On such occasions they raise themselves on their hind-legs, with their jaws wide open, ready to attack their opponent, who must avoid them and endeavour to knock them down with his club. . . . When all the old seals have been dispatched, the men proceed farther into the cavern, where the young ones remain lying on the dry rock, without paying any attention to the people or the lights, and in this manner become an easy prey.'

In the eighteenth century the flesh of seals was not eaten commonly, though it was in the seventeenth; but they were killed for the sake of their skins and oil.

The walrus is a rare winter visitor, and is occasionally killed on the Faroes, especially in Waagoe.

There do not appear to be any terrestrial mammals indigenous to the Faroes. The mountain hare was introduced between twenty and thirty years ago, and has increased greatly; but it is possible that it will be exterminated before very long, as the restrictions formerly put upon its slaughter have lately been removed. Considerable numbers are shot in winter, and the flesh is a wholesome addition to the limited diet of the islanders. The hare has never been so abundant as to cause dearth of pasture for the sheep and cattle. It now exists on Stromoe, Waagoe, Naalsoe, and probably on other islands.

Rats and mice are often so prolific as to do considerable damage to the dried mutton and whale-meat, and when there has been a whale-hunt the rats are said to swarm to the kill. The old black rat appears to have been the common species until the year 1768. At this date the wreck of a Norwegian vessel, which drifted north from Lewis, is stated by Landt to have brought the brown rat, which has practically ousted its predecessor. It is said, I do not know with what truth, that the black rat still exists in some remote localities. Certain of the islands, however, have always been so free from rats that it is even now believed that earth brought from them will kill or scare rats away. There are no rats on Naalsoe, where one is said to have been accidentally brought in a row-boat a few years ago, but to have been promptly captured and killed.

Mice, on the other hand, are extremely common on this little island and reach a great size. Indeed, Mr. W. Eagle Clarke has lately described some specimens from it as a new sub-species, partly owing to their greater bulk and very much stouter feet (probably connected with their rock-climbing habits), and partly because of other less conspicuous differences from the common house mouse. They show certain affinities to the representative of this species from St. Kilda, which has been named *Mus muralis* by Capt. Barrett-Hamilton. The mice of Thorshavn, however, are stated by the natives (to whom I have shown fresh specimens of the Naalsoe form) to be very much smaller; so that it is probable that at least two varieties or species [1] occur in the Faroes. Both in Naalsoe and in Stromoe the mice keep chiefly to the fields in summer-time, only

[1] The mouse of Iceland, *Mus islandicus*, is a local race of *Mus sylvaticus*, not of the house mouse (*Mus musculus*).

occasionally visiting the 'dry-houses' and cellars at this season, but swarming in the houses in winter.

The evolution of a peculiar breed or local race of the house mouse in the Faroes, or, for that matter of several peculiar breeds, need not have taken very long, for we know that this species has great powers of adapting itself to its environment, and that what is practically a new species can be evolved from it in a comparatively short time. For example, it has been shown by Mr. Lyster Jamieson that many of the mice of a little sandy island in Dublin Bay are now distinct in colour from those on the mainland of Ireland, being adapted in a very interesting manner to resemble their surroundings; and yet it can be proved without any doubt whatever that the said island was not in existence as such a century ago. We are still absolutely ignorant, except in a few obvious cases of the kind, what are the results of change of environment in the production of new forms and species of animals under natural conditions.

At present no reason can be given why the mouse should be larger in the Faroes than in Scotland, except on the general principle, which has never received an adequate explanation, that animals which have a wide range often become smaller as they are found nearer the Tropics; for instance, one of the cormorants of Burma or the Malay Peninsula can only be distinguished from our common British species by its very much diminished bulk. Dr. Winge, of Copenhagen, in a letter to Mr. Eagle Clarke, remarks that the mice from the island of Myggenaes, robust as they are, afford the greatest possible contrast to the representatives of the species from Tropical Brazil, which are small and feeble.

Perhaps naturally[1], the Faroemen class the wren with

[1] A similar name occurs in some English folk-songs.

the mouse, calling it *musabródir* or mouse's brother. As a woman said to me on Naalsoe, 'Whatever the mouse spoils, the mouse's brother spoils it too.' The bird differs a little in habits and structure from our own wren, belonging to the Icelandic form, which has been called *Troglodytes borealis*; it is more of a rock bird, rather larger, has stouter legs and feet and a slight difference in plumage. Somewhat local in its distribution in the islands, it is common in certain villages, where it runs about on the walls more like a beast than a bird, and makes its way into the dry-houses and cellars and pecks at the meat and fish stored therein.

In this way it manages to do a certain amount of damage, but not nearly so much as was formerly brought about by the raven, on whose head a price was fixed until comparatively lately. In the seventeenth century, according to Debes, who says that the custom was dying out in his day (1670), 'every man that roweth in a boat must bring at St. *Olaus* Tide, every year into the Session-house, the Beak of a Raven, which beaks are laid on a heap and burn'd, and he that hath brought none must pay a Raven-fine, that is for every one that hath neglected it, one skin, which makes twopence halfpenny.' Its bad character was due to its slaughter of young lambs. The bird is now very scarce, and appears to do little or no harm; a pair are occasionally to be seen in the vicinity of the whaling-stations. Darwin and other naturalists believed that the race or species peculiar to the Faroes was pied black and white, and a number of individuals of this colour certainly were obtained at one time; but Dr. E. Hartert has lately shown that the character is by no means constant in specimens from the Faroes, though all of them have certain peculiarities of the beak and other parts which, in his opinion, entitle them to a special zoological name. Debes says, 'Among those ravens there are found some white, though few; but those that are half white and half black are fit to be taught to speak.' The few that I have seen myself have been black.

The small birds, from the starling [1] downwards, are very strictly preserved in the islands, as it has been recognized that they are beneficial to the islanders, in that they keep within moderate bounds the increase of the larvae of the daddy-longlegs, which have occasionally ruined the hay-harvest by eating the roots of the grass.

Land birds, however, are of comparatively little importance to the Faroemen, who depend, in some of the islands, for their livelihood to a large extent on seafowl. This is especially the case on Myggenaes, the most westerly of the group, on several of the smaller islands in the south and on Naalsoe.

By far the most important bird is the puffin, of which two, or even three hundred are sometimes taken on a favourable day by one fowler. The puffin is captured by means of a triangular net, which is rather loosely stretched between two divergent sticks of about three and a half feet in length; where they meet the sticks are fastened to the end of a pole twelve feet long. In the month of July the puffin season is at its height, for the birds are then breeding in enormous numbers in their burrows among the boulders and grassy slopes above and below the cliffs. During this month and in the first half of August, those birds which have nests of their own and those which have been hatched one or more seasons earlier but have not yet taken on themselves the cares of house-keeping, spend the morning fishing at sea. They are very

[1] The Farish starling is believed by some naturalists to belong to a peculiar sub-species or even species; but the typical form also occurs. It is worth noting that mouse, wren, and starling are all modified in the same directions, viz. increase of bulk and coarsening of the feet.

gregarious, and the surface is often dotted over with flocks of them, each of which appears to keep to itself. About noon they begin to leave the sea and to fly home, those of them which have young ones carrying a number of small fish in their beaks. The fish are always arranged with the greatest exactness, head and tail and tail and head; but how the bird manages to catch them in this position, or to retain those already caught while catching another, is a mystery. Puffins which carry fish in their beaks are always spared by the fowler. There are always plenty of others to be caught which are apparently too young to breed although they have reached their full size.

The fowler seats himself on the cliff at a suitable place, generally behind a boulder or a wall built of rough stones. His net lies on the ground in front of him, and he grasps its pole with both hands. The first few birds he catches are fixed up round him in as lifelike an attitude as possible, so that they may deceive their fellows into a false sense of security. They are fastened in position by means of little pieces of stick, which are stuck at one end into the ground and at the other into the bird's body. The man raises the net as the birds fly over his head and, by a twist of his wrists, entangles them in its meshes. As a rule only one bird is taken at a time; but two or even three are occasionally caught, and even the best fowler makes many a miss. The birds are killed by twisting their necks, and, if they are not wanted as decoys, are immediately tied together in bunches. In some islands the puffins are also taken with a similar net by men who are let down over the edge of a cliff on ropes; but I do not think this is commonly done on Naalsoe. On Myggenaes and the surrounding skerries as many as 90,000 puffins may be taken in a season; on Naalsoe the number is about 30,000.

Besides puffins, fulmar petrels are now taken in large numbers on some of the islands. This species is a comparatively recent arrival in the Faroes, for it was almost unknown a generation ago. About 1839 it first began to breed on the cliffs of Suderoe; thence it spread to the neighbouring islands, and it is now common all over the group. It is a bird which has greatly extended its range in several directions during the last century, and it now breeds on the cliffs of the extreme north of the Scottish mainland (since 1897), though it first arrived in Shetland only as late as 1879. In that year a dead whale reached the island of Foula, having been brought by the currents from the northern seas. On the carcase were a number of fulmars, which found a suitable nesting-ground on the island and did not return northwards. It has been common on St. Kilda for at least three centuries.

The fulmar has not been received with very great favour in the Faroes, for it drives all other sea-fowl but the puffin away from any cliff on which it settles. Numbers of the nearly fledged young, however, are hooked off the ledges on which the eggs are laid, an iron gaff being used for the purpose. Some Faroemen appreciate the oily flesh of the bird as an article of diet, but others will not eat it; it appears to be more favoured by men than by women. Large quantities of oil are made from the fat.

On Myggenaes the gannet is also a fowl of value. The old birds are caught at night, just before the eggs are laid. They are gripped by the neck by men who steal upon them in the dark. The young are killed in September, when they are nearly ready to fly. They are knocked over into the sea with clubs and picked up by boatmen who wait below the cliffs for the purpose.

In 1894 an albatross (*Diomedea melanophys*) was shot

on Myggenaes Holm, where it had lived for thirty-four years with the gannets. The people of Myggenaes called it the 'king of the gannets,' believing it to be actually this, and regarding it with superstitious reverence. They were naturally indignant when it was shot. At least one other specimen, which I saw shortly after it had been killed, has since been sent to the Copenhagen Museum from the Faroes. The natural home of this species is on the east coasts of Africa, America, and Australia; but individuals occasionally stray far from their proper locality. Knud Andersen, one of our chief authorities on the birds of the Faroes, believes that the 'king of the gannets' may have actually bred on Myggenaes Holm, visiting the southern seas in winter and bringing back a mate with it to this northern rock.

The other birds captured in the Faroes are guillemots of three kinds, razorbills, and, occasionally, shearwaters. Collectively they have some value, but not nearly so much as the puffins. A few of them are caught in nets, knocked over by clubs, or taken from their nests; but the majority are shot at sea: it is illegal to fire a gun near the cliff, lest it should scare the birds away, and only holders of land in the islands are allowed to shoot at all. Especially on the little island, in the south of the group, called the Great Diamond, large quantities of sea-birds' eggs are taken every summer, several boats full of them coming annually to Thorshavn; but ordinary birds-nesting is not permitted in the Faroes. One man is appointed in the islands, however, who has the right to collect eggs, for the benefit of public museums or private ornithological investigation.

The right of fowling does not belong to all natives, but only to those who hold land on a peculiar tenure. In

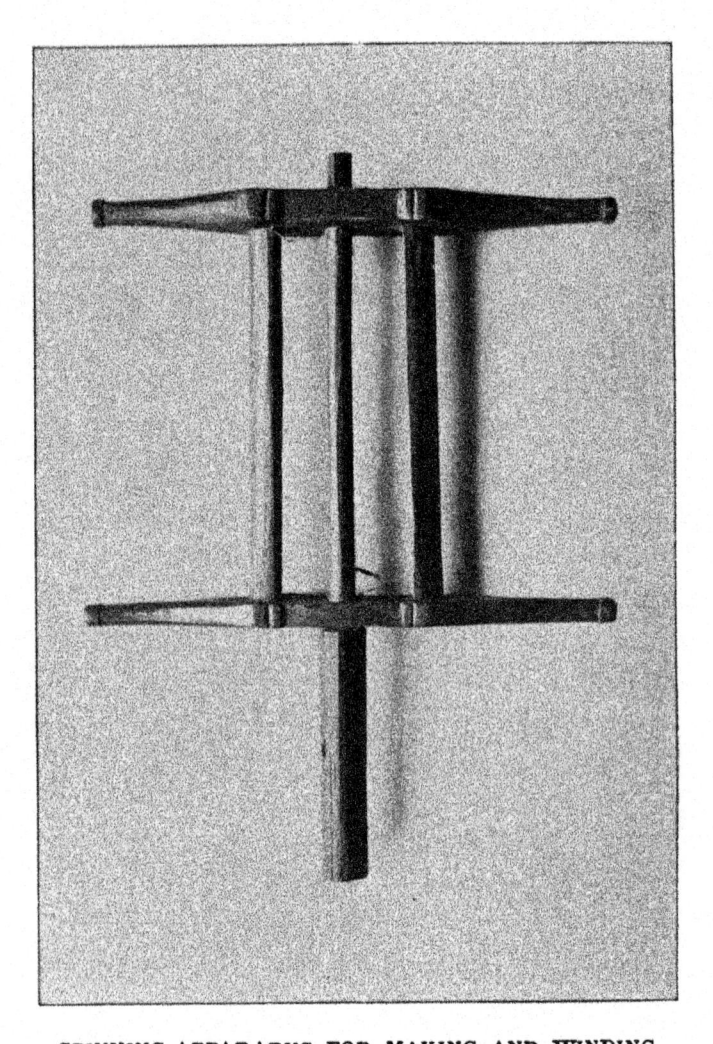

SPINNING-APPARATUS FOR MAKING AND WINDING
HORSEHAIR STRING, FAROES

[*To face p. 57*

some of the islands, for example Naalsoe, where there are a considerable number of such tenants in a comparatively small space, an arrangement is made by which bird-catching is undertaken in rotation, so many of them exercising their rights every year. In a succeeding chapter I have discussed the conditions of the art at greater length as regards the Westman Isles, where I have had more opportunity of observing them personally; for, except during a very brief visit to Myggenaes and a stay of some days on Naalsoe, I have not spent any time in those parts of the Faroes where fowling is practised.

A word or two may be interesting about the ropes used in the Faroes for the purpose, for in the Westman Isles such ropes are all imported. This is often the case in the Faroes too nowadays; but until quite lately considerable quantities of native rope were made in a very rude and primitive manner. The material used was either horsehair or a mixture of horsehair and imported hemp. The fine strands out of which the rope was to be built up were first manufactured by the aid of a hand spindle with a large mushroom-shaped whorl, which was pierced by a staff bearing a metal hook at one end. No distaff was used, but the whorl was rubbed up and down the thigh in the ordinary way. The twine was also produced by the aid of another implement, the mechanism of which it is not so easy to explain. It consisted of an oblong frame of wood, four or seven inches long. Through its main axis passed a staff, which was kept from slipping out by means of a little wooden peg. This projected from it just above the point where it pierced the upper end of the frame. The diameter of this part of the staff, which was not more than about fourteen inches long, was sufficiently small to allow it to rotate easily in the holes in the upper and lower ends of the frame through which it passed. At each corner there was a notch cut in the transverse bar which projected at the sides of the frame. The material to be twisted was fastened to two of the notches, and was stretched out with the left hand and fastened also to a metal hook at the upper end of the staff. The lower part of the staff was then rotated with the right hand, with the result that twine was formed. It was twisted round the frame as it was made, in order to keep it out of the way.

After the separated strands had been twisted they were combined by means of a very clumsy piece of apparatus, which was worked by three men. At one end of a space varying with the length of the rope, each strand was tied to a wooden winch, one extremity of which passed through a piece of board (common to all the winches), which could be easily grasped with two hands. Its exact shape varied considerably. The other extremities of all the winches passed through an upright board fixed in the ground. A man took hold of the first board, and the strands were fastened to the winches on the side of the fixed upright furthest from him. The strands were stretched out to their full length, and were tied together to a single larger winch at the other end. This also passed through a wooden upright, being turned by a second man. A small cylinder of solid wood, with as many grooves running along its surface as there were strands, was fitted in between the strands, in order to ensure evenness, and was pushed along by a third man as the rope was twisted. The men at the two ends turned their winches in opposite directions. The four winches were all shaped alike, having a flat rectangular centre, from two diagonally opposite corners of which a rounded spur projected. The rounded spur passed

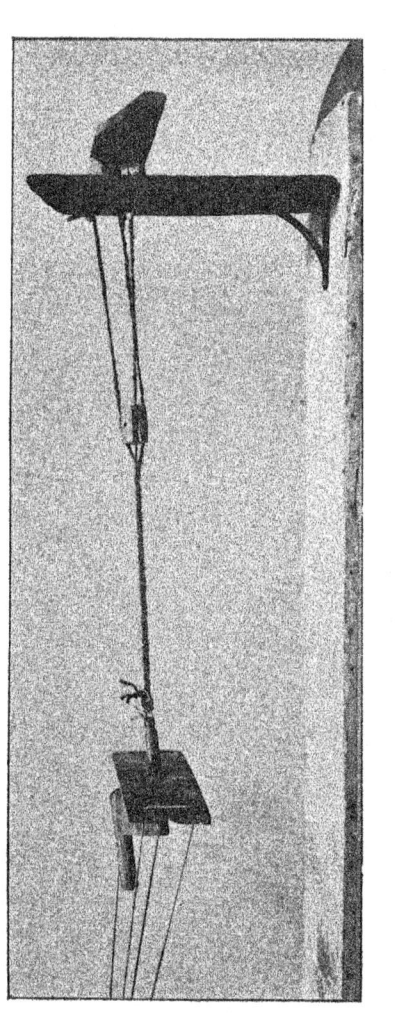

APPARATUS WITH SINGLE AND TRIPLE CRANKS FOR TWISTING HORSEHAIR STRING INTO 3-PLY ROPE, MYGGENAES, FAROES

[*To face p. 58*

through the holes in the uprights and, at one end in the board which held them together.

I have described these implements in the past tense, because I am not quite sure whether they are actually in use to-day; but I have seen them employed within the last five years, and have procured specimens, which are now in the Pitt-Rivers Museum at Oxford. I was told in Myggenaes in 1897 that horsehair ropes made in this way were not only employed in climbing, but were also stretched across certain chasms, which I was shown. Men on their way to the fowling went across these chasms by the aid of the ropes, along which they passed hand over hand, their feet hanging down over the abyss.

It is only recently that the fishings of the Faroes, rich as they are, have undergone any great development, as far as the islanders are concerned. A century ago they were content to use woollen hand-lines, which they twisted themselves with the aid of spindles. Few, if any, of their boats held more than eight men, and they built for rowing, as they still do in most cases, rather than sailing. The deep-sea fishing was in the hands of Dutch and British fishermen, the natives' enterprise being very small. At a very much later date numbers of Shetland fishing-smacks worked immediately round the islands, and young Faroemen still find it more profitable to hire themselves out to smack-owners on the coast of Iceland than to work at home. They are often accompanied by women, who are glad of an engagement as fish-curers in the same country. The Faroes, however, have now a very respectable fishing-fleet of their own, and a great deal of salted fish is annually exported from Thorshavn, some of it going direct to Spain in sailing-vessels.

The natives of the islands do not seem to make this so

important an article of diet as do the Icelanders, probably because they all live on the coast and can obtain fresh fish such as saithe at most times of the year. Indeed, to many of them the saithe is probably a more valuable fish than the cod and the ling, for it can be caught close to shore, often from the rocks, and no expensive tackle is necessary to secure it. It is generally taken by means of a rough fishing-rod, which is actively thrust below the surface of the water from the stern of a small boat, the bait being either a piece of fresh fish or a large artificial fly made of white feathers.

The Faroes are of course visited by many trawlers and steam line-fishers from Great Britain, chiefly from Grimsby; and disputes have constantly arisen between the Danish authorities (who keep a small gunboat to protect the fishing rights of the Faroemen) and these vessels. In 1900 an Englishman, Mr. Montagu Villiers, was appointed British Consul at Thorshavn, largely with a view of settling such disputes. He appears to have been most successful both in protecting the trawlers from aggression on the part of the Danes and also in conciliating the natives, who naturally dislike foreigner fishermen. Information regarding all matters connected with the commercial and legal aspects of the fisheries will be found in his admirable consular report for 1901.

The chief objective of the British line-fishers in Farish waters is the halibut—a truly northern fish, regarding the habits of which naturalists are still very ignorant. It is said to grow fatter on the Faroe Bank than anywhere else in the European seas, though it is perhaps more abundant off the coast of Iceland. Some years ago I had the privilege, thanks to the hospitality of its captain, of spending a day on one of these vessels off the Westman

Isles. It was a boat with tremendously powerful engines, which enabled it to travel at a considerable speed. In the hold there was a large well, into which the water passed through holes in the side of the ship. In this the halibut were brought home alive, all other fish that were taken being either sold or given away locally. The livers of the skate and sharks taken on the hooks were, however, a perquisite of the crew and were preserved in barrels. My friends and I were much struck with the comfort which prevailed on board, and still more so with the character of the captain, who is one of the few British fishermen popular in Iceland, and the crew. They had a wonderfully good library in the cabin and seemed most eager for information of all kinds. They told us that the halibut they took often reached a great size, and one we saw captured was over seven feet long. So stout was it that it hardly looked like a flat fish at all. Such monsters, however, are not welcomed, for their flesh is coarse and they can seldom be got on board without such injuries that it is impossible to keep them alive. Those fish which are pulled up uninjured are tied together in bunches by the tail and suspended from hoops which are hung up in the well. In this position they are sometimes so restless that they may even break off their tails in their attempts to get loose; but as a general rule it is found that they are not only more easy to handle when suspended in this way but also more healthy. Those that are taken off Iceland can even be fattened up by having sprats and other small fish let loose in the well while on the voyage to England; but the Faroe specimens are generally in such splendid condition that they need no fattening. The fishermen can always tell that their catch will be a good one if they see a peculiar pinkish tinge on the bellies of the first few fish they catch, as they believe, apparently with truth, that when the halibut are assembled in large numbers this peculiarity is always noticeable. Possibly it may have some connexion with the breeding habits, of which very little is known. The lines used are of great length, with many hundreds of hooks.

This short account of the halibut-fisher is, I fear, a digression, as it has little or nothing to do with the Faroes, but I must plead the interesting nature of the subject as an excuse, if one is needed. The agriculture and domestic animals of the Faroes and Iceland are discussed in separate chapters.

In the summer months the Faroeman's time is pretty well occupied with the fishing, whaling, fowling, and haymaking; and it is only in winter that he has much leisure for amusing himself. Dreary though the weather must then be, it gives the men, if not the women, a rest from their labours. Then it is that their lack of energy becomes apparent, for, having nothing better to do, they while away the day smoking and talking in the shops; and their wives sit spinning and weaving at home. In the evenings there is often a dance at some farmer's house, and then a certain subdued merriment prevails. There is no instrumental music, however, and people dance to the sound of their own voices. Nowadays concertinas or accordions are occasionally used, but their employment with the old-fashioned dances is not considered at all correct.

The Faroe dance is very peculiar. Some dozen men commence it by joining hands in a circle and slowly stepping round and round, now and then, at irregular intervals, indulging in a few little kicks, and shouting out a ballad about 'Kaisar Karl Magnus' or some other hero of olden times. After a while others (men and women indiscriminately) join the circle, and the dance proceeds and enlarges in this way until the dancers have hardly room to continue it. Sometimes the ballad is changed, but there appears to be no alteration in the steps or figures.

Such is the Faroe dance as it is usually performed nowadays; but the old men tell me that it has lately become very degenerate. Both the words and the tunes of the ballads are fine and spirited; but they are often howled rather than sung, and a lamentable ignorance of the words is frequently displayed.

In his introduction to *The Tale of Thrond of Gate*, also known as the *Færeyinga Saga*, Professor York Powell gives the following description of the dance as it formerly was:—

'The dance-step is thus described: Left, forward scrape and lift, right follows and takes its place (*bis*); right, step back, left follows it (*semel*); and so on *da capo* to $\frac{6}{8}$ time.'

The following is a translation, by the same author, of the first few verses of one of the best-known ballads:—

> In Norway there dwells a christened man,
> *Ye Norway men, dance so fair and free!*
> And Olave Trigasson is his name.
> *Hold your peace, ye good knights! all!*
> *Ye Norway men dance so fair and free!*
>
> King Olave he made a feast so fine
> In honour of God and Mary mild.
>
> The King to his footboys twain gave call,
> Go fetch me Sigmund here in the hall!

This, of course, is one of the older ballads; but it is not thought to be very old, at any rate in its present form.

Another old-fashioned amusement is probably quite obsolete, though it was at one time practised at wedding-feasts and may still be revived occasionally on such occasions. Once it was common, and old men have told me of it. When the company were assembled a friend brought in a lamb's tail on a large dish and set it before one of them. The person so favoured had to improvise a couplet suitable to the occasion and to pass on the lamb's tail to some one else. As the tail went round the board, every one, sooner or later, had an opportunity of testing his own skill and admiring that of his neighbours.

Dramatic entertainments of all kinds are very rare in the islands. Occasionally a travelling company visits Thorshavn in winter, and once at least a play was written in the local dialect and performed by natives in the clubhouse there. The Danes considered this a very vulgar performance; but the Faroemen enjoyed it heartily. It was a comedy or farce, and the custom referred to in the last paragraph was introduced with great effect.

There are a few local festivals. St. Olaf's Day (*Olaidag*) is a holiday; but no peculiar rites or ceremonies now appear to be connected with it. When the last load of hay is brought in a feast is held; but no 'Corn Baby' or other symbolical figure is made, and all the old harvesting ceremonies, which are still preserved in Scandinavia and parts of this country, seem to have quite died out. Even Landt made no mention of them.

Marriages are still conducted in a rather curious manner, at any rate in the remoter islands; though the old marriage costumes have almost entirely disappeared. The bride is conducted to church by two young men, who take hold of her arms. She is received by a party of girls, who range themselves in a row in front of her pew, where they remain standing until she and her maids have passed them. After the religious ceremony a feast is held. It is followed by a dance, in which the whole company form themselves into a circle, or into several concentric circles, and move round towards the left to the sound of a nuptial chant, which they sing together.

When the dance is finished the cup-bearers enter, and summon the bridegroom to bed by giving a loud thump on one of the beams. He takes no notice of the first summons, and half an hour later it is repeated. At intervals it is again repeated, until the couple at last retire. The bride lies down, and weeps; the bridegroom follows her to bed. When they have been seen by the company together the others retire to sing psalms in another apartment.

Next morning the bride and bridegroom hold a reception in bed, and receive presents from the wedding guests. Another feast is held in the evening, at which a rump of beef is brought in with the tail still attached and ornamented with coloured ribbons and the like. The dish is introduced with a poetical oration, and is then passed round, in order that any one who wishes may recite verses, which are generally of a humorous nature, over it. The custom is evidently the same as that mentioned concerning a lamb's tail above.

This description of the marriage customs is almost wholly derived from Landt, as I have not been present at a wedding myself. Landt's description is of course a century old; but I have reason to believe that the old ceremonies are still carried out, though details may have changed. Landt says that among the poorer people weddings are always held in autumn, after the sheep have been slaughtered. A remark of his, contained in a note, would lead one to believe that the wedding ceremony was more frequently anticipated in his day than in ours.

In the foregoing pages I have attempted to sketch, with

certain digressions, the life led by the Faroemen at the present day, except in so far as agriculture and their domestic animals enter into it. Life cannot be ideal for them in winter, whatever romance—probably more apparent to the eyes of the visitor than to those of the native—may invest their summer work. In winter every village becomes a quagmire with the soaking fog and the spray blown up from the sea; the imprisoned air explodes with mighty cannonading in the cliffs all round the coast, and everything is dark, and damp, and gloomy. But even then the native of the isles, accustomed to such gloom, manages to enjoy himself in a sober manner, with dances and an occasional marriage feast. And then, though the nights are long and the gales terrific, there are times when the aurora makes midnight almost as light as day, and the islanders come out to watch the 'Northern Lights' and to listen to them whizzing down the sky.

CHAPTER III

THE ALGERIANS IN ICELAND

'FULL costly and pitiful tidings in Iceland, the which wrought more scath than any of this kind since Norseman first settled the land'—in some such words the annalist Björn of Scardsá, who was alive and writing when they occurred, refers to the events to be set forth in the present chapter. Iceland had been subjected to many disasters, to earthquake, volcanic eruption, pestilence, and civil war, almost since the days of the settling in the ninth century; but it was not until the year 1627 that she experienced the ravages of the African hordes who were then the scourge of Europe. English pirates had landed on her shores, and had sacked her homesteads: but now she was to experience the full horrors of the 'Turkish fiends.'

A story is told in the Westman Isles to the effect that either on June 20, 1740, or, as some say, at the beginning of the nineteenth century, the Algerians returned, and were outwitted by the cunning of the *sýslumadur* or sheriff, a Dane named Johannsen, who, when he saw the corsair approaching Heimey (the 'Home Isle'), drew up all the men who had guns along the shore, bidding all unarmed persons of both sexes march up and down the islands with fowling-clubs, skating-poles, or anything else that might seem in the distance like a gun, upon their shoulders. The pirates, thinking that the island was occupied by an armed force, departed without effecting a raid. Such is the legend, and possibly it may be true; but we are at present concerned with a far more serious, and an earlier, attack, of which several contemporary accounts have been preserved, compiled partly from the statements of survivors and partly from the letters the captives wrote from the land of their captivity. The majority of these accounts were carefully edited and printed in Reykjavik in the middle of the nineteenth century; but they are now difficult to obtain, and I am not aware that any of them have been hitherto translated into English, except in a couple of articles contributed by myself to the *Scotsman* in August, 1901. The most notable are, perhaps, the *Travels of Sir Olaf Egilsson*, and the *Story of the Turkish Raid* by Björn of Scardsá—a respectable Icelandic historian, or rather annalist, who was noted for the bad Icelandic he wrote and for the numerous annals he compiled.

Occurring at a period when the old Icelandic speech had become temporarily debased, and when it was considered correct to be as foreign and as pedantic in diction as possible, these annals are not literature in any sense of the word; but their very close agreement even in minute details regarding the events of the sudden and utterly unexpected disaster with which we are concerned, gives them a practical interest as historical documents. To translate them literally, *in extenso*, could serve no useful purpose, for they abound in repetitions and uninteresting details. One of their most curious characteristics is an almost complete absence of emotion, an almost morbid restraint, which adds a peculiar poignancy to them, only giving way in the extraordinary series of abusive names with which the pirates are branded. As often as possible, I have given a literal translation of the more powerful phrases and passages. In doing so I have been much indebted to the kind assistance of Sysselman Jónsson, of the Westman Isles, and other Icelandic friends on Heimey.

It is of course impossible that even contemporary Icelanders can have had exact and detailed information of the events in Algiers which led to the corsair's attack on a country so remote as Iceland; but their annalists have not hesitated to give a graphic account of these events, as they conceived them to have happened. They state that in the early summer of the year 1627 the chiefs of the Barbary pirates assembled at Algiers to discuss whither they should make their next foray, and that one of the company mentioned 'that island in the north-west sea which is called Iceland.' The eldest of the counsellors, who appears to have been the chairman of the council, ridiculed the rashness of any such suggestion, saying that it would be folly to visit the uttermost inhabited spot on earth for the sake of a few miserable Christians. But it chanced that the slave who waited on the council was a Danish Christian of the name of Paul, who had been taken on some previous raid. Paul was tired of servitude. He made bold to speak, and promised that if his lords would permit him to pilot an expedition to Iceland (which he had already visited on several occasions) they would gain much profit in sheep and men. In return for the success of the voyage, he would beg for his own freedom. After much discussion, this was agreed to, and Paul acted as pilot on board one of the ships which visited Iceland that summer.

Here we may pause in the narrative for a moment to describe the fate that overtook Paul, according to the Icelandic annalists, ere he had long enjoyed the fruits of his treachery. When the expedition returned to Algiers he found that he no longer desired to visit Denmark, and elected rather to become a renegade and to accompany the pirates on future expeditions—no longer as a slave but now as an equal. To this his comrades made no objection, and Paul was one of the crew of the next corsair that sailed out from Algiers to attack the shipping of Christendom. The annalist may now speak for himself, as clearly as a literal translation of the Icelandic will permit him, 'Late one night an evil spirit, such as they had never thought to see, stood on the deck, and called upon Paul with a loud voice, saying, "Paul, thou art mine! Lo, I have come for thee!" And as the words were in the saying, it vanished in a whirlwind over the face of the sea. Next day a Christian ship came out against these bloodthirsty hounds, and fired upon them. And then was Paul shot to hell by these Christians, and his head clipt from him. But no other man, save Paul only, was struck down on that day.'

When we deal with events that happened in Iceland during the summer of 1627, we are on firmer ground, and there is no reason to suspect even a trace of myth in the native accounts of the 'Turkish Raid,' as it is generally called at the present day. I will relate it simply as the Icelandic annals do, making no comment upon the facts as they are told by contemporary scribes.

Four ships of Barbary came to Iceland in this summer, three sailing from the city of Algiers, and one from a port on the Straits of Gibraltar which Icelanders called Kyle. What town exactly this was it is rather hard to say. That it was not the historic Salee, which had then passed its zenith, is proved both by the description of its position and the fact that 'Salee' is also mentioned in the Icelandic records as a city of the pirates. On the whole, it would seem to have been further east than Tangier, and rather to have occupied the position of Ceuta; for it was well within the straits, some little distance from their opening into the

Atlantic. In any case, the Algerian and the Kylean expeditions acted quite independently of one another, and I think it will be best to follow our authorities in treating them severally, dealing with the Kylean vessel first.

The ship from Kyle was under the command of a trio of Moors, named Amorad, Areif, and Beiram, all of whom bore the title *reis*, though Amorad was the superior officer, being also called 'admiral' or captain. It is noted that these men, 'Turks' by birth, were far more merciful in their dealings than the leader of the Algerians, who was a German renegade, and that they restrained their men from illtreating the weak and aged, and even from doing wanton damage to property which they were unable to remove.

On June 15, 1627, they arrived off the coast of Iceland, anchoring at Grindavik, a government trading station near the south-west corner of the island. The district was then (as it still is) but thinly populated, and the only buildings that the pirates could see were the store, a solitary farmhouse, and the residence of the local trading agent. As soon as they had come to anchor they lowered a boat and rowed to a small Danish vessel which lay in the roads, awaiting her cargo of dry fish and wool. To allay suspicion they told her skipper, speaking in German, that they were subjects of the Danish king—whalers who had been out on the high seas for nine months and had run short of provisions. The skipper was surly. (It must be remembered that at this date trade in Iceland was a government monopoly, and that therefore all strange vessels were discouraged from visiting the island.) He replied that he had no provisions to sell them. Meanwhile their arrival had caused some little excitement on shore, and Lauritz Bentsen, the agent, sent out a boat to inquire of the new-comers their business in Iceland; for he evidently suspected them of contraband trading. Bentsen's boatmen were not permitted to return ashore.

The pirates' boat had now returned to their own ship, and the crew proceeded to arm themselves, having first put the agent's nine men in chains. Then thirty of them entered the boat again, taking a supply of guns and scimitars as well as a stock of provisions, and made their way to the Danish trader for the second time—only to find that the skipper was the one man aboard her. Him they bound; and, having taken two more boatmen prisoners who had come out from land to see what they were doing, they rowed ashore.

Bentsen and his assistants fled up country, leaving the store to its fate. The pirates ransacked it, but found very little of worth. The solitary farmhouse next attracted their attention, and in it they seized a woman named Gudrun, Jón's daughter, whom they hurried off towards the sea. On their way to the shore they fell in with a brother of Gudrun, Philip by name, who did his best to save her. He was quite unarmed, and they soon left him bleeding on the ground. Then Hjalmar, a second brother, rode up on horseback, and attacked them with an iron-handled riding-whip; but he too was speedily disabled and overcome. Besides Gudrun, her husband, a third brother named Halldor, and her three sons, were all taken at the farm, as well as a little serving-girl. The eldest of the children was a schoolboy called Jón, and he afterwards became a rather important person in the history of the Icelanders in Barbary, as he wrote home a long letter to his relatives in Iceland, describing the life that the captives led and begging for money to ransom himself and his companions in misfortune. He is said to have finally become a Mohammedan, and to have risen to a high position in the court of the Dey of Algiers. Gudrun's husband, also called Jón, was an old man, of little worth as a slave, and he was permitted to escape by the pirates before they reached the sea.

It is specially mentioned that the Icelandic children made no attempt to run away from their captors, regarding them merely as sheep-stealers, who could have no object in injuring people. As we shall see later, the pirates were mistaken on several occasions for Englishmen, and it may be of interest to point out that the hatred entertained at the present day in Iceland for the English trawlers who frequent Icelandic waters is not wholly due to the belief that the trawls injure the fishing which should properly belong to natives, but also, to some extent, to a remembrance of the marauding habits of English fishermen in the past. The captain of a Grimsby line-fisher who is personally, and rightly, a most popular person in the Westman Islands, has told me that when he was a youth hardly a boat visited Iceland without the crew landing and appropriating sheep, on the principle that the Icelanders had more than they could use themselves and that there was no harm in helping oneself to their surplus. It would even appear that in 1627 the English fishermen entered into league with the pirates.

On the same day on which Amorad reached Grindavik a Danish merchantman sailed past on her way to the west coast. Amorad promptly hoisted the Danish flag and sailed out to meet her. Her captain had no reason to be suspicious of a vessel which came from a government trading station in this guise, and he and his crew were taken practically without a struggle, and were transferred in chains to the corsair's hold. After this, two of the men who had rowed out at Grindavik were set free, being permitted to go ashore in their own boat, why it is not stated.

The Moorish captain had gained information that a ship lay fully laden at Hafnafjord, a small inlet seven miles due south of Reykjavik, which was then a place of no importance. So he rounded the promontory of Reykjaness, taking with him his prize. Before he had sailed far, however, news of his arrival reached Holgeir Rosenkrantz, the Danish Governor of Iceland, who was then stationed at a place called Bessastad, also near the present capital and then the seat of government and of the royal treasury. The Governor was able to send a message to the agents at Hafnafjord and at the neighbouring station of Keflavik, warning them to act on the defensive and to bring in their ships to Seilahöfn — a harbour whose entrance is still rendered difficult by the hidden reefs and sandbanks at its mouth. He himself, at the same time, made what little preparations he was able to defend the country against the pirates, being assisted by several north-country officials, who had come to Bessastad on business, and by the famous Icelandic divine and scholar, Thorlak Skulason, shortly afterwards appointed Bishop of Holar.

The treasury lay on the shore of Seilahöfn, but, apparently, Amorad was not aware of the fact. We are told that he rejoiced when he entered the harbour and saw three ships lying at anchor. Out of pure bravado he fired off several guns—with rather unfortunate effect to himself, for the noise caused all the people of Bessastad, except the Governor and his friends, to rush off into the mountains, where they were practically beyond pursuit. Moreover, Amorad's own ship soon stuck on a sandbank and refused to budge. Meanwhile, the Governor's party had fortified themselves as best they could, and had trained some guns, used generally for firing salutes on birthdays and marriages, upon the pirates. They were not called upon to fire, or did not think they were; but popular opinion in Iceland blamed them for not doing so, and the fact that they made no attack upon the Moors was held a matter for grave comment upon Rosenkrantz in later days. The pirate vessel remained fast on the sandbank through the night, despite the efforts of her crew to relieve her, and early the next morning the prisoners were removed to the prize that had been taken off Grindavik. The ammunition and stores were then transferred also, and on the following day the ship floated off the bank. Amorad, however, did not return to her, but, remaining on board the prize himself, put Beiram in command of her and gave orders to set sail, having made no attempt either to land or to take the three Danish merchantmen which lay behind the bar. He then sailed north, falling in, under the range of mountains known as Snæfellsjökul, with some English fishermen, who warned him that four English men-of-war lay off Vestfjord. This information caused him to change his course, and it is written that he sailed due west for four days; but no mention is made of the coast of Greenland, which he might have been expected to reach, had the wind been anything but adverse. On June 21 the two ships turned southwards, and proceeded home to Africa, reaching Kyle on July 30, exactly five weeks out from Seilahöfn.

The great waves that broke on a sandbank outside the harbour of the Moorish town prevented him from entering for two days, but boats came out on the third day and conducted him in with great rejoicings. On the shore men were stationed to blow bagpipes and trumpets, and all the chief citizens came down to the quay to congratulate Amorad, who had announced the success of his foray by firing a salute of twelve guns as he entered the harbour.

The prisoners were taken ashore on August 2, and were shut up in a house in the town for four days, where they were visited by many Christian captives and others. On the fifth day they were taken out into the market-place, with their heads and feet bare as a sign of degradation, and, after being paraded through the town, were sold by public auction.

We must now return to Iceland and to the three ships which sailed from the city of Algiers, their commander being a German renegade, whose name is variously given as Morad Flamming [1] and Morash Heming. Two of them reached Iceland on July 3, appearing off Berufjord, on the east coast, and sailing up the firth to the anchorage opposite a small farmhouse which stood at its head. Then, without delay, their crews rowed ashore in four boats and looted the farm, breaking up the chests in which the farm people kept their clothing and valuables, and thus obtaining goods to the price of 'six hundreds [2].' They also took possession of some lambs and a new six-oared boat with all its gear, and then began to search for the inhabitants of the farm, who were away haymaking at the *sel* or summer camp in the uplands. Though the pirates were well aware of the probable existence of such a place they did not succeed in finding it, and the farm people escaped capture for the time, some of them being

---

[1] According to Mr. Stanley Lane Poole this was not the famous Algerian captain of that name, but a contemporary.

[2] 'A hundred—i.e. 120 ells of the stuff *wadmal*—a milch cow or six ewes with lambs counted for a hundred,' Cleasby and Vigfusson's *Icelandic Dictionary*.

taken a day or two later. Giving up the search, they then launched their four boats, with the one they had looted, and commenced to row back to their ship. Just as they started, the owner of the farm, a man named Guttorm, chanced to pay a visit to the homestead, and seeing them making off with his property, called out asking why they troubled innocent Iceland folk, who had done them no harm. We are told that he took them for Englishmen. They were very indignant at what they called his insolence in thus addressing them, but the sea was rising and they did not venture to return to the beach, on which tremendous waves were now breaking. They captured him a few days later, and took him with them to Algiers.

The pirates remained on the east coast of Iceland for eight days, during which they took 110 prisoners of all ages and both sexes, several good boats, a large number of sheep, plate belonging to at least one church, a priest's boxes, containing goods to the value of 'thirty hundreds,' and much other booty of a miscellaneous nature. To follow their doings in detail would be tedious and unprofitable, but it was noticed that they exhibited far greater ferocity, and did far more wanton damage, than their colleagues from Kyle.

One example of their cruelty will suffice. At a place called Hál they found a bedridden woman, the wife of a priest, and ordered her to accompany them. This she was physically incapable of doing, but they dragged her out of the house, and when they found that she really could not walk, struck her with the butts of their guns until she fainted, and then left her for dead. After their departure she recovered, and her fate was enviable compared to that which befell not a few of her friends.

Meanwhile the third vessel had arrived, and had joined her consorts at Faskrudsfjord, having been delayed by a storm, in which she had suffered much and had been partially disabled. At best she was old and not very seaworthy. A council of war was held, and it was decided that the three ships should sail at once to the Westman Islands (where the only trading station on the south coast was then situated), and should there exchange their leaking vessel for the Danish trader which they would probably be able to seize. As they sailed along the coast, under Eyjafjallajökul, the 'Island Mountain Glacier,' they came upon an English fishing-smack, manned by ten English fishermen and an Icelandic pilot, who was a native of the Westman Isles. Leaving the captain of the smack to pursue his fishing, they pressed nine Englishmen and the Icelander, whose name was Thorstein, into their service, promising that if Thorstein would safely pilot them into the harbour at Heimey they would leave the ten of them unharmed on the island, where their skipper could call for them later. They seem to have performed their bargain to the letter in the case of the nine Englishmen, but what became of the pilot is not quite clear. He seems to have gone to Algiers with them, very possibly as a renegade.

The people of Heimey, who had already received news of the Algerian's arrival in Iceland, saw the three vessels lying becalmed off the south of their island on the morning of July 16; but the mutual suspicion which existed between the Danes and the Icelanders could not be put to rest even by so terrible a crisis. Each party began to make preparations for defence independently of the other, and while the Danish officials shut themselves up in the agent's house, the natives fled into another building in the village. Public alarm was allayed, at any rate as far as the

Icelanders were concerned, when the pirates hoisted the Danish flag, but so transparent a ruse could not long deceive them, and Bagge, the Danish agent and bailiff of the crown lands, does not appear to have been even temporarily duped. Cleaning the small cannons that stood in front of his house, more as ornaments than as effective weapons, he served out guns to his assistants, who, in all probability, did not number more than half a dozen men, and, when night fell, posted watchers round the island, with orders to bring him news of any movement on the part of the strangers, who were still prevented from landing by contrary winds.

Early on Tuesday morning three large boats full of armed men came ashore at the base of the cliffs which rise almost directly from the sea at the south end of Heimey, and the raiders climbed up on to the island by a secret path, which Thorstein, the pilot of the English fishing-smack, disclosed to them. This path still exists, but it is known to few even of the bird-catchers. A tradition, current in the Westman Isles, has it that the pirates had accidentally got their powder wet, and that they spread it out to dry in a little hollow near the summit of the cliffs called Lingdal. At any rate, they did not proceed to the attack immediately, but danced and yelled for some hours after landing, during which interval Bagge, who had been summoned by his watchers, fired upon them, doing them no harm, and merely exciting their derision.

Before continuing the narrative of the Algerians' raid on Heimey—by far the most disastrous part of their Icelandic expedition—it may be well to consider the scene of this incident in some little detail, as it is one which offers many peculiarities, and a knowledge of which serves to explain certain subsidiary events. The Westman Isles, of which

Heimey alone is inhabited, lie about seven miles off the south coast of Iceland, from which they are separated by a strait full of devious and erratic currents. The coastline opposite them is one of the most inhospitable in northern Europe, on account of the vast level stretches of black volcanic dust, known as the Rangar Sands, which fringe it, and on which a tremendous surf breaks almost continually. It is only possible for even small boats to land on this part of Iceland when the wind is from the north, driving back the surf from the shore. The writer has been delayed for three weeks on Heimey, in early autumn, before it was possible to cross the strait. Heimey itself has an area of about four square miles, or rather less, and at present supports some five hundred and twenty inhabitants, who live on the proceeds of fishing and fowling, the latter industry being of great importance to them. The majority of the people, now as in the seventeenth century, live together near the northern extremity of the island, their village being built on the south shore of a narrow bay, which still affords a harbour to small vessels, though its mouth is dangerous, owing to the rocks which beset it, in anything but very calm weather. This bay is only separated from the strait by a line of magnificent bird-cliffs, which cling on to the rest of the island in a very curious way by a level isthmus, not much more than a hundred yards wide, almost opposite the village. Behind the houses, the land slopes gently up to the flanks of Helga Fell, a shapely cone of scoriae and ashes whose lower parts produce a scanty vegetation, contrasting with the naked blackness of the peak. Further inland, uneven, hummocky pasturage, wild moors, with jagged lumps of lava protruding at every turn, and patches swept bare by the wind, combine to form a dreary and somewhat desolate landscape, unshadowed by trees, un-

HEIMARKLETTEN FROM HELGAFELL, WESTMAN ISLANDS

[To face p. 80

PINNACLE ROCKS ON NORTH SIDE, WESTMAN ISLANDS

[*To face p. 81*

watered by streams. Where the lava has been removed from the soil and on the summit of the cliffs, which have been fertilized by countless generations of puffins and fulmars, the grass is very green; for the climate is moist and Heimey enjoys the highest mean temperature in Iceland. All round the coast of the 'Home Isle,' precipitous cliffs, worn and fretted into the most fantastic shapes, alternate with coal-black shores and banks of volcanic ash, while the other islands of the groups are mere rocks and skerries, which offer a resting-place to myriads of sea-fowl, and in some instances produce sufficient vegetation on their summit to feed a few sheep throughout the year. On some of them a company of fowlers camp out during the fowling season, and all of them are visited, should the weather permit, at least once a year, in order that birds or eggs may be taken on them.

But to return to the Algerians. While Bagge and the men who had landed were demonstrating against one another, Morad's ship was making its way round the island to the harbour, the wind having suddenly changed, as it frequently does in the Westman Isles. When this was discovered, the Danes determined on flight. Bagge spiked his cannons and made off with his family in a small boat which happened to be launched in the bay. Henrik Thomsen, the captain of the Danish ship that lay at anchor, waiting its cargo (but Björn of Scardsá calls it a war-ship), attempted in vain to sink it, and then followed the other fugitives in a yawl. Morad fired upon them, but without hitting either boat, and they reached the Rangar Sands, on which their boats were overturned in the surf and their oars broken, so that they escaped alive with difficulty.

After demonstrating for some hours, the raiders who had

already landed divided themselves into three parties, the largest of which is variously computed by different eye-witnesses to have numbered 150 or 200 men. The first company marched right across the island to the village, and seized the house wherein the Danes had shut themselves. They bound all their prisoners, and hurried on. Another company looted the Landakírk or Parish Church, and amused themselves by ringing the bells, dressing up in the priest's vestments, and finally setting fire to the church. The third company visited the manse of the priest Olaf Eigilsson[1], to whose 'Travels' I have referred, and, having seized and bound him, his wife and his family, hurried them all off to the Danish agent's house, in which there were already many prisoners. Olaf, rather ungenerously, blames his wife as the cause of his captivity, for he says that they would have permitted him to go free, as he was an old man and made no attempt to defend himself, had not she foolishly begged to be allowed to remain with him. He says also that he thought that the raiders were Englishmen, until he noticed their turbans.

The man-hunt now became scattered, for the island of Heimey, small as it is, contains many hiding-places, especially in certain peculiar caves, or rather tunnels, which open to the surface in the wilder parts of the island by more or less perpendicular shafts. They are of various sizes and appear to be due to the action of gases bursting forth in some ancient volcanic disturbance, their mouths being often surrounded with fantastically contorted lava rocks. The cliffs, too, provide many a ledge which none but a man exercised in the hazardous art of the fowler

---

[1] At that date there were two priests in the island, now there is only one.

BEE-HIVE HUT, FORMERLY USED FOR DRYING STOCKFISH, ICELAND

[*To face p. 83*

could reach in safety; but the pirates, being seamen bred, could climb better than most people, and did not hesitate to shoot down those natives who had scrambled beyond their reach. On such a ledge, on the face of the cliff called Dalfjall, the ruins of a small beehive-shaped hut, in which the people of the island formerly dried their stockfish beyond the range of the flies that swarm round the houses, are still pointed out as the scene of several murders of the kind. One of the larger tunnels, on the other hand, is known as the 'Cave of the Hundred Men,' because a hundred persons are said to have remained hidden in it for the three days in which the raid was consummated. It consists of two narrow passages, now so blocked with sand that it is impossible to stand upright in either, the one eighty feet in length and the other about forty, and opening to the surface at an incline by a common mouth, which is so well concealed by the rocks surrounding it that it can only be discovered by a most careful comparison of prominent points in the neighbouring cliffs.

Another cave is shown as the scene of the murder of the priest Jón Thorsteinsson—the 'Martyr,' as he is still called—whose psalms and sacred songs are much admired in Iceland. Björn's account of his death is so direct and so simple that I cannot do better than give a literal translation of it:

'The other priest,' he says, 'who was that famous bard Jón Thorsteinsson, fled from his homestead at Kirkeboe, with his wife Margrjet and his daughters and his son and all his family, to a certain pile of rocks by the sea, into a cave below the cliff. And when he was come therein he read to his folk, and exhorted them and comforted them; and at length he read a litany. Among these folks was an old man, named Snorri Eyjolfsson[1], who had given the priest charge over his property. He would not go into the cave, though the priest bade him in, but remained ever before its mouth. After a while, the priest went to the outer part of the cave, and there he saw that blood ran in at the opening; and then he hied him out, and saw that Snorri lay headless at the door of the cave; for the raiders had seen him and had shot off his head, and he had been to them a signal to the cave. Then Jón went within again, telling this hap; and he bade his folk beseech Almighty God to succour them. Forthwith thereafter these noisy hounds stood over the cave, so that he heard their footfall. "Margrjet, they are coming," he said, "Lo, I will go to meet them without fear!" He prayed that God's grace might not leave her. But while the words were in the saying, the bloodthirsty hounds came to the cave's mouth and would search it, but the priest went out to meet them. Now when they saw him, one of them said, "Why art thou here, Sir Jón? Ought'st not to be at home in thy church?" He answered, "I was there this morning." Then said the murderer, "Thou wilt not be there to-morrow morning," and thereafter he cut him on the head to the bone. The priest stretched out his hand and said, "I commit me to my God. That thou doest, do freely!" The wretch then struck him another blow. At this he cried out, saying, "I commit me to my Lord Jesus Christ." Then Margrjet, the priest's wife, cast herself at the feet of the tyrant, and clung to them, thinking that his heart would be softened; but there was no pity in these monsters. Then the scoundrel struck

---

[1] It was formerly the custom in Iceland for aged persons to give over all their property to the care of some responsible person, who undertook in return to provide them with the necessaries of life and a comfortable home. Snorri had done this to Sira Olaf.

a third blow. The priest said, "That is enough. Lord Jesus receive my soul!" Then the foul men cleft his skull asunder. Thus he lost his life. His wife took the linen cloth from his head and kissed his brow, but they dragged her and her daughter from the corpse, and bound her son with the other folk that were there, and hurried them to the Danish house. There was a little rift, higher up in the cliff than where these folk lay, and two women were hidden therein, who saw and heard all these things.'

There can be little doubt that Jón Thorsteinsson's murderer was the Icelander Thorstein, who had acted as guide to the raiders, though Björn hesitated to brand an Iceland traitor by name. The anonymous editor of the Reykjavik edition of Björn's 'Story of the Turkish Raid' adds a note to his author's account of the murder, to the effect that Thorstein had been the priest's servant, and, having been rebuked by him for immorality, had sworn to be revenged upon him. Björn himself tells us that on board Morad's ship a man confessed to Margrjet that he had been her husband's bane, and that it was noticed that during the voyage the guilty wretch was continually begging for water from the prisoners' allowance in which to wash his hands. 'As if washing could cleanse him from so great a sin,' the annalist indignantly exclaims.

During July 17 and 18 some two hundred and forty prisoners were taken on Heimey, and thirty-four persons were killed, being either shot on the cliffs or burned in their houses. As a rule, children were treated kindly; for the Moors did not wish to prejudice them against a free profession of Islam; but a few infants were thrust into the fires which were consuming their homes.

On the morning of the nineteenth the priest Olaf Eigilsson was taken on board Morad's ship, and was questioned about a treasure which was said to have been hidden on Heimey. He declared that his people had no money, but was savagely bastinadoed to make him confess. Probably Morad had heard some rumour of the legendary 'Herjolf's gold,' for which the people of Heimey still search whenever they have nothing else to do. The story goes that a certain Herjolf, the first Norse settler on the Westman Isles, had gained large sums of money by selling the water of the only spring on Heimey, of which he had taken possession, to his neighbours during a drought. He had a daughter named Vilborg, who was as charitable as he was avaricious, and who used to give away the water to poor people without his knowledge. Vilborg had a tame raven, which she had found wounded and had cared for until it recovered its powers of flight; and one day, while she was sitting outside her father's house and making hide shoes, this raven seized a shoe which she had just finished and flew off with it, alighting a short distance away. Vilborg pursued the bird, which always flew on just as she had nearly rescued her handiwork, until she had gone a considerable distance from home. Then there was an earthquake, and her father was buried beneath a cliff, which fell on his house, with all his illgotten treasure; but the daughter was preserved on account of her charity. The rocks among which Herjolf is said to have stabled his ponies are still shown, and the only perennial spring on Heimey, or rather the pool in which it comes to the surface, is still called Vilpá, after Vilborg.

So much for the Westman treasure, which the raiders did not find. On July 19 they gave up the search and sailed for Algiers, having first captured a Danish vessel, which sailed into the harbour as they left it, and having transferred their prisoners to her hold.

THE ALGERIANS IN ICELAND 87

On the voyage Asta, the wife of Einar Loptsson (a man who has left an account of his sufferings in captivity), gave birth to a son, who was christened Jón, in memory of the Martyr, by the priest Olaf. When the pirates heard the baby cry they were much amused, and gave its mother two old skirts to make it clothes. Two other babies were born before they reached Algiers; two women died, and a man hanged himself. Off the coast of Spain six other Moorish vessels were spoken, and they all entered the Straits of Gibraltar together on September 11, reaching their destination either on the seventeenth or the nineteenth of the same month. The Icelandic captives were sold in the city of Algiers, very much in the same way as their fellows had been sold in Kyle two months earlier; but before the sale the Pasha of Algiers chose out eight women and children, and Morad received two slaves, either women or children.

Many of the Icelanders suffered persecution for their religion in Algiers; being chained in insupportable positions, beaten on the hands and faces, exposed naked in public places, and again beaten until they lost the power of speech. Under these torments over a hundred persons, many of whom were children, renounced the faith of their fathers. Others, who were not publicly misused, suffered much hardship at the hands of their masters, or more commonly at those of their mistresses; for, as Cervantes observed when he was a prisoner among the Moors, the Algerian women were allowed far greater liberty in the presence of Christian slaves than in that of men of their own creed. Many of the prisoners, however, were bought by persons who treated them kindly, permitting them to work or beg in their spare time to obtain money with which to purchase their freedom. Among these more fortunate ones was Einar Loptsson, whose account of his 'misery and oppression' has been preserved. His master was a Moor named Abraham, who was fond of him and treated him well. Abraham had a concubine of whose existence his wife was unaware; and, unfortunately for Einar, he gave him to this woman. She bade him draw water from a certain fountain, which, as she had forgotten, no Christian was permitted to approach, the punishment for any but a Mahommedan who went under an iron chain that hung over the entrance of the courtyard being death.

Thinking no harm, Einar entered the forbidden courtyard, where he was seized by a soldier on guard and dragged before the Council, which was then sitting in the palace to which the courtyard belonged. When it was understood that the prisoner was an ignorant Icelander, who knew no language but his own, he was reprieved from the legal penalty of his offence and was cast into prison, where he was chained to a heavy log of wood. For five days he was persecuted by the gaoler and a French renegade, who endeavoured to make him an apostate by very forcible means. Finally, finding it impossible to pervert his faith, the renegade was persuaded to cut off his nose with a sword and otherwise to mutilate his face. They then gathered up the pieces of flesh that had been severed and rubbed them over his naked shoulders. Thus disfigured, he was paraded through the streets and then given back to his master Abraham.

It is pleasant to learn that Einar, in spite of his disfigurement, not only returned to the Westman Isles, but married, on the very day on which he landed on Heimey, a woman who had shared his captivity in Algiers; his first wife having died shortly after they reached Africa. Moreover, he was able to exult over the fate of the guard who arrested him, and even over that of the prison in which he was confined, though the gaoler and the French renegade appear to have gone unpunished. He tells us that shortly after his arrest the guard was convicted of assault on a little Moorish boy, and was condemned to have all his limbs broken and to be exposed for two nights; while the prison was blown up with gunpowder in a riot caused by the unauthorized return of certain renegades, who had been banished from the city for talking treason over their cups.

In the five years of captivity which followed Einar's return to his master's house he managed to save one hundred and twenty rix-dollars, with which he purchased his freedom. He had also laid by a further sum as a provision for the journey home; but this he lost by imprudently lending it to an Englishman, and so was forced to wait for another five years before an opportunity of going back to Iceland occurred to him. During this period he made a living in Algiers by knitting woollen caps and by distilling brandy. His position as a freedman also gave him an opportunity of befriending other Icelandic captives less fortunate than himself, and he persuaded his old master to take into his house an old Icelandic lady, who had been cast out into the streets to die, no longer fit for work.

Einar was not the first of the prisoners to return to Iceland, for in the year following the raid, the priest Olaf Eigilsson, of the Westman Isles, was permitted to leave Algiers on board an Italian ship, in order to carry a petition to the King of Denmark begging for one thousand two hundred rix-dollars, for which sum the Algerians had agreed to set all their Icelandic captives free. He has left a most curious account of his time in Algiers (and especially of his visit to Italy on his way to Copenhagen), in which he dwells at considerable length upon the green marble churches and the religious processions of Leghorn, and upon the dress and luxury of the Italian women and the destitution of the Italian beggars. Like a true Icelander, he compares the Algerian with the Icelandic ponies; but he tells us very little about Algiers itself. The 'Turks' gave him a letter, bidding any of their captains who might chance to capture the vessel in which he sailed not to molest him. He expresses astonishment that not even the Archbishop of Copenhagen could read this epistle, which was probably kept as an heirloom in his family, and may very possibly still exist in some Icelandic farmhouse occupied by his descendants.

In the year 1633, at Whitsuntide, the schoolboy Jón Jónsson, who had been taken prisoner at Grindavik by the Kyleans, wrote home from Algiers, whither he had been brought from Kyle, describing his life in Africa and begging his friends to ransom himself and his brothers; his mother and his uncles having already obtained their liberty through a Dutchman's generosity. The letter was sent to Iceland in care of a man named Bededicsson, who had been captured on board a Hamburg ship and had been ransomed by his people.

One passage from Jón's letter is worth translating, as showing the Moors' opinion of the Icelanders. It runs as follows:—'The Turks say that Iceland folk are better than other folk, least given to rascality of all men, obedient and true to their masters. Therefore have their captains consulted together to take only young persons of about twenty years, of which captains that poisonous dragon, Morad Flamming, whose memory remains in hell, is the most blood-and-soul-thirsty. Formerly he took folk in the west country and on the Isles, and now, in the year 1632 of our Lord, was this said captain come on his way to

Iceland with two other ships; but because he took a strong ship off England, he turned back, and so, by God's grace, was stayed from his purpose.'

Meanwhile a public subscription was being raised in Iceland, and the King of Denmark had contributed a large sum of money towards the ransoming of Icelandic prisoners in the Barbary States. So, in the summer of 1637, thirty-four persons were set at liberty, out of between three and four hundred who had been captured in Iceland. Of these thirty-four persons, six died on the way home.

Such was the 'Turkish Raid on Iceland,' as it was depicted by the sufferers and their contemporaries and friends; even at the present day it has lost little of its horror in the eyes of their descendants. During six weeks' stay on Heimey in 1898 my friend and I heard almost daily of it.

It is sometimes said that the dark-skinned, black-haired element in the populations of Iceland and the Faroes is due to intermixture with the Barbary pirates; but there does not appear to be one particle of evidence for any such theory. In the first place, we must remember that there was a dark strain in the Scandinavians, probably due to marriage with the aboriginal inhabitants of what now is the coast of Norway, from the earliest historical times, and, in the second, that the Scandinavian chieftains who colonized Iceland and the Faroes had certainly mixed to a great extent with the peoples of Ireland and the Hebrides before Iceland was discovered. As I have shown in a former chapter, it is further probable that members of some 'Iberian' race reached the Faroes at a later date. And even if the Algerians, as is probable, did make a few of the Icelandic women their wives or concubines, it is practically impossible that this could have affected the population of Iceland at the present day. It is extremely unlikely that the few Icelandic women who returned from captivity to their native land, would have been permitted to take with them their children by Mahommedan fathers, and even supposing that they were allowed to do so, nearly all these women belonged to the Westman Isles, where hardly a baby survived for a fortnight after its birth until quite recent times. It is only within the last few decades that proper sanitary precautions put a stop to the fearful mortality from infantile lockjaw which formerly occurred in many of the small islands of north-western Europe and was especially rife on Heimey.

As regards the Faroes, there are several legends of a 'Turkish' raid current among the people. It is said that the corsairs visited Naalsoe once when all the men were away at sea. They took the women and hurried them aboard their ships, but the women preferred to die and cast themselves into the waves. Then the 'Turks' drew their swords and cut off the women's breasts in the water, so that they sank and died, and the sea was red with their blood when their men came home. But I cannot find any proof that any such event really occurred.

We may say, therefore, that it is most improbable that any trace of Algerian blood exists in the Icelander or the Faroeman of to-day, though it is quite possible that, as a result of the Algerians' raid on Iceland and the capture of occasional Icelanders in other ways, there is a small Icelandic element in the very mixed population of Algeria, in which individuals of almost all the races of modern Europe must have lived and married, in addition to the native Berbers and the Arab conquerors, not to mention the Romans and other peoples of antiquity.

CHAPTER IV

THE BIRD-CLIFFS OF THE WESTMAN ISLES

The position and extent of the Westman Isles or Vestmannaeyjar have been noted already; the present chapter deals with their most remarkable feature—the marine cliffs on which the islanders practise the art of fowling for a livelihood.

Of course these islanders are also fishermen; but even now their fisheries are still undeveloped, and it is only a few years since, long lines with a number of hooks were introduced to their notice by the captain of an English steam liner. Before this they had only hand-lines, with which they caught quite sufficient fish for their own wants, with some over for preservation and export and for the preparation of oil.

They have also a considerable number of sheep, a few cows, and a few horses; but of these the sheep are the only animals of real importance to them, for the cows, owing to the poor pasturage on the level ground (which is all they can reach), afford little milk, and the distances on the only inhabited island are too short to make pack or riding-ponies more than a luxury to them.

The population is concentrated in the village near the north end of Heimey, of which an account will be given later, but there are a few farms, including the priest's, near the other end of the island. The history of the people has been a peculiar one, for few if any of the older generation are island-born. Until recent years brought with them some knowledge of sanitary laws, the children born on Heimey died, as I have noted, almost without exception, of infantile tetanus within a few days of their birth, and the population was constantly recruited from the north of Iceland. That the colonists came from the north is recorded not only in documents but also in the local dialect, for the islanders still talk of a visit to Reykjavik, which lies almost due north of their present abode, as ' going south.' It was probably the custom for certain families in the north of Iceland to send some of their members to catch birds in the Westman Isles, and there were other reasons why the resident population should be derived from this part of the country.

The people of the district of Rangarval, which lies exactly opposite Heimey, are very poor and obtain a large part of their supply of cods' heads, which they are sometimes forced to eat in winter instead of bread, from the Westman folk; but constant intercourse is prevented, though the distance is short, by the peculiarity of the coast alluded to in the preceding chapter. It is girt by vast stretches of fine black sand, thrown out at one time or another by Hecla and other volcanoes. These stretches are nearly flat, being only raised sufficiently for a heavy surf to break upon them; and they are constantly changing in position and extent. At many points they do not actually constitute part of the beach, but are separated from it by a shallow lagoon. To walk and wade through them and the lagoon is an exertion which one can only appreciate by experience, and to drag a boat down to the sea entails enormous labour; but the Rangarval fishermen must endure the labour whenever a chance of fishing occurs. This is only possible when a north wind is blowing, as the surf is then calmed down and kept away from the sands. Such difficulties, then, have proved sufficiently great to put a stop to frequent visits from the island to the mainland, and the cods' heads are only carried across the straits when there is some additional reason for attempting the voyage; for example, when a party of women are to be ferried over to help their neighbours in Rangarval with their hay or their shearing. A party of the kind goes over yearly, and returns with the wages it earns. These are paid in kind, often in sheep, mutton, or wool.

There is more frequent intercourse between Heimey and the east coast of Iceland, which is visited yearly by a large proportion of the younger men and women, who go to assist in the fisheries and fish-curing. There they meet large numbers of Faroemen, from whom they learn to sing the Farish ballads; but racial antipathy seems too strong to allow intermarriage, for the Icelanders have long regarded the Faroemen as socially inferior to themselves, calling them by such opprobrious names as 'island-shaggies.' Probably the rich smack-owners of the mainland look down almost equally on the young people from the Westman Isles; at any rate they have their own concerns and do not go to Heimey. Local patriotism is a strong influence in Icelandic life and politics, and emigration to America often seems less of a wrench than leaving one district of the home country for another.

The people of Heimey are very simple in their lives and manners, but their houses are generally both cleaner and more comfortable than those of the natives of many parts of the mainland. This may be due in part to the fact that a higher standard of culture has prevailed from the earliest times in the north country than the south, probably because the early settlers who found a home in the north of Iceland belonged to a better class than the adventurers who preceded them and occupied the south of the island. But it is also due to the easy circumstances of the Westman folks themselves, arising from the wealth of life which nature provides on the cliffs of Heimey and the other islands of the group.

In summer time it is the business and in good weather the pleasure of most of the men to be out on the bird-cliffs. All through the day the raucous chatter of the fulmars on the cliff's face mingles with the groans of the puffins, which sit above among the white blossoms of 'Balder's Brow' (a kind of feverfew), forget-me-nots, and the spreading foliage of the angelica, and the guillemots bow to one another solemnly along the ledges. For the bird-cliff must be more than a great crag. The crag must form its base—high, naked, and full of holes and crannies, with wider ridges for some of the birds: above there must be earth and vegetation, among which puffins and shearwaters dig their burrows with beak and claw; below there should be loose stones on the sea-side and moor on the land, for Eider-ducks will breed in either situation. Special conditions there may be for other birds such as the Stormy and Fork-tailed petrels; but these hardly occupy the fowler's thoughts, as they are not of sufficient value to cause him to risk his life in their capture.

With one exception, the bird-cliffs are the property of the Danish Crown. They are rented annually by the richer inhabitants of the island, some few of whom are wealthy enough to take a whole cliff, while others combine to take one through a syndicate of several members. The rents are not very high, for a good cliff, with which a considerable amount of pasturage for sheep is included, can be had for some 200 krone (between £12 and £13) a year. The only expense in connexion with it but the

CLIFFS ON SOUTH SIDE OF HEIMEY, WESTMAN ISLANDS

[*To face p. 96*

rent is the cost of ropes, and this varies greatly with the height and other characters of the crag.

On most of the cliffs a number of hired fowlers are employed; but they receive their wages entirely in kind, getting one-third of all the birds but fulmars that they kill, and two-thirds of the fulmars.

The one rock which belongs to the community is an isolated skerry called Sulnasker (Gannet Skerry) or Almenningasker; the latter name explains itself. The birds from this skerry, which is rarely visited more than twice, or at most three times, in a year, are distributed as follows:—They are divided into sixty equal shares, of which forty-eight go to the crown tenants on Heimey, the priest, in virtue of his glebe, ranking as equal to four ordinary tenants; four go to the fowlers who climb the rock, four to the boatmen who take them to its base, two to the poor, and two to the two constables, who are appointed by the sheriff to keep order in the village and to wake up those who are to start early for the bird-cliffs or the fishing.

Some seven years ago strict laws were made limiting the season and methods of capture in the case of different birds, and it was enacted that a list of the numbers of each species which were killed should be provided by the fowlers for the sake of reference. The last part of the law is followed in the letter rather than the spirit; a list is provided but it is not a true one—not because of any intentional falsification, but merely because many birds are omitted through carelessness on the part of the islanders, who consider the making of an accurate list a quite unnecessary piece of labour. I have been obliged to rely, unless when it is otherwise stated, on these official lists in giving the number of each kind taken annually, but it is probable that my figures are in such cases much below the true number.

The one offence against the Icelandic bird laws which a native cannot commit with impunity is the slaughter of an Eider-duck. This valuable bird is strictly protected in all Scandinavian countries, and it is specially stated in the Icelandic Act that a man who is actually starving, and can see no other way of obtaining food, may kill and eat one. The fine imposed under any other circumstances is 40 krone—a large sum for an Icelandic farmer or fisherman. What is more important than many laws, namely public opinion, protects the species; and there seems to be a sentimental interest in it which cannot be explained solely by the fact that it is of great commercial value to a comparatively few members of the community: probably it is due in part to the great tameness of the bird, which appears actually to seek the vicinity of a human dwelling for its nesting-place and to frequent those parts of the coast which are most frequented by man.

The drake is a very handsome bird in his nuptial dress, which he only wears for a small part of the year; but at other seasons he is, like the female and young at all times, sober and inconspicuous in his plumage. When the duck is on her nest, especially if it is situated among loose stones, it is almost impossible to detect her, as her back is of exactly the right shade of grey to match her habitual environment, and she crouches very low upon her eggs. The pale grey down, with which we stuff our bed-quilts, is quite hidden beneath the coarser and stiffer feathers which cover it, and probably protects the bird herself during the time she spends on the surface of the sea, besides retaining the warmth round her eggs, of which she lays a considerable number in a clutch. The young birds only stay among it for a time which probably might be numbered in minutes, and the drake has also a waistcoat of similar, if coarser and darker, down upon his breast.

It is illegal to sell Eider-ducks' eggs in Iceland, but they may be collected by the tenant of a bird-cliff or other land, and may be given away. This law is openly violated, and the eggs are usually sold on Heimey for 10 öre each. They have rather a fishy taste, but are esteemed a luxury in Iceland. It would really be difficult to tell the difference, from a gastronomic point of view, between them and the eggs of domestic ducks which had been allowed to find a living for themselves on the sea-shore. The Icelanders, however, declare them altogether superior.

The eggs and down are collected at a few points at the base of the Heimey cliffs every summer; but there is no regular cider-farm, like those which exist in other parts of Iceland, on the Westman Isles. It is well known that the Eider-duck makes its nest out of the down from its own breast; forming a circular mound, beautifully regular in shape, out of this substance, which has the property of retaining heat in a marked degree. She plucks out the down with her beak. If it is removed she provides a second, sometimes even a third supply in the same manner and from the same source, which then becomes exhausted. When this occurs the drake gives his down, which can be distinguished by its colour. It was formerly the custom to take away all the down supplied by the female; but this practice was said to lead to great mortality among the ducks through exhaustion, and nowadays each nest is generally rifled only once before the eggs are hatched, and then again after the young birds have left it.

The Icelandic cider-farms are frequently situated on

little islands off the coast. The most favourable situations are those which are not liable to be flooded, but in which the ground is covered with the low hummocks so characteristic of unworked land in Iceland. Small circular or oblong erections of rough stones are made among these hummocks, to protect the brooding ducks from wind and driving rain, and bells are sometimes suspended near them, under the belief that their sound, as they are rung by the wind, attracts the birds.

All the seafowl on these farms become exceedingly tame, as no gun is allowed to be fired and everything liable to disturb the ducks is carefully banished. Those who know how to handle them can even stroke the backs of the ducks as they sit on their eggs. I have seen a body of Arctic terns, which nested among the pebbles on the shore of an eider-farm near Reykjavik, attacking some cows which had wandered near their nests. They even darted down and pecked at the beasts' backs and legs. The same birds swooped down on the party to which I belonged with such violence that we were obliged to protect our eyes with our hands; they struck our heads both with their wings and their beaks. The very Phalaropes, generally among the shyest of sea-birds, allowed us to approach quite close to them on this island.

On such farms there is a separate building or large room entirely devoted to cleaning the down. The apparatus consists of a series of oblong wooden frames, which may be either fixed in a horizontal position or held in the hand. Their number and size varies greatly, but in all cases the principle is the same, depending on the tenacity with which the down clings to anything on which it is thrown, partly because of its lightness and partly because of the structure of the individual feathers which compose it.

Along the frames are stretched, rather loosely, a number of strings which may be either of twine or of thongs of leather. The down is cast on to these near one end, and a spatula of wood or bone is drawn briskly backwards and forwards over the other end. The down still clings to the strings, but all impurities, such as pieces of seaweed or grass, small stones, or coarse feathers, fall through to the ground.

The lightness of cider-down is well known, this quality, combined with its power of retaining heat, giving it commercial value. A number of nests are therefore necessary to produce even a small quantity, and the storekeeper on Heimey will give as much as 8 krone[1] a Danish pound for well-cleaned down, while it fetches even larger prices in other parts of Iceland and is much more expensive in Great Britain.

The form of the Eider-duck, but always with some slight difference, is believed on Heimey to be one of the shapes taken by the *sjóskrimsli* or sea-goblins, which are still said to come ashore at night to fight with men, having the power of taking any appearance they please or even of remaining invisible. Debes tells a story of a girl who was decoyed away to the spirits by an apparition of a duck in the Faroes.

The Eider-duck is not a very common bird in the Westman Isles, and the puffin or Sea-parrot is very much more important to the islanders. According to the official lists as many as thirty-one or thirty-two thousand puffins are killed every summer in the Westman Isles, and it would probably be safe to estimate their true number as nearer forty thousand.

The puffin is a stout little bird, black above and white below. In the breeding-season it has very bright red legs

[1] 100 öre = 1 krone = 1s. 1½d. ; 9 Danish pounds = 10 lb. avoir.

and its beak is very large and brilliantly coloured. In autumn, however, the ornamental part of the beak is cast off bodily. This must materially alter the appearance of the bird, but as it goes far away from land as soon as the breeding-season is over, specimens not in full breeding plumage or in an altogether immature condition, in which the beak is still quite small, are very rarely seen, and are scarce even in our best museums.

Through June, July, and August the puffins sit in tens of thousands all along the tops of the cliffs and on the little hummocks which cover the slopes above the crags. It is necessary for them to choose an exalted position, because the length of their wings prevents them from raising themselves into the air directly. By the end of September, when the young are fledged, they are away to sea, and hardly a specimen remains on the islands.

In foggy weather one can approach them and even sit down among them above the crags; but when the day is clear they are far more alert. Bolt upright they sit, many of them still holding little rows of fishes in their beaks; and they groan together audibly. Should a man intrude upon them on a fine day, they begin to look self-conscious at once. They turn their heads in a furtive way and glance sideways at the intruder, and then they turn them away again as if nothing was the matter; they stretch their wings just as a tired man stretches his arms, they preen their feathers, they become silent, they put forward their little red legs and strut and waddle up and down in a more and more agitated way. Then, suddenly, as he comes very near, they launch themselves and flit round in bat-like circles. If he remains very still, they soon settle down again; but the slightest movement causes a repetition of the little drama, which is ludicrously human, in the earlier stages of alarm, in its apparent pretence of unconcern. At length the birds become so thoroughly scared that they dash away without looking where they are going; not infrequently they fly straight into a rock, and occasionally do so with such violence that they kill themselves.

When a flock of puffins is surprised on the surface of the sea, the birds are just as much alarmed. If they have a little time to escape, they dive and swim away under the water; but if a steamer comes upon them suddenly, they seem to be unable to make up their minds to this course, and they attempt to fly. The only way that they can do so is to swim along, using their wings as paddles as well as their legs, until they can gain sufficient impetus to raise them into the air. At least this is what appears to take place, for it is probable that they do not intend to use their wings as paddles, but that the length of these organs causes the tips to touch the surface at every stroke until they happen to strike it sufficiently hard, or perhaps rather at the right angle, to lift the unwieldy body to which they are attached. Very often the puffins, after progressing for some distance over the sea in this quadripedal manner, change their minds and dive instead of flying; but equally often they succeed in flying at last.

It is interesting to watch them attempting to reach their burrows from the sea on a windy day. After they have once risen from the surface they are quite at the mercy of the wind and are driven in all directions as it eddies round the cliffs. Under these circumstances they exhibit more skill than would be imagined from their other movements. They take advantage of every lull, and often follow what is by no means the most direct, though it is under the circumstances the easiest, line of approach to their goal. They attempt every possible way, however roundabout, and at length succeed in their purpose through sheer perseverance and pluck, scuttling down their burrows with what looks very like an air of triumph.

The puffin is known both in the Faroes and in the Westman Isles by the old Norse name of *lunda*, from which are probably derived such English place-names as Lundy Island—from *lunda*, a puffin, and *ey*, an island.

It is not difficult to catch this bird. Formerly, before the new laws came into force, the nestlings were hooked out of their holes by means of an iron gaff, and the adults were taken in long nets, which were stretched at night over a large extent of their nesting-ground, so that they flew into them when they came out of their burrows in the morning. These methods are both illegal now, and no one is allowed to kill a young puffin. How important the nestlings were, however, is shown by the fact that there is a special word in southern Icelandic for a young puffin, viz. *pýsjur*; and a considerable amount of poaching undoubtedly still goes on as regards them. They are to the eye mere balls of black down, with narrow black beaks in no way remarkable.

About twenty years ago the storekeeper on Heimey introduced the hand-net (which has been described in a previous chapter) from the Faroes; and it has become the only recognized implement in puffin-catching. It is called *háf* in Icelandic.

The puffin season in the Westman Isles is in June and July, terminating legally at the end of the latter month. During the greater part of it special camps are set up on the less accessible cliffs on Heimey and on some of the other islands, and the fowlers live for some weeks in tents.

THE FOWLING-NET, HEIMEY, WESTMAN ISLANDS

[*To face p. 104*

PUFFIN-CATCHING, ON CLIFFS ABOVE THRAELA-EYDI, HEIMEY, WESTMAN ISLANDS; SHOWING ISTHMUS CONNECTING TWO PARTS OF THE ISLAND, WITH CIRCULAR SHEEP-FOLD UPON IT

[To face p. 105

Each man has his own station at the edge of the cliff, and he catches the birds which fly over him in exactly the same way as the Faroemen do; but he takes all that he can, not excepting those with fish in their beaks, and does not use decoys. His method of killing them is also rather different, for instead of twisting the neck he holds the head in his right hand and rapidly jerks the bird across his chest. The effect is of course the same, the neck being dislocated in either case.

There is generally a little boy in each puffin camp whose duty it is to collect the birds as they are killed and to tie them together by the neck in bunches. Every few days some of the party return to the village, to carry down the birds and to obtain supplies.

As soon as the puffins are brought home the women take them in hand. They are first plucked and then the breastbone with the flesh that adheres to it is cut off, this being the only part of the bird considered edible. All the breasts that are not wanted for immediate consumption are salted and stored in barrels for winter use. The wings, backs, heads and legs are strung together on long ropes and hung in festoons along the garden walls or between poles set up in the gardens. They are thus dried, and when dry are used as fuel. The feathers are carefully dried on trays or mats; some are used locally in making bed-quilts, but the majority are sold for export to the storekeeper, who practically controls all commercial transactions in the island.

A puffin in its natural condition is worth from 5 to 6 öre; after being plucked it is sold for 3 öre. The storekeeper gives from 50 öre to 1 krone a pound, according to its condition, for the down. A pound is produced by about twenty birds.

The Westman folk believe that the puffins are an organized community, with a king, a queen, princes and princesses. The king is pure white and the queen white and yellow, while the princes and princesses are black and white. All these varieties actually occur, representing different degrees of albinoism, and the capture of any of them, especially of a 'puffin king,' is regarded as lucky. I do not think that exactly this superstition exists in the Faroes; indeed, Colonel Fielden tells a totally different story regarding the belief held about white puffins on the island of Skuoe, where he says that they are, or were, protected because they were supposed to have each been the saviour of a man's life. When a man was left on the bird-cliff owing to the sea rising and the boat which brought him being obliged to sheer off, he caught a puffin, plucked it, tied a cord to it, and threw it into the sea. Being cold without its feathers it swam to the boat, and his companions were able to assist him on board with a rope tied to the other end of the string. It was thought that the bird's feathers would be white when they grew in again. In any case, whatever may be the explanation for the superstitious feeling as regards albino puffins in one or other of the islands, it is undoubtedly an interesting instance of that reverence for abnormally white animals which occurs among many different races, one of its most notorious manifestations being the worship paid to the so-called white elephant in Burma and Siam.

To the Westman folk the Fulmar petrel is hardly second in importance even to the puffin. In 1898, according to statistics collected daily throughout the season, 24,229 young birds of this species were taken in the Westman Isles, and this does not include stray nestlings taken by children. Great emulation exists on this point among the little boys, one of whom, to my own knowledge, brought home over fifty young fulmars in a single season. Moreover, the season of 1898 was a very bad one, for the amount of rain which fell that summer rendered some of the cliffs so slippery that they could not be properly worked. It is probable that quite 30,000 of this species are taken in a good year, including a few which are captured at mid-winter (when they become very tame) in the hand-net.

The fulmar differs in every respect, equally in structure, appearance, and habits, from the puffin. At first sight it may easily be taken for a gull, as its back is grey and its belly white, but a glance at the wings, which are longer in proportion to the girth of the body, or at the abrupt posterior termination of the tail, will readily distinguish between them. An even more important distinction, which cannot always be seen when the birds are on the wing, is that the nostrils of the fulmar, instead of being mere slits, are enclosed in a pair of tubular chambers—a characteristic feature of the petrels and their allies the albatrosses. Some naturalists recognize two kinds of fulmars as occurring in the north-west Atlantic, one of them having darker plumage on the back than the other; but they are probably mere varieties of the same species, or the difference may be due to age. Both are common in the Westman Isles.

Even in the Westman Isles there are traditions that the fulmar was not always an indigene.

In early summer the female lays a pair of eggs, one of which is frequently addled, on the bare cliff, generally in such a position that the young bird can retire for shelter from the elements into some cranny in the rock. It is fed by the parents, which put their beaks down its throat and regurgitate the food they have swallowed.

As it approaches maturity, the parents leave it much to

itself, deserting it to circle gracefully round the crags, alighting now and then upon some jutting rock to screech and chatter with outstretched neck and gaping beak. Not infrequently it takes the opportunity of their absence to flutter over the edge of the cliff. Sometimes it is drowned or dashed to pieces, but more often it lands in safety and is caught by the children, who hunt stray birds of the kind with dogs.

The best way to observe the old fulmars on Heimey at their ease is to go out in a boat on the bay to the north of Thraela-eydi. In this bay Norwegian whalers are in the habit of anchoring the whales they have killed, until it may be convenient to tow them to their whaling station on the mainland of Iceland; and these whales form a great attraction to the fulmars, which drive away any other birds that might wish to share the feast provided for them. They cannot pierce the whale's skin to get at the blubber which they seem to know it covers, but it is all scored with their attempts. The wound of the harpoon, which is often exposed as the whales float belly upwards, gives them an advantage, and they scoop up the oily exudation from the surface of the water. They are peculiarly attracted by the blubber, for they are so fond of any food of an oily nature that they are said to be obliged to eat a kind of sorrel, which usually grows on the cliffs they haunt, in order to counteract the physiological effects of a diet consisting wholly or mainly of fatty substances. The story appears to be founded on the authority of ornithologists, but I cannot vouch for it personally.

When the fulmars cannot get at the whale itself they are obliged to content themselves with the parasites which infest it.

These are of several kinds, depending in some cases on

the species of the whale; for barnacles flourish on some species and will not grow on others. On those whales which are favourable for their development there are usually two kinds of barnacles, which are especially numerous on the chin. Only one of them is directly parasitic on the whale, while the other is parasitic on the parasite, or at any rate grows often upon it. The former is the crown barnacle (*Coronula diadema*), which in appearance somewhat resembles the acorn barnacles common on rocks in the sea, except that it reaches about two and a half inches in diameter. It has no stalk, but consists, so far as can be seen when it is out of water, of a dull white shell, opening by a fleshy bag above and having its base firmly adherent to and even embedded in the skin of the whale. The other barnacle is the eared species known to zoologists as *Conchoderma auritum*. It only grows on the shell of the crown barnacle, never directly on the whale's skin, but sometimes on that of large fish. It consists of a stalk, which hangs down in the water, and of a head, in which most of the important organs of the animal are contained; externally the head is provided with a pair of ear-like processes. The function of these structures is unknown[1]; they hang down below and on each side of the opening through which the barnacle extends the arms that catch the organisms on which it feeds.

As the barnacles die in the sun, both species begin to spread out their arms, and the fulmars then have a chance of pulling them from their shells and devouring them. The shell of the eared form has a leathery consistency, with hard plates embedded in it. The integument is of a very dark purplish brown, mottled with white and glazed with a peculiar blue iridescence.

[1] Darwin suggests that they aid in respiration.

Another whale parasite on which the fulmars feed is the so-called whale-louse or *Cyamus*, a small, pallid, angular crustacean, which clings firmly to the smoothest surface by means of its sharp claws, especially affecting the deep folds beneath the chin of many kinds of whales. The birds become so intent upon searching it out that they can often be driven from the whale only by blows.

Sometimes, on the same bay as that in which the whales are anchored, they have an opportunity of indulging in a feast so bountiful that they can afford to share it with other seafowl. The bay gives on the straits which separate Heimey from Rangarval, and when certain conditions prevail in these straits enormous numbers of small crustaceans, known to science as *Euthemisto crassicornis*, are churned up to the surface, on which they float—still living, but unable to sink owing to the expanded gases in their tissues. They belong to the same group as the sand-hoppers and are identical with a form dredged up by Professor Sars from a considerable depth off the coast of Norway. There are specimens in the University Museum at Cambridge which I procured at Thraela-eydi, and which Mr. A. O. Walker and Dr. H. J. Hanson have kindly examined. What factors influence their appearance I do not know; the Heimey people say that it depends upon the condition of the wind, but possibly it may be due to submarine volcanic activity, which is known to exist in the neighbourhood. Possibly, however, it may be brought about solely by the meeting of currents in the straits, for a somewhat analogous phenomenon occurs in the Straits of Messina, where it has been properly investigated. Deep-sea fish [1] with luminous organs and other peculiar forms have also been found floating off the Westman Isles.

[1] See note at end of volume.

When the crustaceans come up the whole sea appears as if covered by the cast down of young sea-fowls. It is of a pale yellow colour, with which the grey beach is tinged as the tide goes out; amongst the mass the staring red eyes of the little animals can be distinguished on a close inspection, the remainder being composed of their bodies and limbs.

Fulmars, Kittiwakes, Eider-ducks, and 'Odin's chickens' (*Phalaropus hyperboreus*) swarm to the bay to partake of the heaven-sent feast, and soon entirely hide the surface of the water with their bodies. But, sooner or later, a Robber-gull or Great skua descends among them; and then the Eider-ducks swim off, followed by their ducklings, the Phalaropes and Kittiwakes take to their wings, and only the fulmars are left to share with it; for the 'foul-gull'— and this is the literal meaning of *ful-mar*—fears no bird of the air or the sea.

The origin of its name and its immunity from attack is a peculiar habit which it shares with many other petrels, namely that of spitting at any aggressor a large quantity of oily liquid with an extremely disagreeable and penetrating odour, which resembles that of a mixture of putrid fish and cod-liver oil. This power it exercises, to all appearance, not only on members of its own species (and on men who interfere with it) but even on smaller birds such as puffins. I have often seen both fulmars and puffins with the breasts of the peculiar yellow which the substance produces on white feathers, and have watched the old fulmars fighting with one another.

The fulmar is too active and powerful a bird, at any rate in summer, to be netted, and the young are taken from the nest just before they would leave it in the natural course of events. This critical period in their history is reached about the middle of August, the season only lasting for about a fortnight or three weeks, as they all appear to be hatched about the same time and are only in good condition for a brief period. The implements used in killing them are a wooden club, locally called *kjepp*, and ropes. The club somewhat resembles a policeman's baton, but is longer; at its base it is provided with a leather thong, by means of which it is suspended from the belt or the wrist of the fowler, leaving him at full liberty to use both hands in climbing. At one time an iron gaff was often fixed to one end of the club and was used in hooking out young birds of different kinds from holes and burrows; but this is not done now. The ropes are of great length, made of the best hemp, and all imported.

On Heimey it is usual for six or seven men to go out to kill fulmars together, and on the other islands the party is often larger. In all cases several of the fowlers carry the ropes wound round their bodies, and each man has his *kjepp*. On account of the disgusting habits of the bird special garments are worn, which are more picturesque than is usually the case with the clothes of Icelandic men. They are always made of woollen cloth or knitted material, tight-fitting, old and often ragged, stained in yellow patches with the fulmar's oil, very malodorous. The most peculiar part of the outfit is the mittens worn by the men when handling ropes, whether at sea or on the cliff. They are shaped like a baby's mittens, with one compartment for the four fingers and another for the thumb; but the curious thing about them is that they have two thumb-stalls placed on opposite sides, one in front and one behind, at diagonally opposite corners. They are made in this way because it is found that the thumb-stall wears out before the rest of the mitten, and they can be turned round and worn with what was originally the back on the palm of the hand. They are knitted out of very soft wool which is usually of a brown colour, and are sometimes exported to the Faroes, where this peculiar shape is not in vogue among the local knitters.

When the fulmar-catchers reach the top of the cliff on which they are to work—and they can generally do this from the land side without much difficulty—they separate into smaller parties of from two to six men. Each of these parties works a certain part of the cliff's face, and there is frequently an old man posted at some part where he can see them all, in order that he may call out to them where the most fulmars are and where the rock is rotten. The number in each party depends on the character of the crag, most precautions being necessary where the ledges are covered with vegetation (such as coarse grass, sedum, angelica, feverfew, forget-me-nots, and scurvy grass), which often conceals loose stones but offers a tempting and precarious foothold.

Suppose that they are working in pairs: one man of each pair sits down at the edge of the cliff and manages the rope which assists his comrade, using his body as a stake round which to wind it as he pulls it in and twisting the loose end round his waist for the sake of greater security. The climber may be tied to the rope, or, if he is experienced, may simply swarm up and down it, especially if there are no loose stones on the cliff. As a rule it is twisted round his waist and then round each thigh, and sometimes it is further secured to a leather strap which passes diagonally across his chest. When this is done it is necessary for three or four men to hold the rope above, as the whole of the climber's weight may be suddenly thrown upon it at any moment. Occasionally it is further secured round a stake driven into the ground, or even to an iron staple permanently fixed for the purpose. Should the cliff be very high, the whole party sometimes make their way down it from above, to save the extreme labour of climbing up again after they have descended. In this case the last man to go down must climb without the aid of a rope; but the one just in front of him helps him by guiding his feet on to the ledges and prominences on which he must find a foothold. When this is done the fulmars are thrown over the edge as they are killed, to be gathered up below after the descent, or to be picked off the surface of the water by the boatmen, who wait there for the purpose when the crag rises straight from the sea.

An ingenious, but exhausting manœuvre is practised by climbers whom it is necessary to haul up for any distance. They do not remain passive or attempt to climb as their fellows above drag in the rope, but swing themselves as far as possible off the rock with their feet; and it is only when they have swung out as far as they can that the rope is drawn taut. When this is done over and over again the labour of hauling in is very much decreased.

When the young fulmars see the men approaching them they either flutter over the edge of the rock or else prepare to defend themselves. Those which take the former course are frequently drowned or dashed to pieces, but a large proportion reach the ground in safety, as they are very nearly able to fly. The children and the dogs, should the cliff have a beach at its base, wait to receive them, killing them by biting through the backs of their skulls. Whether the children have learnt from the dogs that this is the best way to kill a fulmar, I do not know; it is certainly reckoned the correct way in the Westman Isles, if only one can approach the birds from behind. This the fowlers can seldom do, and they aim at stunning

YOUNG FULMAR ON THE DEFENSIVE

[*To face p* 115

them before they can spit; for the young birds defend themselves in the same way as the adults and can eject their oil violently to the distance of several feet. Before doing so, however, they puff themselves out in such a way that their apparent size is much increased, they stretch their necks, hiss like snakes, quiver, gurgle and splutter, and finally open their beaks widely, as photographs show—and then out comes the oil.

When the day's fowling is over, that is to say when it is dinner time (about 3 p.m.), the fulmars which have been killed are tied together and brought down to the village, ponies often being sent up to carry them. The women receive them, pluck and clean them, and cut off their heads, wings, and legs. They are then split open, and the fat from the interior of the body is carefully scraped out. When this has been done, a few of the bodies are smoked over a fire of driftwood and are then salted; but the majority are simply packed in casks between layers of salt. Prepared in the former way they are regarded as a great delicacy and form the chief dish at a feast which is held at the end of the birding season. The ones preserved in the more simple manner are mostly kept for winter consumption, and a few are eaten fresh.

The fat is used mainly in two ways, being either boiled down to form oil or, salted and flavoured with spices, eaten with bread instead of butter. It naturally contains a large proportion of water, and though each bird yields (partly under the skin and partly in the inside of the body) what seems a very great amount of fat, ten good fulmars are required to produce a litre of pure oil.

The oil is chiefly used in native-made lamps, a twist of cotton or linen forming the wick. These lamps resemble the Scottish 'crusie' very closely, but are generally rather deeper. The great majority are made of brass; iron, however, is occasionally used. They are sometimes made in the Westman Isles, where there is one in every kitchen, but are frequently brought over from the mainland of Iceland. They give a very poor and flickering light; but it is an interesting fact, of which we had many proofs while on Heimey, that the Icelanders can see better in the dark than we can do. Probably this is due to individual experience gained during the long nights of winter in a country where efficient lighting apparatus is seldom to be got and proper illuminants are costly.

The skin of the fulmar, freshly removed, is said to form an excellent dressing for either cuts, burns, or bruises. The entrails, heads, legs, and feet are carefully dried to be used as fuel. On account of the oil they contain they are valuable for this purpose, especially on an island like Heimey, where there is neither peat nor brushwood and practically all the indigenous fuel is of animal origin—droppings of the sheep and cattle, birds' remains, bones of sharks, skates, and other fishes, and the residue that is over after fish-liver oil has been extracted. Women may sometimes be seen searching along the beach at low tide for the bodies of any fulmars or other petrels which the waves may have cast ashore, in order to use them for this purpose.

The feathers of the fulmar can rarely be freed from all taint of oil, and are therefore of less value than those of the puffin: they are mostly used locally. When clean they are worth from 30 to 50 öre a pound. The birds themselves, plucked, sell for from 10 to 12 öre.

White fulmars, like white puffins, sometimes occur. They are also called 'kings,' and are believed to portend good fortune to their captors.

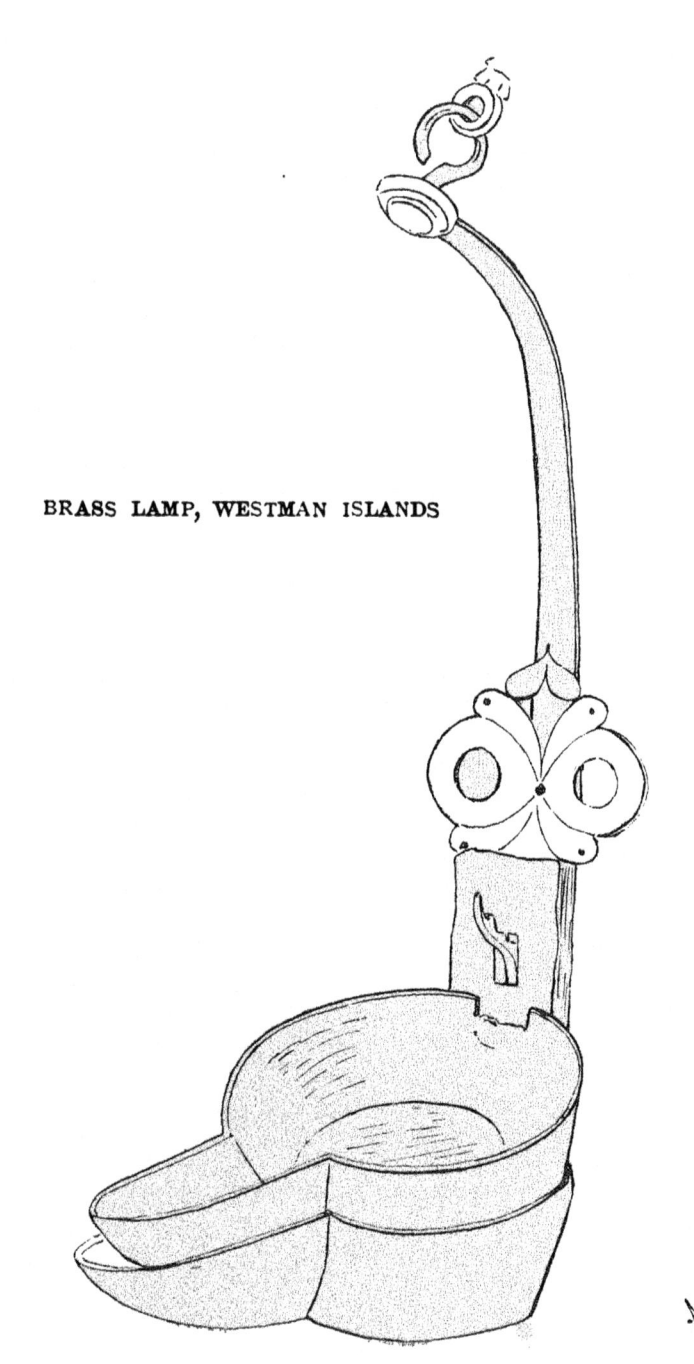

BRASS LAMP, WESTMAN ISLANDS

[*To face p. 116*

HOME FROM SULNASKER, WESTMAN ISLANDS

[To face p. 117

More fulmars are generally killed on Sulnasker than on any other cliff. This skerry, as its name implies, is also a favourite nesting-place of the gannet or Solan-goose, which breeds in large numbers on the Bass Rock and other isolated islets off the coast of Scotland. It does not now nest on Heimey or any of the larger islands of the Westman group, but is confined to a few remote skerries, the most distant of which is Sulnasker.

The rock rises sheer out of the sea some hours' sail, with a good wind, from Heimey, and is regarded as the most dangerous and at the same time the most prolific bird-cliff in the islands. Its being the property of the community causes it to be regarded with considerable sentiment, and it is the focus of some interesting customs and superstitions. The man who climbs it for the first time is bound to treat his comrades on their return, and also to deposit an offering, which usually takes the form of a small coin or an iron nail, in a cairn on the summit. This cairn is called the 'Skerry Priest,' and its legend is as follows:—

Once upon a time two men climbed Sulnasker. They were the first to do so. When they reached the top of the crag they threw themselves down on the grass to rest, and one of them said, 'It is by God's grace that we have come hither!' His comrade replied, 'I had come, whether God willed it or no!' An earthquake immediately shook the impious climber into the sea, but the pious man was held fast by a giant, who was the Skerry Priest. The Skerry Priest then showed him the easiest way to descend, helped him to make a track up the crag, and promised to aid him with his fowling. When the right time came to take the birds the giant would beckon to the people on Heimey; but if they came without his invitation some misfortune overtook them and they got no luck. Every New Year's Eve he came over to Heimey in a stone boat and took supper with the priest at Ofenleiti on the island.

The legend is interesting from several points of view. In the first place it illustrates the truth that similar conditions give rise to similar folklore, no matter how far apart two districts or peoples may be. In other countries where pumice is seen floating on the water legends of stone boats occur, and even in Tahiti one of the native gods was supposed to travel in a craft which was actually a piece of pumice. The similarity of birding customs all over the world is also illustrated. In the edible birds-nest islands of Lower Siam I have seen the fowlers making offerings of a portion of their take—not in a cairn, but before conical stones of a very similar form—and ensuring the neutrality or protection of the spirit of the caves by dedicating to it food and wax tapers before entering them.

There is no preliminary propitiation of the rock spirit in the Westman Isles, new-comers being merely introduced to his favourable notice; but a custom which may be a christianized relic of some such practice persists; for the fowlers, before climbing the crag, recite a special prayer for guidance and safety on the rock. What Victor Hugo says about the rocks off the coast of Brittany in his *Toilers of the Sea* may be considered in this respect, and it may be recalled that in certain of the Outer Hebrides the birding season began with an elaborate ceremony, in which a procession, evidently for the purpose of driving off the spirits, formed an important part. The fine which those who climb a steeple for the first time in Lancashire and other parts of England have to pay also has its bearing on the subject; while the legend of

Trolshoved in the Faroes and of the bullock which haunted it after the death of the troll whose head it was, is worthy of note in the same connexion.

The young gannets are taken on Sulnasker on the first calm day in the third week after the completion of the fulmar season. This usually falls towards the end of September. Owing to the distance of the rock from the Home Isle, it is necessary for the fowlers to start very early in the morning; and the two constables go their rounds calling them and the boatmen long before daybreak. As soon as it is light a boat containing the party sets off from the village, containing, besides the men, fowling and fishing-tackle and rakes, which will be employed in picking up the dead birds from the surface of the sea. A prayer is said for safety on the sea by the helmsman as the boat gets clear of land; all doff their caps and cross themselves, and then resume conversation. A song is often started—generally either the Farish ballad of King Olaf Trigasson or else an Icelandic version of some English music-hall ditty. It is a curious sign of the times how songs of the latter kind fly all round the world. A favourite of the natives of the Malay peninsula, even in remote Patani, is a translation of 'A Bicycle Built for Two,' which is also appreciated by these Westman fowlers, having been adopted into Icelandic as well as Malay.

In the boat there are two men to every oar, one to relieve the other after a short spell of work; and, if the wind be favourable, the sail is soon set. Icelandic seamen, however, prefer, like the Faroemen, to row rather than sail, on account of the treacherous nature of the winds among the islands.

If it is low tide when they reach Sulnasker a party is

landed on a little strip of slippery seaweed at its base, with their clubs and ropes. Should the tide be high, great difficulty is experienced in landing at all. When this has been done, in one way or another, the boat sheers off and its occupants fish round the rock, or even underneath it—for it forms a huge natural arch, under which very large halibut are often taken—while their comrades are upon it. The latter scramble up as best they can to a ledge on which there is room for them to sit in comfort. There they take off their shoes, which are tied up into a bundle with the clubs at one end of their rope. The prayer for safety on the cliff is then said.

The most expert climber goes first, dragging up the rope, with the clubs and shoes tied to it, behind him. It is fastened at the other end round his waist. As soon as he reaches a ledge he seats himself in a firm position, grasps the rope tightly, and assists his fellows with it to follow him, calling out directions to them. Going along the ledges they are all roped together. Thus, by slow stages, the summit is attained. The ascent takes at least two hours if there are inexperienced men of the party, though the cliff is not more than 200 feet in height.

The top of Sulnasker is not level, but slopes down towards one side. A far more serious difficulty to progression upon it lies in the little hummocks of vegetation and the puffins' holes with which it is covered; indeed, one has to watch one's feet very carefully to avoid tripping. The slope is explained by the earthquake in the legend of the rock, which is believed to have been at one time flat. Very probably it is really due to a landslip or an earthquake, which would be paralleled by some disturbance which greatly altered its shape a few years ago, largely destroying the symmetry of the natural tunnel under it, though this tunnel is not a mere superficial cave, but contains water of great depth; so great, indeed, that native fishermen say that it has no bottom.

The bare rock crops up on the surface only in two patches, each of which is about fifty yards square. It is on them that the gannets breed. Here they sit in hundreds, cackling like a flock of real geese, the slightly shriller cry of the young birds being easily distinguishable from that of the adults. Each nest consists of a little pile of grass, seaweed, and dirt, to which the old birds add continually throughout the nesting season; they may often be noted even as late as the end of September flying about with seaweed for the purpose in their beaks. Some of the nestlings are still covered with white down at the time of the fowlers' visit, on some this down is partly replaced by speckled feathers, and in the case of a few it has completely disappeared.

As the heads of the fowlers are seen coming above the edge of the cliff, the cackling is redoubled. They range themselves in line, walking round the nestlings with uplifted clubs, so as to get between them and the edge. Then they advance, thrust the old birds out of the way, and knock the young ones on the head. Few of the old birds take to flight, but they remain cackling angrily on the grass until the slaughter is consummated. Some of them have already assumed the adult plumage of white— now sadly besmirched—with black tips to the wings and a pale yellow tinge on the head and neck; but many still show a greater or less admixture of black in their feathers; for the gannet breeds before it assumes its final dress, the complete change of plumage taking several years. Other birds, roused from their nests on the cliff's face, wheel round and round in the air, adding their quota to the babel on the top. In five minutes all is over; the ground is slippery with blood and with the young fish which the birds have disgorged; a few nestlings, not quite stunned, sob and cackle feebly; others breathe heavily like a person asleep; the old birds make occasional ineffective dabs with their formidable beaks at the men, and flap their wings with wrath. Only those nestlings which are on the ledges below the summit escape; and a few of them are killed earlier in the year, together with the fulmars.

When all have been dispatched the bodies are gathered to the edge at a point where the rock ascends sheer from the sea. Then, together with the clubs, they are pitched over, each one striking the surface with a noise like the report of a gun. The boat below is in waiting, and the birds and clubs are raked into it.

When any newcomer has paid his tribute to the Skerry Priest, the descent, which is even more difficult than the ascent, begins. Often the boat cannot now approach quite close to the landing-place, as the sea rarely remains absolutely calm for any period and the tide has probably risen in the interval since the landing. When Mr. Eustace Gurney and I went up Sulnasker in 1898 this happened while we were on the rock, and a slight swell had come on. There was some difficulty in getting into the boat, which had to keep a yard or two away, for fear of being dashed violently against the cliff. It needed all the skill of the boatmen to manage her, and the climbers were much perplexed as to what to do with inexperienced persons like ourselves. At last they tied me up with a rope, the loose end of which they passed through an iron ring permanently fixed in the rock. Then, without saying anything, they took me up and threw me across to the boatmen, who caught me easily. My friend was not so light as I, and he was forced to trust more to his own activity. The fowlers followed us one by one, until the last man was left. He tied the rope round his waist, passed it through the iron ring, and threw the loose end across to the boat, where it was firmly held. Then, leaping into the sea, he reached the boat with a very few strokes; the rope was untied, pulled in, and we started homewards.

As we entered the bay at Heimey a white flag was hoisted, to show that there had been no disaster. The whole population quickly congregated on the shore, the women bringing hot coffee for their men-kind in little metal flasks. Each fowler and boatman chose out a single bird for his supper, and then the remainder were distributed in the way described above, the sheriff presiding.

In the month of September of that year 662 young gannets were killed in the Westman Isles; 560 of these coming from Sulnasker on the one day on which we visited it. Each bird is worth 35 öre, as it provides a considerable amount of edible matter; but the feathers are valueless, being too stiff for stuffing cushions or other purposes of the kind. The bodies furnish very little oil, though a small quantity is obtained by boiling the skins; for the place of fat appears to be taken in the gannet to a large extent by an elaborate system of air spaces. These probably act as a warm jacket round the bird, very much as the fat does in the case of the fulmar or shearwater.

Both Brünnich's and the Common guillemot, and also a few Razorbills, are taken on Heimey and the other islands while they are sitting on their eggs in June. These birds all belong to the family of the auks, of which the puffin is a member also; they lay on the broader ledges of the cliffs, sitting together in rows and bowing towards one another in a most curious way. They are snared from above by a running noose of fine wire or twine which is slipped over their necks, a long pole, to which it is attached at one end, enabling the fowlers to reach them more easily. Only a few hundreds of each species, however, are taken annually, and they are not individually more valuable than puffins, though they are larger birds. They yield just about the same weight of feathers, and the feathers are of the same value and quality.

A certain number of the Black guillemot (an allied bird which differs more markedly as to its plumage in different seasons of the year than most sea-fowl do) are also shot at sea, both during the breeding season and also later in autumn, when their black colour is beginning to be mottled with white.

Shearwaters are birds of the petrel family which are largely nocturnal in their habits, nesting at the end of very long burrows, which run chiefly in a horizontal direction. The young nestlings are extremely fat, and often fetch as much as 50 öre each, because of the labour of digging them out; but only a comparatively small number are taken in a year. The species that breeds in the Westman Isles is probably the Manx shearwater (*Puffinus anglorum*).

The shearwater completes the list of the birds which are taken in any considerable numbers for food; but Kittiwakes and gulls are occasionally eaten, being caught by children, chiefly for the sake of their feathers, by means of baited fish-hooks and a line. A few other birds, such as cormorants, are sometimes shot for culinary purposes. The Stormy and the Fork-tailed petrels are captured alive in the few islands where they breed, in order that they may be used in playing a practical joke on any one who has annoyed the fowlers. The men listen until they hear the birds 'purring [1]' in the burrow in which they nest, and catch them in a sack placed over the mouth of the hole. When a number have been taken in this way they are surreptitiously let loose at night in the house of the obnoxious person. The birds have a peculiar darting flight, which has, in conjunction with their shape, caused them to be called 'sea-swallow' in Icelandic; they are mostly black or dark grey in colour, but have a very conspicuous white patch above the rump; their cry of alarm, which is quite different from the 'purring' noise they make in their burrows, is weird and uncanny. As they dart about in the dark inside the house the white patch alone is visible, and they cry continually, alarming the person on whom the joke has been played in a very efficacious manner; indeed, it is not to be wondered that he thinks that his house is haunted.

A bird which should not pass without mention is the Little auk, though it does not breed and is not captured in the Westman Isles. Essentially a northern species, it only nests within the Arctic circle, its most southerly breeding-place being the little island of Grimsey, which lies, just within the Arctic circle, off the north coast of Iceland. In winter, however, it comes south, often visiting Great Britain in considerable numbers, but varying from year to year in the extent and character of its migrations. It is one of the smallest and most delicate-looking of true sea-birds, and its appearance in their seas has caused the Westman folk, who know nothing of its real habits, to speculate as to its breeding and origin. By a process of thought not altogether incomprehensible they have come to confuse it with the

---

[1] The word used to express the purring of a cat on Heimey means literally to grind corn, the sound produced by the hand-querns in common use being very similar to a purr.

Halcyon of the Greeks, and its only name in south Iceland is now *halkjon*. With the name of this fabulous bird it has also assumed the legend, being thought to build a floating nest on the sea with its own feathers, without, however, so far as the Westman people know, enjoying 'halcyon days' during the period of incubation.

The Westman men are regarded as the most skilful fowlers in all Iceland, and they have even extended their dominion beyond their own islands. Off the west coast of Iceland there is a solitary rock known as the 'Meal Sack' on account of its covering of white guano, which is due to countless generations of gannets and other birds having nested upon it. Until a few years ago no one had ever climbed this rock, and it was considered quite inaccessible. The King of Denmark, to whom it belonged, offered it to any one who could scale it, and two men from Heimey succeeded in doing so. They have fixed chains and cut steps in the cliff, rendering it comparatively easy of ascent, and now reap what is considered locally a handsome income from the gannets they kill upon it.

Of course fowling, like every other trade, has its misfortunes; but these are not nearly so great or so frequent as they would appear likely to be. A cool head, a keen eye, a steady arm, and a sure foot reduce the dangers to a minimum, while these very dangers are so obvious that they keep the mind alert. Every year some accident occurs; but fowling accidents are generally not very serious; only rarely do they prove fatal. The two things which the fowlers fear are loose stones and slippery grass, and probably more men are hurt by stones which their companions have dislodged than by falls. Wonderful stories are told of those who have fallen over cliffs even as high as several hundred feet without any great injury to themselves. In fact, it is affirmed that if a man in this fearful predicament does not lose his presence of mind, he may save himself alive by doubling up his knees to his chin and clasping them with his two hands while he is falling, especially if he happens to have on a loose coat which will help to support him in the air. It is only if he falls into the sea, however, that this manœuvre could avail him much; it would not save him from being dashed to pieces against the stones of the beach. I am inclined to believe that a man whose head was strong enough to enable him to perform an action of the kind while in the very act of falling, would not be likely to fall at all; but I am only telling what I have been told by the fowlers themselves.

A word or two may not be out of place as to a diet of seafowl's flesh. The Icelanders and we 'Europeans' (as they call us) naturally approach the question from two entirely different points of view, which doubtless have in each case a physiological basis. We abhor anything that tastes of oil; the Icelanders revel in such flavours, as all Arctic and sub-Arctic peoples would seem to do. It is probable that this is not solely due to the rigours of the climate to which they are subjected, but partly to a something, possibly vegetable substances [1], lacking in their food, and partly to cultural or even racial causes. Darwin has noted that in certain parts of South America the Gauchos of the Pampas, who have no opportunity of obtaining vegetable food, can eat fat in a way which would cause nausea in a European, and I have been much struck myself with the difference in this respect between Siamese cookery and that of the Malays. The

[1] This is Darwin's view, but it seems to have very little physiological justification. See the *Naturalist's Voyage*, p. 117 (1870 ed.).

difference can be noted in the same district, even in the same village; but it would here seem to be a cultural rather than a physiological one, seeing that the Malays and Siamese in the country where it was remarked are not racially distinct, but chiefly divided by religion. I well remember the gusto with which a Siamese youth remarked in my hearing that he liked duck 'because there was much fat,' and the scorn with which the Malays, to whom he was speaking, received the statement. Possibly, in this case, the disgust expressed for fat arose primarily from the dislike felt by all Mahommedans for anything connected with the pig, as lard is commonly employed in the cookery of the Siamese, who are Buddhists; but it appears to have become more or less of a fixed principle, at any rate with the more civilized Malays, that fat is itself disgusting as an article of diet.

Even to a British palate several of the Icelandic sea-fowl provide good eating, especially the puffin and the Black guillemot; but they are preferable when the skin and as much as possible of the fat have been removed before cooking. To the Icelander, on the other hand, the skin, which contains a very great deal of fat, is the best part of the bird. The fulmar cannot be cooked in such a way as to deprive it altogether of oiliness: except for the young shearwater, which is if anything more oily, it is the Icelander's favourite. During the six weeks we spent on Heimey we could often get no meat but fulmar's flesh, and at first welcomed it as a relief from the tastelessness of boiled cod. Every time the dish appeared, however—and it could always be smelt before it was seen—it became more and more repugnant, until at last it was only with difficulty that we could eat it at all.

A diet of sea-fowl's flesh evidently agrees, in the case of

adults, with the Westman folk, who appear to be healthier both in mind and body than their neighbours on the mainland; for they are certainly more robust, and seem to be far less morbid and gloomy in their outlook on life. Leprosy is extremely rare among them, though it is common in many Icelandic districts, and it is interesting to notice in this connexion that they make less use of salted fish than do the Icelanders of the mainland, having salted birds to take its place. They would never think themselves of eating the dried cods' heads which they sell, chiefly as winter fodder for cattle and ponies but also for human consumption, to the people of Rangarval. In 1898 there was one leper on Heimey—a little boy whose mother had died of the same disease. So peculiar was this thought that it was believed that the woman had been made ill by some medicine the local doctor had given her and had transmitted her illness to her son, as no other case had been known for a long time previously. I am not arguing that badly prepared fish is the cause of leprosy, as some maintain; for I have no special knowledge of the question. I merely put this fact on record. Both sexes suffer on the island from a kind of eczema.

CHAPTER V

MODERN ICELAND

The first discoverers of America, the earliest Arctic explorers, poets and historians (named and nameless) innumerable, warriors and scholars not a few, were born of old in Iceland; now her glory has departed, leaving some score of grave-mounds in a remote and desolate island, echoed by an aimless longing in the heart of a poor and isolated race. If anything of the old viking spirit lives on in the world, Iceland is not its home.

The Faroeman will readily confess that his country has not progressed as greater countries have done; but he cannot understand that Iceland is, in essentials, but little more advanced than the Faroes, and that where she has gone forward she is often less worthy of praise. In his eyes Reykjavik's iron mansions are very palaces, not quite so magnificent as the stone houses of Lerwick or Kirkwall, maybe; but fine indeed. Leith and Copenhagen are yet more wonderful, but they belong to a different world—to Europe, as the Faroeman himself would say. The attractions of Reykjavik, with its hideous 'tin' houses, its sham modernity, will, in his opinion, offer to the 'European' attractions superior to anything that the Faroes can provide—and the Faroeman is right, chiefly because there are agents in Iceland who will provide, for a price, the majority of those conveniences which are so attractive to the man who travels because it is the correct thing to do, or because he must, and so irritating to him the object of whose journeys is a true holiday—a change of scene and atmosphere.

Be this as it may, the attractions of Iceland are not always pre-eminent, for while a Farish cottage is generally clean, an Icelandic farmhouse is almost as often airless, filthy, and verminous. A mediaeval monk described Iceland, in summer time, as a country which was so light that a man could see to pick the lice off his shirt at midnight, and, in this respect at any rate, it has changed very little. The modern Icelandic peasant is curiously devoid of all conception of cleanliness of person, home, and food; at the Hot Springs, which act as a public wash-house for Reykjavik, it is no uncommon sight to see a woman fill her coffee-pot from a tiny pool in which the dirty clothes of several households are steeping. For this neglect of ordinary precautions the Icelanders suffer in what they call the 'liver plague,' a disease of parasitic origin, caused by the immature stage of a tapeworm derived from the dogs which share their homes.

If scenery, again, be taken as a criterion, that of the Faroes is quite unique, chiefly because of the marvellous effects of mist and sunshine, brilliant flower-strewn slope and barren rock, and the weird avenues of pyramidical hills which embrace the fjords so closely. Icelandic scenery also has its marvels—its table-lands of cinders, its broad green valleys, the white steam of its hot springs and geysers, and, above all, the brief autumnal glory of its diminutive forests of dwarf willow, dwarf birch and blaeberry. Yet in Iceland there is something wanting; the highest hills lack boldness of outline, the glaciers, which are the largest in Europe, are tame compared with those of Norway or the Alps, and the verdure of the valleys lacks the exquisite freshness of the Farish hillsides—it is the rank growth of swamps. It is characteristic of Iceland that the place of the daisy, which is common enough in the Faroes but absent from the larger island, is largely taken by the Grass of Parnassus—a plant which does not grow save in boggy land. Nor is the human element in the landscape picturesque, the farms and churches being almost invisible, owing to their covering of turf, or standing boldly forth in all the glory of new 'tin.'

A well-known journalist and lawyer of Reykjavik once remarked in my hearing that the only true thing an Icelander could say was that all Icelanders were liars—a remark which probably possessed more cleverness than truth, though a stranger who had only heard the Icelanders talking for effect, as they are too fond of doing, might well agree. The ordinary Icelander, when he talks to a 'European' is often so conscious of the glory of his ancestors, and of the present intellectual and moral state of Iceland, that he is apt to indulge in hyperbole—the ancient Icelanders were the greatest heroes, the greatest poets, and the greatest explorers that ever were; they taught Columbus[1] how to discover America, their literature was infinitely the greatest that ever was written; they themselves were the bravest men that the world has ever seen; Thorwaldsen was an Icelander, and he was the finest artist that Europe ever produced; it is horrible for an Icelander to contemplate the immorality of London; look at the morality of Reykjavik (the purity of which, it must be confessed, is open to doubt): and so on. Or sometimes, especially when he is not sober, the Icelander affects

[1] It is an historical fact that Columbus visited Iceland during the year before the commencement of his great voyage; but we have no information as to whether or no he examined the documents or traditions then in the island concerning the long-lost Icelandic colony in 'Vineland' (Labrador?).

a deprecatory mood, whining that Iceland is a poor miserable little place, devoid of everything, inferior in its ponies to Shetland. In both of these moods I have seen and heard him repeatedly; but I am inclined to think that he reserves them largely for the 'European's' sympathetic ear.

When, however, he begins to talk against the ponies of his country, he has sunk very low in his own estimation, and the foreigner is inclined to wonder; for to the majority of those who visit Iceland (not being salmon-fishers or historians absorbed in the past, but merely tourists), the ponies are the one feature of the country which makes it worthy of a visit. The charm of Iceland is the freedom from the petty cares and worries of business or study that it offers, the absence of society, newspapers, and letters. It is the ponies alone that make such freedom endurable to the ordinary man, harassed by that peculiar disease of our civilization—an insatiable hatred of sitting still. The ponies are not particularly fast; they are rarely even spirited; a child or an old woman could ride them, but they have certain attractive qualities, due perhaps rather to their environment than to themselves. Now galloping over the plain, now fording a glacier stream, now chasing the ever-errant pack ponies up a slope so steep that it almost seems as if rider and steed would be precipitated backwards, the busy man can forget all else and enjoy only the excitement of the moment. The discomfort of the night before is forgotten, and the horror of the night to come fades in the vivid anticipation of supper. Riding from one farm with a name that he can only pronounce with difficulty to another, the traveller feels that he goes from nowhere to nowhere, and the inconsequence of his journey is delightful. Should he travel in luxury with a tent, the uncomfortable nights need not be a reality to him.

Not less valuable to the native than to the tourist, the Icelandic ponies are so strong that no work appears too great or too prolonged for their exertions. Grass is their only summer food; hay, and when that fails, dried cods' heads, all they have in winter, even when they are not obliged to fend for themselves. Those that are small and miserable are exported to England to work in the mines, but those that remain in Iceland reach no great size, and few have any beauty of form or motion. During the summer in Iceland, the cost of keeping a pony is about a farthing a day, though in a bad winter it may be considerably more. Everybody rides. To walk is considered to be deficient in personal dignity, to pay a call on foot in the country, or even to dismount uninvited at a farm-house door, is looked upon as a breach of good manners. The very beggars are men who, through laziness, bad management, or misfortune, are unable to produce sufficient on their own farms to support their families, and who ride round to their neighbours with a large bag, in which they receive broken meats and cast-off clothing. Without the ponies it would be impossible for the lowest savage to exist in Iceland, except directly on the coast; for without food from the sea, if not from abroad, there would be nothing to eat. Every luxury, every article above the necessities of primitive man, every plank of wood, every piece of metal, every pound of corn, must come from the outside; the land produces sheep and a few miserable potatoes, the sea and the rivers produce fish; every other kind of food is exotic, and the materials for so foreign an article of diet as bread must come oversea. Still influenced by the ban of the Christian missionaries who came to Iceland from Germany in the early days of her history, the majority of Icelanders refuse to eat the flesh of horses;

but there are farms, both in the north and the south of the island, where this wholesome addition to a monotonous diet is not despised. Yet, though these modern *hippophagi* are few in number, the food supply of the whole population is entirely dependent on the ponies, which carry in the hay, transport the wool to the coast, and bring fish to the farms which are not near the sea. Indifferent as to their track, sure-footed as goats, they trot along through marshes, over mountains, across rivers, in single file, sometimes herded by a dog like sheep, sometimes tied tail to head, often almost hidden by their load. Given time and numbers, they will carry anything from a man to the wood and metal for a house; it is largely thanks to them that there are no villages on the mainland of Iceland, but only towns and farmsteads; and it must be remembered that Iceland is an island about one-fifth larger than Ireland.

The distinction between town and village may seem, at first sight, an arbitrary one, for an Icelandic town need not consist of more than half a dozen houses; but in Iceland such a collection of dwellings has none of the common rural life that one finds in the villages of the Faroes. This is because it has originated as a Danish trading-station, being always on the coast, while the Farish village is a natural outcome of the resources of the country. The Icelandic coast town is essentially a 'cheaping-stead,' a place where the people of the surrounding district may sell their goods or exchange them for foreign produce, a point on the coast where a wharf for small ships has been built. In the heroic age almost every Icelander who had the means became a trader, visiting Europe in search of warlike pleasure and commercial supplies. What he took in his viking raids, or what he bought in Norway or Denmark, he brought home to Iceland with him. Then he held a sale at his stead, or procured what goods he wished from his neighbours by a system of exchange. Indeed, so thoroughly is Icelandic commerce imbued with the idea of barter, that, even in the present age, land is theoretically reckoned according to its value in ells of *wadmal*, a coarse frieze of home manufacture. The practice introduced by the Danish Government, when the Danes became possessed of the relics of the old Norwegian empire, was very different, for under the new régime the government claimed an absolute monopoly of trade. Commerce of all kinds was restricted to the traffic which took place in definite trading-stations, each of which was occupied by a crown agent; all goods of every sort must pass through his hands, and a law was even passed which made it a capital crime to buy or sell with any one else. By far the most important event in modern Icelandic history has been the repeal of this pernicious system (in 1856), for the restoration of the ancient parliament, the Althing, has done little more than give an opportunity for talk and bombastic phraseology.

At the end of the eighteenth century, if not earlier, other houses began to grow up round the Danish trading-stations, and the process has continued with increased facilities of foreign communication, until towns like Reykjavik and Akureyri (the latter of which is often said to be the true Icelandic, as distinct from the Danish, capital) have arisen, each with several thousand inhabitants. The important places in mediaeval Iceland were not towns, but theological colleges such as Hólardal, where a famous printing-press existed, and Skalholt, the see of a bishop until the beginning of the nineteenth century. It does not appear that these colleges were ever housed in buildings of any architectural pretensions, and in all cases their sites are

MODERN ICELAND

now occupied merely by a small church and by the residence of a farmer-priest; yet some of them retain their place on the map of Europe, even in modern atlases, as if they were still important places. In the year 1801 the Danish Government proclaimed Reykjavik the capital of Iceland in place of Skalholt, an inland steading which had formerly been considered the centre of national life. Reykjavik had been founded, as a steading, at the end of the ninth century, but when Columbus visited it in the fifteenth it was still a farm. It is not even marked on the map in Horrebow's *Natural History of Iceland* (the work in which the famous chapter on the snakes of Iceland occurs), and pictures of Reykjavik dating from the first decade of the nineteenth century represent it as a little cluster of wooden houses gathered round a wooden church—not more than one-tenth the size of the corrugated-iron town that now bears its name.

Taking all in all, Reykjavik is probably the ugliest town in Europe, if the Icelanders will recognize it as appertaining to our wicked continent. It boasts some streets and a square, but the material of which most of the buildings are made, or, to speak more accurately, in which they are encased, is corrugated iron—a substance which does not lend itself to architectural beauty. The Althinghuus or Parliament House, which is of stone, can boast a certain solidity—a merit which the Cathedral lacks. A large apothecary's shop in the square is typical of much that is vicious in modern Iceland, for its Greek deities in plaster are singularly out of place in a country which had so splendid a mythology of its own, and whose people boast so frequently of their patriotism.

Akureyri, situated in the north of Iceland, is not so hideous as the southern capital, for it contains a larger proportion of wooden buildings, but in essentials it is little more refined. Isafjord and the other smaller towns partake of the same character, and are more picturesque simply because they are less extensive.

So much for the Icelandic towns; they are almost entirely foreign institutions, and the real life of the people is still lived in isolated farmhouses, just as it was in the old days, when men rode from all districts of the island to the annual *Thing* at Thingvallir, the ' Fields of Assembly,' not only to settle matters of state, but also to get them wives, to see their friends, to do their private business. When they came to the vast lava-flow whereon the people assembled, they built their temporary booths (the foundations of which, by a strange irony of fate, may still be seen); and when their business, public and private, was over, each man rode home to his steading. Thus, the modern farmer visits Reykjavik, or some other town, once a year in early summer, to sell his wool, and too often to break an enforced abstinence by an orgy of steady drinking of a peculiarly monotonous and uneventful kind. When his money is spent, he returns to the country, and often keeps sober until the following summer brings again the opportunity of excess. On a few of the small islands off the coast, however, such as Grimsey in the north and Heimey in the south, villages came of necessity into being centuries ago, as the space was very limited and the fowling on the cliffs led people to settle.

The village on Heimey is probably the largest indigenous Icelandic community, sheltering nearly five hundred souls, but still retaining much of its primitive simplicity. It is built by a narrow bay, the opposite shore of which consists of two gigantic bird-cliffs, rising precipitous from the sea. Along the beach stands a row of little wooden fish-houses, in which the salted cod is stored at night, and in front of each of them is a table on which the fish are cleaned and salted. They have little wooden shutters in the place where the windows would be in an ordinary house, and a cross is often marked with chalk upon their doors, probably for a superstitious reason, though I could never ascertain its significance. In front of the fish-houses there is a pathway roughly paved with cobbles, alongside which a few poles are erected, in order that lamps may be hung upon them when the fishermen are out at sea after dark. At one end of the pathway a jetty runs out for a short distance into the bay, and above it towers the store, which is the one building of hewn stone upon the island. It is surrounded by a number of warehouses built of tarred wood. The dwellings stand further back, most of them in small gardens, in which potatoes, a few carrots perhaps, turnips, rhubarb and even a lettuce or two succeed in growing, while the native angelica, relegated to a corner, flourishes and overtops all other vegetation. The walls of the gardens are constructed of rough stones, and are often festooned with strings of drying cods' heads and puffins' backs. At night the former give out weird gleams of light, which sometimes increase to a regular illumination, though, as we have seen, this is not the purpose for which they are being preserved. The houses themselves range from two-roomed huts roughly piled together with stones and turf, dark save for a tiny window at one side, to neat two-storied residences of wood or corrugated iron, occasionally even with slates on the roof, though turf is still more common. These latter houses are dignified with the names of cities in Denmark or of the capitals of Europe, one being called London, another Paris, another Elsinore, and so on. A characteristic feature of the village is the presence of great black vats in which the livers of a variety of fish—shark, dog-fish, skate, cod, halibut and saithe—are allowed to soak until the finer quality of their oil oozes out from them by a natural process. It is thus that the 'cold-drawn' cod-liver oil of commerce is obtained, though the variety of its constituents may not be so great.

The farm in which the Icelander of the mainland lives is a curiously inconspicuous dwelling, unless, of course, he has recently built a new dwelling of corrugated iron or brightly painted wood. Imagine a row of small mounds, their bases rising together, and then diverging to form as many separate ridges, some of them capped by little boxes whence smoke is seen to issue—here you have the side view of the homestead. Nor is the front view much superior. Each mound is faced with wood, and pierced above and below with holes in which panes of glass are set; and there are several larger apertures that are fitted with stout doors and lead into inner darkness. The middle entrance is the main door of the dwelling, and opens into a long, narrow passage, built of alternate layers of turf and unhewn stones, and at the end gleams a smoky light, the kitchen fire. To the right and to the left, shorter passages lead to the living-rooms. The other entrances open directly into the harness-room, the cow-byre, and the forge, which have no direct communication with the rest of the house. A number of low sheds, constructed almost entirely of turf, and used as winter stables for the ponies and the sheep, surround the main building, and the whole is enclosed in a wall of turf, through which a narrow lane, generally churned to mud by the passage of many hoofs, conducts to the entrance of the house. In many cases where a modern farmhouse, constructed of wood or wood and metal, has taken the place of this peculiar dwelling, the latter remains in the capacity of storehouse and byre but is no longer used as a residence.

Even in the older farms, the living rooms might be fairly comfortable, were they clean and was the ventilation good; but as a rule it is impossible to open the windows, and very often the only method of admitting air is to extract a small plug of wood, about as big as a beer-bottle cork, inserted into one of the window-panes. Even this is never left out for long. The mound-like appearance of the buildings is due to an external coating of turf, which covers the woodwork inside and produces what may be considered excessive warmth. The furniture in the rooms is not elaborate, but consists chiefly of large wooden chests, the older specimens of which—now very rare—are beautifully carved, while those made to-day or yesterday are gaudily painted, often with a crude picture of a ship.

The decoration of the rooms is either tawdry or gloomy in the extreme. Those farmhouses which can boast a parlour often rejoice in an extraordinary collection of cheap oleographs and other pictures of a similar nature, with which are sometimes mingled a series of English theatrical posters of the blood-and-thunder style. These share the walls of the parlour with pockets in ugly woollen embroidery, made at home, and photographs of friends and relatives, especially those who have emigrated to Canada.

A favourite decorative device in less modern households is to hang the walls with 'in memoriam' notices of deceased members of the family. I have seen some of these which were painted on boards; but the majority are neatly printed and framed, with the usual mortuary symbols, such as skulls, cherubim and the like, coarsely engraved above them. The wording is generally in verse; but the matter is often of a most commonplace nature, dealing with the age, place of birth and death, and the number of children of the dead friend.

In the older farms a whole mound is usually devoted to a large dormitory for the farm servants; but one end may be partitioned off to serve as a bedroom for the farmer and his family. This dormitory is common to all who live on the farm, men and women alike; there can be no privacy and very little decency in it, for the beds are not even surrounded with curtains—a good thing from a sanitary point of view. It is difficult to exaggerate the squalor that often prevails in such dormitories. The beds are mere chests without a cover, filled with worn-out or disused clothes, among which the people sleep, swarming with vermin. The walls and floor are black with dirt, littered with women's gear and men's implements, absolutely without decoration. The milk is often kept in covered wooden vessels, which may be delicately carved if one could see them, beneath the beds; and the sides of the beds themselves may be also carved and even tastefully painted to emphasize the carving, if they are old. In any case the ornamentation is often obscured by dirt.

One of the most curious things in modern Iceland is the way in which the taste for decorative design, once so prevalent in the country, appears to have died out completely within the last ten or twenty years. Its only common manifestation to-day is in the making of horn spoons with floral and other patterns, generally including the initials of the maker, engraved upon the handle; and even these, except in very remote districts, are now chiefly manufactured to sell to tourists. They are exact reproductions of the spoons which have been carved for centuries in the island. There is a specimen which was dug up in the Westman Isles now in the Pitt-Rivers Museum at

Oxford, and the only difference between it and modern examples is the seventeenth century date carved upon it. Practically everything in the island which has any artistic merit has already been secured for the National Museum at Reykjavik, or else sold to travellers; and there is no desire to produce more work of a similar kind among the natives, who are fonder of boasting of this Museum than of profiting by it.

Of course Iceland never produced a great art, or even a great artist. The sculptor Thorwaldsen is regarded as a national hero; his statue stands in front of the Althinghuus at Reykjavik, and there is a font in the Cathedral sculptured by him, with an inscription in which he acknowledges Icelandic descent. Yet Thorwaldsen was only half an Icelander, his mother having been a Dane; he was born at sea, never saw Iceland, and owed his art to Italy; he neither was the founder of a new school nor the culminating point of an indigenous one, for his merit lay in introducing the sculpture of Southern Europe to the Teutonic peoples. Nevertheless, his manual skill at any rate was probably hereditary, for his father, like many another Icelander, was an expert wood-carver.

Purely decorative as was the genius of the true Icelandic artist, he could only become ridiculous when he attempted to portray anything of the nature of a scene, whether that scene was real or imaginary. His art carried him no further than the utterly conventional representation of flowers, dragons, entwined cords (which often cannot be distinguished from the dragons), and purely 'geometrical' designs. These, judging by the analogy of other primitive art, had, at any rate in many cases, at one time a mystical meaning, and may even have been the lineal descendants of what were once intended for real pictures. Time, innumerable copyists (many of whom were ignorant of the thing depicted), and perhaps that curious fear of producing anything too near perfection which has influenced many primitive races, have conventionalized and debased such pictures, until we no longer know that they are pictures at all, only guessing at their meaning in the rare cases where a traditional name or a traditional explanation has remained attached to them in folklore or popular tradition, or when it is possible to obtain a series of specimens [1] which actually shows the retrogression.

Since Norsemen first settled in Iceland there has been but little evolution in the patterns with which they have decorated their household implements and their clothing. It is only a religious motive which has proved strong enough to bring them back to the primitive desire, so well exemplified by the Palaeolithic man of Southern France, of reproducing what they saw or imagined to occur. In some of the older Icelandic churches there is over the altar, in the place of the modern Danish painting which usually occupies this position, a crude painted and sculptured representation of some Bible story, and the virtues and fertility of some old bishop or priest may occasionally be commemorated by a similar effigy of himself and his children. A still more curious work of art—and one in execution of a far higher order—is preserved in the National Museum at Reykjavik, dating from pre-Reformation times. It is the vestment of a bishop, elaborately brocaded and embroidered, harmonious and rich in colour. On the back

---

[1] For example, I believe that it would be possible, by means of specimens in the Reykjavik Museum, to trace a connexion between designs representing two birds sitting on a tree, as in the tapestry now in the Edinburgh Museum, and the purely conventional design on the back of the Icelandic brass lamps.

LID OF CARVED BOX, DATED 1767, BELONGING TO A WOMAN,
A— L—'S DAUGHTER (DÓTTIR), ICELAND

[*To face p. 145*

the rescue of a storm-tossed ship by the apparition of a saint is depicted in needlework. The ship is small and quite impossible; its mast is broken, its sails are gone, it rocks on a conventional sea. In the middle, by the mast, stands the saint, in ecclesiastic robes, with a mitre and crosier. He floats in the air rather than treads the deck. A sailor kneels in adoration before him; another sailor is being seasick, in the most realistic manner possible, over the edge.

Until a few years ago much silver jewellery, wood-work engraved and beaten brass-work, and embroidery, was produced upon the farms. The lids of the bickers in which the haymakers carried their luncheon to the fields were always tastefully carved; the women's sweethearts or husbands carved them boxes to hold their knitting-needles and embroidered collars, or elaborate hand-mangles with which to smooth the clothes they washed. The beds had carved, and often painted, boards along their sides; the churches were bright with work of a more ambitious nature; for a peculiarity of Icelandic wood-carving was that it attempted to combine colour with form—often with great success, so long as no copy of natural things was aimed at or desired; the patterns being emphasized by the use of bright paints harmoniously combined. The work, however, was often marred by the unsuitable character of the material used and by the artist's lack of skill in joinery. The wood at his disposal frequently consisted of several small pieces, which had to be fitted together in order that the design might be completed; but in many cases this was done clumsily, leaving wide cracks between the pieces. This was due in large measure to the lack of metal, whether in the form of tools or for the making of nails. Neither iron nor copper is worked in Iceland, and both these metals are still hard to obtain in most parts of the island, though scrap iron is actually exported from Heimey, where it is derived from wrecks. The Icelandic workman, moreover, still finds it easier to work with copper or brass rather than with iron. Even to-day he often makes his nails, hinges, and the like, of one of the first two of these substances, or even of bronze derived from coins; and neither copper nor its compound can be employed in delicate joiner's work with the same success as iron. It is evident, too, in many examples of Icelandic carving that the carver possessed no metal at all except his knife; for the parts are fitted together either with little wooden pegs or with lashings of the roots of blaeberry and dwarf willow, which pass through holes bored in the wood.

The silver jewellery which was formerly made in Iceland closely resembles that of other Scandinavian countries. What is now manufactured mostly follows traditional designs, but is produced by professional silversmiths in the towns—no longer by the men on the farms. Embroidery, being women's work, has naturally become less decadent. It is still every woman's ambition, at any rate in some remote districts, to have a wedding-dress of black velvet, embroidered with gold or silver thread; and she can only make it herself, with the aid of her friends. The wall-hangings of tapestry, however, which were once common in the living-rooms of the farm, have completely disappeared. Many of them, some of which are preserved in the Reykjavik Museum, were ancient, having been handed down as heirlooms in the family; but some of them were certainly made last century. One of the most interesting specimens now in existence is in the Museum of Science and Art at Edinburgh. It once adorned the tent in which the Althing was held at Thingvallir between the date when the national assembly ceased to be held in the open air and 1800 (when

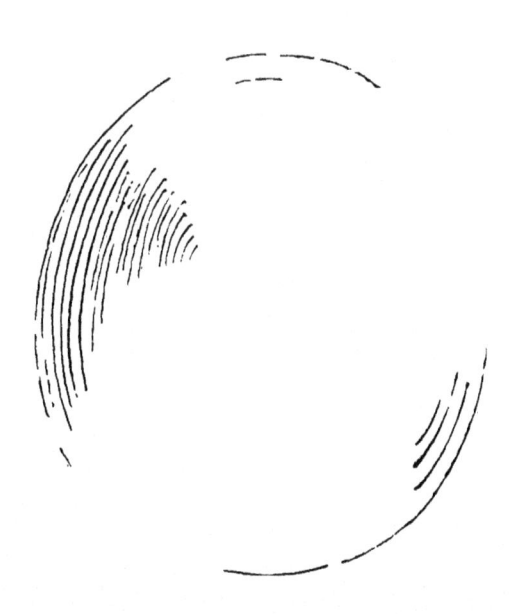

MODERN ICELANDIC HORN SPOON,
WITH INITIALS OF A MAN,
G— S—'S SON

ICELANDIC TAPESTRY (EDINBURGH MUSEUM)

it was removed to Reykjavik). The hangings are in two parts, one worked by nuns in pre-Reformation times, the other of rather more modern date. The embroidery upon them takes the form of conventional patterns, which, in the older portion, evidently represent trees with birds sitting upon them, and of inscriptions in old Icelandic lettering, with certain borders and other ornaments of a less complex character. The colours [1] are now faded and dull, and the thing has little beauty; it is difficult to say what it can have been like in the days of its prime.

But such things do not belong to modern Iceland. The Althinghuus is now hung with modern pictures, many of them representing scenes in Egypt and elsewhere; few have any connexion with Iceland, and very few have any great artistic merit. Many of them were presented by continental artists, to whom an appeal was issued some years ago. There is no hope that this 'National Gallery,' as it is proudly called, will stem the current of artistic decadence or stimulate a new taste in the country, and it is hardly to be wished that it should rouse a spirit of emulation.

In spite of artistic decay—always a sign of degeneracy among an essentially primitive people—there is still much that is archaic in the social life of Iceland, though a great part of this archaism seems to be due rather to an affected patriotism than to real simplicity. Take, for example, the system of personal names. In Iceland there are a few

---

[1] The material is a coarse linen (once white) and roughly spun wool. Most of the wool in both parts has been dyed dark blue, crimson, or black. A bright yellow also appears and a dull fawn, the latter being a natural tint. The stitching is very simple, the wool being merely drawn through the linen in such a way that very little is wasted on the back of the fabric. No attempt has been made to cover the whole fabric.

recognized surnames, mostly of foreign origin; but the vast majority of the people have only a Christian name and a patronymic, a man being called, for example, Gisli Jóusson, and a woman Asta Jónsdóttir. Gisli Jónsson's son might be Magnus Gislasson, and his daughter Margrjet Gislasdóttir; for the patronymic is still in its primitive stage and has not crystallized out into a surname. Even when a woman marries she is still called so-and-so so-and-so's daughter; but her children are known as sons or daughters of their father. Of course she is frequently spoken of as so-and-so's daughter so-and-so's wife, and may even be addressed in this way; but it does not appear that the addition of her husband's name is so common as it is in those parts of Scandinavia where a similar practice still prevails. In the Faroes the system has been very much modified, and in many cases what were originally patronymics, for example, Petersen or Mikklesen, have become regular family names, which are transmitted from generation to generation irrespective of the Christian name of a man or a woman's father. As long ago as the end of the seventeenth century it appears to have been the custom, at any rate in official documents, for a woman to take her husband's patronymic on marriage; but the fixing of this patronymic as a family name is of far more recent origin. The names of places of birth are sometimes still adopted as surnames in the Faroes, in the place of patronymics.

The Icelanders are quite aware how awkward this system of nomenclature is, and those of them who have much intercourse with Scotland or the Continent generally adopt their individual patronymics as a family surname, the wife taking her husband's as a matter of convenience. Many persons, however, who are quite in a position to appreciate what a clumsy and confusing plan the native one is, cling to it simply because it is native; and in remote localities it is still universal.

Perhaps one of the factors which have caused its perpetuation for so long is the frequency of adoption; people who have no children and yet are in a position to support a son or daughter very often taking a child of some poorer neighbour or relative, generally a boy, into their family and treating him as if he were their own. The same custom prevails in the Faroes and is characteristically Scandinavian. Under such circumstances, if the boy retains his real father's name, a distinction is made between adopted children and those really born into the family. Fosterage, by which a son is given into the charge of a family other than his own until he comes to years of discretion, is also practised, and may have had a similar tendency.

One characteristic of the social system in Iceland, which may be mentioned at the same time as these (though possibly it has no real connexion with them), is the fact that men very frequently marry women a good deal older than themselves, who may have had several children by them, or even by other fathers, before marriage. A glance through the inscriptions on the tombstones in the cemetery at Reykjavik or any other place in Iceland where the cemetery is at all large will show how very common it is for wives to have been at least ten years older than their husbands; and a common answer to a question as to whether a man or a woman is married is, 'No, but he (or she) probably will be soon. He (or she) has several children.'

The whole social system on the farms is conducive to irregular unions, and there is much in it that is patriarchal in other ways. Each farm is obliged to be a community which is, or can be, self-sufficient. Even if it is not far distant from the next community of the kind, it may be liable to be completely shut off from all intercourse by snow in winter or by floods in autumn and spring. It is necessary, therefore, for a considerable body of men and women to inhabit it. These men and women belong to two quite distinct classes, though they have much of their life in common—masters and servants. The masters have probably been masters for generations, and the servants, servants—always on the same farm; but the servant class is constantly being recruited from that of the masters who have become so impoverished by misfortune or sloth that they have been forced to declare themselves paupers. In this case they are given out as servants to some more fortunate farmer. If they are too old or otherwise incapacitated for work the state gives their master an allowance for their keep; but the farmers are generally compassionate in such cases, however much they may grumble, and expend more upon them than the allowance would strictly justify.

In the same way, on an old-fashioned Icelandic farm, no servant is ever turned away because he or she is too old for work. Servants form part of the family, and when they marry they bring their wives to their master's home. Their children grow up beneath his roof, many of them never so much as seeing even a copper coin until they are quite adult, though they are fed and clothed, often educated, and have their services paid for in kind. Sons of the master may also stay on in the homestead with their wives and families, if there is room for them; or they may go off and either buy a new farm or else occupy ownerless land, of which there is plenty in the island.

The common life of the community is spent in the big

dormitory to which allusion has been made. Here in many cases the whole community sleeps during the summer season, except when some of its members are away gathering in the wild hay of the uplands or fishing at sea; and here in winter the greater part of the day is spent as well as the night. Ebenezer Henderson, who spent a year in Iceland about ninety years ago, describes how the people occupied themselves during the long, dark days and evenings of winter in his time.

'The domestic employments of this time,' he says, 'are multiplied and various. The men are occupied in fabricating necessary implements of iron, copper, wood, &c.; and some of them are wonderfully expert, as silversmiths; they also prepare hides for shoes; make ropes of hair or wool; and full woollen stuffs. . . . Besides preparing the food, the females employ their time in spinning, which is most commonly done with a spindle and distaff; knitting stockings, mittens, shirts, &c.; as also in embroidering bed-covers, saddle-cloths, and cushions, which they execute with much taste, interspersing flowers and figures of various colours.

'A winter evening in an Icelandic family presents a scene in the highest degree interesting and pleasing. Between three and four o'clock the lamp is hung up in the *badstofa*, or principal apartment, which answers the double purpose of a bed-chamber and sitting-room, and all the members of the family take their station, with their work in their hands, on their respective beds, which face one another. The master and mistress, together with their children, or other relations, occupy the beds at the inner end of the room; the rest are filled by the servants.

'The work is no sooner begun, than one of the family, selected on purpose, advances to a seat near the lamp, and commences the evening lecture, which generally consists of some old saga, or such other histories as are to be obtained on the island. Being but badly supplied with printed books, the Icelanders are under the necessity of copying such as they can get a loan of, which sufficiently accounts for the fact, that most of them write a hand equal in beauty to that of the ablest writing-master in other parts of Europe. The reader is frequently interrupted, either by the head, or some of the more intelligent members of the family, who make remarks on various parts of the story, and propose questions, with a view to exercise the ingenuity of the children and servants. In some houses the sagas are repeated by such as have them by heart; and instances are not uncommon of itinerating historians, who gain a livelihood during winter, by staying at different farms till they have exhausted their stock of literary knowledge.'

I have purposely quoted Henderson at some length, in order to give another man's view of the common dormitory of the Icelandic farm, in which I, who have only seen it in summer, saw nothing but a scene of squalor and ugliness. Possibly there have been changes since Henderson's time, but, so far as can be learnt from the Icelanders, the customs regarding its winter use have not changed very greatly since he visited Iceland, at any rate in some districts. The spread of cheap literature from the printing-presses of Reykjavik and other centres has doubtless rendered both the custom of reading aloud and a superlatively fine penmanship less common in the rising generation; while the decay of artistic workmanship has removed an important employment for men and women. It is now frequently cheaper to buy the few implements necessary for agriculture ready-made than to obtain the metal and make them, cheap goods being imported in large quantities without restrictions such as the monopoly at one time put upon their introduction. Those implements which are still made on the farms are often of a nature so very simple that little time can be occupied in their production, now that the desire to render them ornamental as well as useful has perished. The spread of education has also had its effect on winter life, or rather the conditions of winter life and the spread of education have acted and reacted on one another in a way which is probably more complex than it appears at first sight to be.

It is only lately that there have been elementary schools in Iceland; the education of the people, which has been of a high order for the last seven or eight centuries, was commenced in the family; but throughout the period indicated (that is to say, since the monks became a power in the land) there have existed centres of learning where it was possible for any boy to gain a wider knowledge. The Reformation was, on the whole, peaceful, and wrought but a small change in the life of the Icelandic people, though it was universally accepted: the theological colleges still remained, now turned Protestant (Lutheran). Seeing that there was very little for the young men and boys to do in the winter, their thoughts naturally turned to learning, chiefly classical and literary, as affording them a relief from the terrible monotony of an idle existence in a climate that calls for employment or else profoundest melancholy. Since the attainment of a modified home rule in 1874[1], and largely owing to the patriotic endeavours of Jón Sigurdursson— indirectly if not directly — the number of schools,

---

[1] In 1903 Iceland was granted a new constitution, which made the Althing directly responsible to the king of Denmark through a minister for Iceland—a native of the island who spends the summer at Reykjavik and the winter in Denmark.

elementary as well as advanced, has been greatly increased, and there are now educational establishments of one kind or another in almost all the towns. Even on Heimey the priest teaches the rudiments to the children of the island during winter. Moreover, special advantages are offered to Icelandic students at the University of Copenhagen, including exemption from college fees and even free board in certain cases, provided that they have acquired the necessary qualifications at one of the colleges in Iceland. The chief of these is the Latin School at Reykjavik, where there is also a Medical School. There are theological colleges, in which a student may qualify for ordination by the bishop, at several places in the island.

The result of the system of education has been little short of disastrous. Not only is the decay of art attributable directly to it, but far more serious results have occurred. In winter boys and youths flock to all the educational centres. Most of them are very poor and have to work between their lectures in order to gain their living. They are under no supervision out of school, and it is no one's business to take an interest in them. As a natural consequence many of them, often led astray by older companions, contract the habits of intemperance which are so prevalent in those parts of Iceland where it is possible to get liquor, but which were formerly confined, through necessity, to the population living in the neighbourhood of the trading-stations. Those farmers who lived in remote localities had only the opportunity to get drunk once a year, while their servants never learnt the taste of alcohol. Drunkenness is now a very common vice, the psychological effects of which are characteristic; for a drunken Icelander is rarely quarrelsome or merry, he merely drinks and drinks until he is stupid.

To remedy this state of matters the Salvation Army (which has a strong following in Iceland) and the Good Templars have worked hard. Strict drink laws have come into force, and a young Icelandic graduate of Cambridge has started a crusade in favour of athletic sports among the youth of his country. The last enterprise seems more likely to succeed than either the religious or the legal remedies; for temperance legislation can never be of much avail unless it is backed up by popular opinion, and it is fashionable in the island to believe in nothing, or rather to view everything except the greatness and virtue of Iceland with scepticism. Indeed, even the local patriotism often assumes a cynical tinge in the conversation of the best-educated islanders. Religious piety appears to have completely perished, and even superstitions are openly scoffed at, though in secret they may be fondly cherished.

Nothing shows this better than the condition of the material fabric of the churches. Through the week the church is very frequently used by the priest and his family as a store-room. Dirty wool is piled up in the corners and even in the pews, the ends of which serve as pegs on which they hang their wardrobe; an empty beer-bottle with a candle stuck in its neck stands either on the altar or on a window-ledge, often beside magnificent old brass candlesticks; a gallery is occupied by a mangle and a pile of dirty sheets. On Sundays the litter is hastily thrust on one side to make room for the congregation, which consists almost entirely of women. Going to church is their only opportunity of meeting their neighbours. Formerly the churches, by a very sensible usage, were used as sleeping-places for travellers; but some English tourists took it into their heads, having left their British respectability at home, to extinguish the candle which had been placed to light them on the altar, by throwing their boots at it, and so damaged the picture suspended above. This was brought to the notice of the bishop, who forbade the use of churches as sleeping-places. His injunction is not always obeyed, but it is hoped that the foreigners who profit by its contravention may make a less scandalous use of the privilege in future.

How far the modern scepticism of the Icelanders is due to their education is hard to say. It is certainly due in some measure to the social position of the clergy. Some few of them have been educated in Denmark and attempt by their example to produce an effect on the lives as well as the opinions of their parishioners; but the majority are in no respect superior to many of the farmers. In fact, they are farmers themselves, with their priestly functions superadded. A priest who does not work with his hands is despised; the stipends of the priests (often not more than £5 or £6 a year) make it necessary for them to produce a livelihood for themselves and their families out of their farms; their churches, of which each priest has several, are generally scattered over a large area; after a man has conducted the necessary services in several scattered churches, each of which he must visit so many times a year, and has finished working among the labourers on his farm, there is very little time for him to acquire a wide culture or an extraordinary influence among his neighbours. It is to be feared that the number of priests who even attempt to do so is very small, and that the number of those who spend the winter—their only time of even comparative leisure—in sloth, if not in drunkenness, is large.

As a rule the doctors are men of wider interests, for the

great majority of them have studied for some time on the Continent [1]; but they are few in number, greatly overworked, and often quite exhausted by their labours. They are government officials, each having a huge district under his charge.

There is thus, apart from the professional men in the towns and the official class (the members of which are often considered to be apeing the Danes by their compatriots), no body of men to whom the populace looks up. Local patriotism prevents a wider culture, fearing to reduce Icelanders to the level of 'Europeans.' In Iceland *studia non abeunt in mores*—at least this is the impression of a foreigner who has visited the island. It is, however, very hard for a 'European'—and perhaps especially hard for a graduate of one of the older English Universities—to appreciate the squalid culture of these northern peoples at its true value. How much of its squalor is merely superficial? The Icelandic farmers are no longer simple peasants; some of them are learned men, even scholars. Yet they live in a state bordering, so far as external conditions go, upon savagery, being, apparently, unable to make any practical use of their studies. Like the anchorites of old they seem to make a virtue of squalor—not, like the anchorites, a religious virtue, but a patriotic virtue. Our ancestors were dirty, they seem to say; we will be dirty too. Of course this contention is not true, if the inquirer goes far enough back in history; for the ancient Norsemen were not dirty, and almost the only hot bath that now exists in Iceland is one which was made at one of the hot springs by an early settler; but primitive simplicity and

[1] It is possible for them to qualify by spending one term at the University of Copenhagen after passing through the College at Reykjavik; but most of them stay longer abroad.

dirt often go hand in hand, and it is to be feared that cleanliness is essentially a civilized virtue, which died out in Iceland, as a result of civil war and other disasters culminating in intellectual degeneracy, centuries ago. The excuses of poverty and a bad climate may be brought forward, but these excuses are not valid beyond a certain point; for the climate is often very good through part of the year, and there is always a superfluity of water free. The Faroe people manage to use the scrubbing-brush.

In the foregoing pages I have attempted to sketch from a cultural standpoint—merely to sketch, for to do more would be impossible without staying a winter in the country—the conditions which prevail in Iceland at the present day; but of course factors wholly physical have played their part in the evolution of the Icelandic people, man being primarily an animal and only in the second place a cultured being. Unfortunately, exact data, which would probably be of extreme interest, are still lacking as regards the physical anthropology of the Icelandic race, and what I can say on the matter is only of the nature of a traveller's impressions. I have thought it better to defer mention of the agriculture and livestock of the people, and of those industries which arise from the keeping of livestock, and to deal with them in separate chapters, comparing them in detail with similar practices and industries in the Faroes, and going into the history of the domestic animals of the islands at some length.

In spite of centuries of poverty and exposure and disaster, of isolation for a thousand years and consequent in-breeding, the Icelandic people is not physically degenerate. Many persons attain a good old age; the majority are strong and capable of endurance; the chief diseases are those which can be traced directly, in the case of the individual, to dirt and insanitary conditions. Why is this? Perhaps an answer is to be found in the very misfortunes and discomforts to which the race has been exposed. The epidemics which raged throughout the Middle Ages at not very infrequent intervals, the earlier civil wars, the famines consequent upon volcanic devastation at all periods of Icelandic history, the rigours of the climate, the very filth in which the children are nurtured—all these have eliminated the weak, leaving the strong to perpetuate their race and transmit their characters to their descendants. Even the voyage to Iceland in the days of the Settling may have caused not a few to perish. If this is so, it may be asked, why is it that the slum population of our own great cities is not eliminated? Surely the conditions of their life are sufficiently unhealthy, surely they are sufficiently weak (in body if not in mind), and yet they increase and multiply? This is very true, but whatever weakening there may be in the slums there is far less actual elimination. The people of the slums lead a most unhealthy life; but not one which slays the adult individual. They are not exposed to storm and tempest on the sea, to the hazards of snow and precipice on the mountain, to the intense cold of an all but Arctic winter, to the terrors and exertion of a flight from the glowing lava stream or the cloud of black volcanic dust. Their search for food does not subject them to risk of life and limb, keeping them hardy and fit at the very time when their children are produced. They are protected by a beneficent and careful State against the risk of infection from the germs of those very diseases, such as plague, smallpox, and hydatids, which have again and again killed off the weaklings in Iceland; but they live in a condition of semi-starvation which renders them incapable of giving birth to healthy offspring. Strength of body or strength of intellect —unless it be abnormally great, sufficiently great to raise its possessor out of the abyss—are not the qualities which ensure success—and by 'success' I mean the power to live and to leave children behind—in the poverty-stricken world of the European slums; for a strong man or an ingenious man needs good and abundant food to feed his muscles or his brain, while a weakly man may be incapable of assimilating the same amount of nourishment, may, indeed, be better able to live when nourishment is scanty than the strong man, may survive when he would perish. In Iceland there is no room for men who are physically weak; the race, through the experience of a thousand years, has become adapted to obtain the greatest good possible from the victuals which the country provides; for all those who could not obtain a living from such nourishment were doomed to perish for want of any other. But in the slums the food of the people has changed from generation to generation, still remaining capable of supporting life, giving a chance of existence and persistence with every alteration to some new kind of decrepitude or strength—and the chance of its being a decrepitude is very great. In short, the Icelander has become adapted, through elimination of the unfit, to an environment which demands physical strength; the slum-dweller is probably in the course of adaptation to an environment wherein physical weakness, or at least its concomitant characters, are more suitable than strength. We do not say that the mouse is unfit because it has not the strength of an elephant, or that the race of the dwarfs of the Central African forest is less capable of surviving than that of the tall Patagonians. We have even seen that the mice of the northern islands are less weakly than those of the Tropics; but this does not mean that they are more prolific, for the species survives both in equatorial and sub-Arctic climes.

It is probable, therefore, that the Icelander has become physically changed in all the generations through which he has been isolated and exposed to peculiar dangers. It may even be that the change is so great as to be visible to our eyes. The best way to inquire if this be so will be to describe the physical characters of the race and to compare them with those of another race which we know to be of similar descent. Let us compare the Icelanders with their nearest neighbours the Faroemen. In the main the ancestry of the two peoples has been the same. Both originated, in the ninth century or a little later, from a stock which was mainly Teutonic but had in it another element of a very distinct kind—short, dark, and possibly with a longer head. As we shall see presently, a third element also went to form the breed. In Iceland this stock was preserved practically free from intermixture, while it is probable that in the Faroes additional blood akin to that of the second element was introduced at a later period. It is also possible that there may have been some intermixture between the Faroemen and the different races of the neighbouring countries of Scotland and Norway at a time subsequent to the original settling. Nowadays a very marked racial difference exists between the Icelanders and the Faroemen, which is not of the nature their history would lead us to expect, if we rely in our investigations solely on ancestral history since the islands were discovered. Of course this does not mean that it would be possible in the case of every individual to say ' This is an Icelander,' or 'This is a Faroeman,' with absolute certainty; but it could be done in a large proportion, probably in the majority of cases.

As we have seen, two very distinct types have persisted among the Faroemen, one, so far as general appearance goes, closely similar to the type commonly called Scandinavian; the other, short, dark, and alien-looking. Two types also persist in Iceland, of which one is closely similar to the second Farish type—it may produce great beauty among the women and a certain bold and even majestic look in the men, the features having even something of a Semitic cast. The second Icelandic type is often very different from the Scandinavian, though it fades by insensible gradations into it. It probably exists also in the Faroes, but is very rare; it may be called the 'Icelandic' type for the sake of simplicity, though only a proportion of the Icelanders belong definitely to it, a few being of the 'Iberian' type, while others belong to the 'Scandinavian' or to varieties intermediate between the 'Scandinavian' and the 'Icelandic.' Unfortunately no statistics are yet to hand which show the relative proportions of the different types in the population; I should say myself that the Iberian type is probably rarer than in Stromoe, certainly rarer than in Suderoe, and that it is about equally distributed in all parts of Iceland—but this is merely an impression, for which I can bring forward no statistical evidence.

The men of the 'Icelandic' type are probably taller in the majority of cases than the Faroemen of either kind; they are more stoutly built, less graceful, squarer and broader; their eyes are pale blue or grey; they may be almost albinoes as regards their hair, which is generally smooth and lank, less abundant and less rough than that of the

Iberians; their beards are as a rule scanty, and do not appear until late. But the most remarkable character they exhibit is the shape of their faces and the form of their features; unfortunately I have no information regarding the shape of their heads, but this is perhaps not so important a matter as some would have us believe. We have seen that the Faroeman's face, to whichever type he belongs, is usually narrow and oval, by no means flat, with delicate and well-marked features, which are less delicate and more prominent in dark individuals. The face of the 'Icelandic' type has very different characters; for it is short, broad, square, and flat, often with prominent cheekbones, with small, deep-set eyes, a short, broad, nose, and a very large mouth; the complexion is pale, lacking the ruddy colouring of the typical Scandinavian skin.

In fact, in form but not in colour, the 'Icelandic' face exhibits peculiarities which are generally associated with the great Mongol stock, especially with that offshoot of this stock which is usually known in England as the Lapps. The Lapps are not so dark as those who may be called Mongolians more strictly; their hair is frequently brown, though not so light as that of many Icelanders. That this resemblance is not entirely due to my own imagination—for I can bring forward no measurements to prove it—is shown by an examination of a picture of Icelandic types reproduced in 1810 by McKenzie in his excellent *Travels in the Island of Iceland*. The figure numbered five in his plate is as good a representative of the 'Icelandic' type as any photograph could reproduce, the peculiar 'wooden' look being not entirely due to the artist's lack of skill but actually true to nature.

Now it is a historic fact that in the ninth century and earlier the Scandinavians intermarried with the Lapps or

'Finns,' as they were originally called, whether or no we are willing to accept the evidence brought forward by Mr. David MacRitchie as proof positive that there were colonies of 'Finnmen' as late as the eighteenth century in parts of Europe where no Mongolians or semi-Mongolians now exist, and that these colonies were an important element in the ancestry of north-western Europe. Moreover Beddoe, than whom we could have no safer guide in physical anthropology, believes that physical traces of Mongolian ancestry can be detected in the Shetlanders. Is then the Lapp element reasserting itself in the Icelandic race, after having been seemingly swamped for generations, just as the 'Indian' element is said to be reasserting itself over the 'Latin' in certain parts of Central and South America? The difference in colour would not be an insuperable objection to some such theory, for we know that lack of pigment may have some connexion with a diminution of vitality in one direction; and the Lapps would appear to have been eminently adapted to a climate and conditions of life like those to which the Icelanders are exposed, for many centuries before Iceland was discovered. Is it not possible that those individuals in whom the Lapp element predominated may have been better able to survive in the struggle for existence, which must have far freer play in a country like Iceland than in one more highly civilized? Such suggestions must be printed with a note of interrogation, for our knowledge is still too scanty to state them as actual explanations of the facts before us; but they are at least worthy of consideration.

Before quitting the subject of the Icelandic people it may be interesting to glance at a few statistics regarding the population of the island, which has fluctuated much at different periods, owing to civil strife, epidemics, famines, volcanic outbursts, and, latterly, to emigration. In 1703 it numbered 50,444; in 1770 it had sunk to 46,201; in 1783 it was 47,287; in 1801 it was slightly lowered, being 47,207; by 1804 it had sunk again to 46,349. Nearly a century later, in 1901, it had risen to 78,470; but since 1901 it has probably sunk considerably through emigration to Canada and the United States. In foreign countries, however, the Icelanders exhibit a thrift and an energy which have no outlet at home, and many of the emigrants return, before reaching middle age, with what is regarded as a fortune in the land of their birth, for which they show a passionate affection. It is said that the old customs are even more jealously guarded from change in the Icelandic communities in America than they are in Iceland.

CHAPTER VI

DOMESTIC ANIMALS IN ICELAND AND THE FAROES

THE animals which the Icelanders and the Faroemen keep in their houses include both the dog and the cat. In the Faroes poultry and ducks are reared in considerable numbers, but mostly find their own food, roosting at night in the cellars which form the base of almost all the dwellings. In Iceland fowls are only kept in the farms which are on the coast or in the vicinity of the larger trading-stations. There is nothing peculiar about their breed in any of the islands, so far as I am aware, except their small size. At certain places in Iceland, however, I have noticed that the hens seem particularly liable to polydactylism or the growth of extra toes, and, seeing that this peculiarity appears also to exist among the Icelandic dogs, a question of some interest to naturalists is raised—is this due, directly or indirectly, to environment? I have no statistics to rely upon; but it would be worth any observer's while to note whether my impression is borne out by facts, for a few coincidences are apt to warp a traveller's mind on such a question, unless he has studied it in some detail.

Neither cat nor dog (that is to say, wolf) is indigenous to the island, but the true Icelandic cat is peculiar. It is of a dark blue-grey, in which certain lights enable darker markings to be detected. The fur is very short and thick; the size is small, and the form is slight. Good specimens of the breed are now becoming scarce, as a great deal of intermixture has taken place with ships' cats and others imported into the islands. There are few cat-fanciers in Iceland, and the Icelandic cat will probably soon be extinct. I believe that it has become fashionable in France as a rarity; but, curiously enough—possibly as an indirect result of in-breeding—it is extremely delicate and rarely survives removal from Iceland for long. A specimen formerly in my possession could hardly be induced to take milk or cream when brought to Edinburgh, but fed almost entirely on fish. It was stolen almost immediately; so evidently it must have been considered to be of some value by experts in Scotland. Probably the breed is highly specialized and so admirably adapted to its habitual environment that it is delicate in any other.

The Icelanders attribute the peculiar colour of their native cats to the fact that they prefer to breed out among volcanic rocks of a similar colour to themselves rather than in the houses, and that the kittens born under such conditions, like Jacob's ring-straked goats, are affected by maternal impressions. Even supposing the asserted fact to be true, it is most improbable that it is the real origin of their colour; though the question of maternal impressions is one which cannot be said to have been finally settled. It would rather seem that a peculiar smoky blue is associated with the climate of Arctic and sub-Arctic districts, whether directly or through its fitness and consequent perpetuation, it is difficult to say with certainty. That it is probably fixed by transmission through a considerable number of generations is, however, indicated by its imperfect development in cats of mixed breed born in Iceland. It is found, in a more or less marked degree, in many animals which live in cold climates; for example, it occurs, though not so intensely, in the summer pelage of the northern 'Blue' hare (*Lepus timidus*), in the fur of the 'Blue' foxes of Iceland and Greenland (which are merely a variety of the white Arctic fox (*Canis lagopus*), found both in Iceland[1] and especially in more strictly Arctic countries); occasionally, as a slight tinge, in that of the Icelandic and Esquimo dog, in the hair of northern cattle (even, as my friend Mr. Muir Stewart tells me, as far south as the northern Hebrides), and possibly in the hair of many Icelanders, which has a peculiar silvery grey tinge, especially in early youth. Moreover, a breed of 'blue' cats (of which I have seen specimens brought to Leith by sailors), is found in the extreme north of Russia that is in all respects similar to the Icelandic breed. Possibly it exists also in Norway, and in any case it was probably brought to Iceland from Scandinavia. It does not occur spontaneously in the Faroes, so far as I can discover; but Icelandic cats have, to my knowledge, been imported into Thorshavn, and individuals of the peculiar coloration are occasionally seen both on Stromoe and on other islands of the group.

The Icelandic dog was originally a representative of that curious northern stock which reaches its finest development in the Chow breed of Manchuria and the sledge dogs of the Esquimos. It is characterized by a pointed nose, prick ears, thick fur, and a curly tail, which is carried bent upwards over the back: obviously it is a near relative of the wolf, with which it frequently interbreeds. In Iceland, as in Norway, the type is reproduced on a small

---

[1] White skins, said to be of native origin, can frequently be bought in Reykjavik, and the older authors mention both white and blue foxes as occurring in Iceland. It has been stated, however, that only the blue variety inhabits the island. (See Lydekker's *Mostly Mammals*, p. 212.)

scale, and its representatives are of a comparatively feeble build. The eyes are often blue, and this peculiarity is perpetuated, in an instance which has lately come under my notice, in a half-breed, the father of which was a Scotch collie and the mother an Icelandic one, though in other respects the dog resembles its British parent. The breed, like that of the cats, is now rapidly disappearing, having been much crossed with Scotch collies. This has been done with the object of increasing its intelligence; but it is doubtful whether the desired effect has been produced.

A few years ago regulations were passed in Iceland about the keeping of dogs, especially as regards the towns; for it has been found that almost all of them are infested with a small tapeworm (*Echinococcus*), the eggs of which give rise to very serious consequences. The worm itself is too small to do much injury to the dog, being only a fraction of an inch in length; but should the eggs, which pass out of the dog's body, gain entry into a man's interior through his mouth, they may produce, in his liver or in some other organ, enormous cysts full of liquid which cause the very greatest disturbance and even death. Hydatids, as these cysts are called, are the cause of a large part of the normal mortality in Iceland, owing to the close association between the Icelander and his dog; and a similar condition of affairs produces a similar prevalence of the disease, though perhaps not quite so great a mortality, in some parts of Australia.

Dogs are an absolute necessity in Iceland; without them it would be impossible to gather the sheep or herd the ponies; it would seem more practical, if possibly less practicable, to improve the sanitary conditions on the farms than to restrict the keeping of dogs in the towns. A scene to the point is in my mind. A friend and I had reached what was probably the filthiest human dwelling that either of us had ever seen—a farm in Rangarval. We were very hungry, having crossed that morning without a proper breakfast from the Westman Isles; but we had great difficulty in getting anything to eat, as all the people on the farm except an old man and an old woman were away at the haymaking. After a good deal of talk the old man agreed to get us some milk. He took us into the dormitory, and from under a bed he produced the milk in a wooden bicker. A dog followed sniffing at our heels, and we noticed another in an outhouse licking the big iron pot in which the haymakers' breakfast had been prepared. The milk was too filthy, hungry as we were, to be taken in its natural state, and the divinity student who was accompanying us as a guide to Reykjavik persuaded the old woman to boil it for us. We had disturbed her in the act of grubbing up potatoes with her hands from a plot in front of the farm, and she had merely rubbed off the loose earth with her apron. She took down the pot from a shelf without any further cleansing of her person. When the milk was ready she brought it to us in a jug. There was a black scum on its surface, and when we objected to this she plunged her dirty hand, still contaminated with earth and all it may have contained, into the milk and pulled out the scum. Under such conditions the spread of disease is not surprising.

In the Faroes I do not think that the prevalence of 'liver plague' is nearly so great; but the people keep fewer dogs and do not live in such close association with them. (Their superior cleanliness appears also to have protected them against the infantile tetanus which once wrought so much havoc among newly born children in some parts of Iceland.)

The dogs in these islands are of a different kind from those of Iceland. They formerly belonged to three very distinct breeds, of which Landt, writing, it will be remembered, rather over a century ago, says as follows:—'those which seem to be of the oldest breed have a somewhat long-pointed muzzle, and short erect ears; but most of them have their ears half or entirely hanging down, stand pretty high on their legs, and are smooth-haired. A smaller kind of dogs are kept for driving the sheep from the enclosures, when they jump over the fences (walls) in summer; the principal property of these dogs is to bark.'

Landt's breed with the short erect ears was probably identical with the Icelandic dogs; but he is wrong in considering it the oldest indigenous breed, for Debes, writing in the seventeenth century, describes the Farish dogs of his day as 'long and small, almost like Greyhounds.' The wolf-like stock is now practically extinct in the islands; I have seen one individual of the type in Suderoe, but it may have been brought from Iceland. The smooth-haired dog with hanging ears still persists in some of the islands, especially on Naalsoe; it has a head something like that of a pointer, rather long legs, and a short coat, which is usually of a dark colour. The third breed is also common side by side with the preceding; and there is little chance of intermixture owing to difference in size and shape. It is small, curly-haired and with short legs, somewhat resembling the griffon dogs of the Continent. Its principal property certainly is its bark; but it is a very cowardly little beast.

An interesting thing has happened to the dogs in the immediate neighbourhood of Thorshavn. Some ten years ago a former amtmand introduced from Denmark a well-bred dachshund dog, which apparently interbred with a large number of native bitches. Now hardly a dog can be seen in the place which has not got the bandy legs and other peculiarities of the dachshund in more or less marked degree. This shows that the foreign dog has proved 'prepotent,' in other words that it has been able to transmit its characters to its descendants in such a way that they have dominated those of the other parent. We might have expected that this would have been the case if dog-breeders' views are correct; for a dog having the characters of a peculiar breed in a well-marked degree is likely to be in-bred, that is to say, to have a comparatively small number of individual ancestors in its pedigree; and it has been deduced from their experience by breeders that in-bred animals are frequently prepotent. Landt's remarks about the Faroe dogs, on the other hand, show that the native breed was decidedly mixed as long ago as the end of the eighteenth century.

Neither in Iceland nor in the Faroes have the dogs the intelligence and training of the British sheep-dogs. Their duty is not so much to marshal a flock of sheep as to single out individuals which stray from the others and to bring them in by seizing hold of them. They are trained not to bark when the sheep are being collected; but at other times they have a wonderful nose for strangers and act as very efficient protectors of a house, so far as making a noise can go. They are also able to trace the sheep which have got covered up with snow and to dig them out. In Iceland they are employed in herding horses on a journey. When a man is travelling with a train of pack ponies he drives them on in front of him; but they take every opportunity of running away, unless there is a dog to bark at their heels and keep them in single file.

The history and present condition of the horses of

Iceland and the Faroes have lately been dealt with in a paper by my friend Mr. Francis H. A. Marshall and myself, and many of the facts to be here set forth are derived from this source. For zoological information especially I am indebted to Mr. Marshall, who was my companion on my last visit to the Faroes. In our account of the ponies we begin by describing in brief the history of the islands. This will be unnecessary in the present chapter, but one or two points may be noted, although most of them could be deduced from what has been said previously.

We know as a historical fact that Iceland was occupied at the end of the ninth century by two distinct bodies of men, who belonged to rather different social classes, so far as social classes could then be said to exist among the free-born. The first colonists were adventurers or vikings, whose calling was that of pirates and who owed what they had to what they took. Many of them were of good blood, had gathered round them by their prowess a band of followers and obtained by their expeditions much material wealth. Of those who came to Iceland the first settled definitely in the island in the year 874 A.D. The majority of the settlers belonging to this group had already had homes for at least a generation in the British Isles, though they called themselves Norsemen and were of Norwegian extraction. This is proved by the *Landnáma-bóc*, which has been called the 'Domesday Book of Iceland,' containing as it does an ancient record of all the early colonists of the islands and of their lands and parentage. Moreover, we know that some of them brought with them a considerable number of 'Westmen' slaves, some of whom, as we have seen, enjoyed a brief period of freedom on the islets afterwards called Vestmannaeyjar.

About twenty years after the first settling another body

of colonists arrived. Partly because the south of the islands was already occupied, and partly for superstitious reasons[1], they settled in the north, where, at any rate in later times, the climate was better. This second batch of colonists belonged to a higher class than the first, for they numbered among them some of the most powerful families in Norway. King Harald Fairhair, the paramount sovereign of that country, had determined to reduce to order the chaos of warring factions that occupied the land, and so to make himself a king in fact as in name. Wise though this course undoubtedly was, and successful in the end, it naturally proved obnoxious to the chiefs his vassals, whose power and pretensions he was determined to reduce. He was a mighty man of war; they fled before him to the north of Scotland and Ireland, the Hebrides and the Orkneys, were pursued, beaten and decimated; their survivors found rest at last in the remotest islands of the north-west sea. Many of them, therefore, came to Iceland not direct from Norway, but after a sojourn in what are now the northern Scottish islands.

The history of the colonization of the Faroes was evidently similar, though precise details are lacking. Professor York Powell shows that many of the early settlers were related to those of Iceland by blood and marriage, and we know that all of what has been called, somewhat loosely, the old Norse Empire was knit together by frequent though unorganized intercourse in the early times.

It is no great assumption, therefore, to assume that the settlers of both parties brought with them to Iceland and the Faroes a considerable proportion of Hebridean or Irish livestock, though it is only reasonable to believe that

[1] They followed the house-pillars which they brought with them from Norway and cast into the sea off the Icelandic coast.

a proportion had also originated from Scandinavia and possibly from countries further afield. After they had settled in Iceland, moreover, their predatory expeditions did not cease for some centuries, and many of the young men visited Jerusalem on pilgrimages after the introduction of Christianity at the beginning of the eleventh century, while others took service for a period in the bodyguard of the Emperors at Constantinople. They may well have brought back horses with them, and it is worthy of remark that Olaf Eigilsson noted in 1627 a resemblance between the horses of Algiers which were employed in working cornmills and those of Iceland. In short, it is probable that the original breed of horses in Iceland and the Faroes was of mixed origin, in which the Hebridean and the Scandinavian stocks predominated, though blood from South Europe or even from the African and Asiatic coasts of the Mediterranean may have also contributed to its formation.

Now, as Professor Ewart has shown, it is possible even now, after centuries of interbreeding, to distinguish at least two main types among the horses of the British Isles and the north-west of Europe. These two types he has named the 'Celtic pony' and the 'cart-horse' types. At the present day the Norwegian horses belong mostly to the latter, the Faroe and Icelandic horses to the former.

The peculiar characters of Professor Ewart's so-called Celtic pony, which he has found as an important element in the equine population of certain of the more remote and isolated of the Hebrides (for example, Barra), of parts of North Ireland, and of Iceland and the Faroes, are its small size, small head and slender limbs, the absence or reduction of the hock callosities or chestnuts on the hind legs—the wrist callosities of the fore-limbs persist—and the short hairs in the upper part of the tail. The typical cart-horse, on the other hand, is usually larger (though some very small horses belong to this type), is always of stouter build, has a larger and coarser head, a tail in which the hairs of the upper part are mostly of the same length as those lower down, and very large hock callosities. These differences in structure are not of a kind, so far as we know, which is likely to be the result of environment, except perhaps the short hairs in the upper part of the tail, of which Professor Ewart has lately discovered the function from observations on the living animals[1]. The chestnuts at any rate are probably vestigial, that is to say, they are the remnants of structures which had a use far back in the history of the race, but appear to be functionless in all breeds of modern horses, just as the appendix, of which we hear so much nowadays, is probably functionless in the adult human being. They have quite disappeared in the asses and zebras, but are large in the true wild horse of Central Asia.

Mr. Marshall's examination of a number of Icelandic and Faroe ponies shows very clearly that these breeds belong essentially to the 'Celtic' type, despite the facts of their mixed origin in early times and of the great admixture with Norwegian blood that has taken place in the Faroes within the last few years. Of course all of them are not equally good representatives of the type, and a few, which are half or three-quarters Norwegian, have the characters of the 'cart-horse' breeds well developed. Moreover, there is no breed now in existence in which the characters of either type are absolutely uniform, and this is especially true of the 'Celtic' characters. Prjevalsky's horse, the wild species of Central Asia, is the only genuine wild horse

[1] See the second paper referred to under his name in the bibliography; also Mr. Marshall's appendix at the end of this volume.

which still survives, and although it was probably not this species, approximates to the 'cart-horse type' rather than the 'Celtic pony.' Some twenty thousand years ago, however, the two types are believed to have existed as separate forms or species in Southern France, for not only have their skeletons been unearthed, but even their portraits, scratched on the walls of caves by Palaeolithic man, remain intact. Of course neither skeletons nor portraits can bear on the question of the chestnuts; but both illustrate the difference in other respects very clearly. The wonder is that after thousands of years of inter-breeding the two types should remain at all distinct, not that they should often have become confused. The facts are most instructive as illustrating the peculiar persistence of certain zoological species and the way in which well-defined types may survive the effects of cross-breeding and environment, being, perhaps, in themselves well adapted to a variety of conditions and therefore having an advantage over forms which are more highly specialized. The fact that the Icelandic and Faroe breed has proved prepotent over a continental stock in modern times, after having been isolated for wellnigh a thousand years, is also of interest; for there is more chance of a form shut up in remote islands being in-bred than one from a continent. Indeed, it is even possible that the Norwegian breed has had in the past an extremely wide range, and therefore great opportunities for cross-breeding, for it is similar in many respects to the Mongol ponies (which must not be confused with the wild horse) of Central Asia, and it is possible that this type may still exist all over the European and Asiatic mainland of the sub-Arctic zone. The dogs in the Faroes, which did not belong to an isolated breed, have, as we have seen, not proved prepotent when foreign blood was introduced even through a single individual belonging to an in-bred race; but the ponies of these islands, having become in-bred, have proved very distinctly prepotent, even when the amount of foreign blood brought into the race has been considerable. It is possible that there is not a single purebred Faroe pony now existing, and yet the Faroe breed remains quite distinct from the Norwegian.

So far I have taken it for granted that the Icelandic and the Faroe ponies are identical; and, as regards their general type, this is the case. There are, however, certain local differences in the different districts of Iceland, as may be well seen from the statements in the *Voyage en Islande* published at Paris in 1802. This book is a French translation of a very full report on the different districts of Iceland. It was made to the then King of Denmark by two commissioners named Olafsen and Poulsen, of whom the former was an Icelander born, the latter a Dane resident in the island as a doctor. I have not been able to see a copy of the original report; but the translation gives a detailed account of the livestock, and though it does not deal with matters of purely biological interest as regards the ponies, it shows that local differences in the breed did exist in the eighteenth century, as I believe they still do. In the seventeenth century the ponies of Suderoe in the Faroes are said to have been lighter and swifter than those of the other islands. Moreover, there appears to have been a difference in colour between those of Faroe and those of Iceland; for Landt says that the former were in his day mostly 'fox colour' and occasionally black; while the majority of the pure Icelandic breed are either very pale dun, with a dark stripe down the centre of the back and often with dark cross-bars on the limbs, or else piebald. The red colour, which is still common in the Faroes, is the typical colour of the Hebridean ponies, and Martin, who visited St. Kilda in the seventeenth century, says that the few horses then on the island, where now there are none, were red. It is therefore possible that the Faroe ponies, in this particular, have remained truer representatives of the 'Celtic' type than those of Iceland, which may possibly have been more strictly guarded from the introduction of fresh Hebridean blood during the course of their history. In other words, it is possible that, in the matter of colour, evolution has been more active in Iceland than the Faroes. It is also possible that this may have been due to the greater rigour of the climate in Iceland, and therefore the necessity for higher specialization in an isolated race. Professor Ewart, however, believes that dun, the colour of many desert animals, was that not only of the primaeval horse itself, but also of the 'Celtic' pony.

A question naturally arises as to the Shetland ponies, which most of us at least know by sight—are they identical with the Icelandic and Faroe breeds? It is probable that they once were; but Shetland has not been isolated like the Faroes and Iceland; for centuries it has been subject to Scottish colonization, and foreign blood has thus been introduced among the livestock in very large quantities, as has also been the case with the population. Accordingly we find that the Shetland ponies of to-day belong to a mixed breed, some representatives of which exhibit the 'Celtic' characters while others do not. In 1839 a Danish official named Ployen, who was then amtmand of the Faroes, visited Shetland with a view of investigating the agricultural conditions in what he acknowledges to be the more advanced group of islands. In his account of his visit, which has been translated into English, he only mentions horses incidentally. He notes, however, that the Shetland breed in his day was even smaller than that of the Faroes, but was strong and sturdy. Nowadays, of course, it is frequently bred for small size combined with strength, and is used in traction; but Ployen remarks that, while in Orkney he rode in a gig with a strong Scotch horse, in Shetland he could generally travel on a pony with a good saddle along a riding-path, and in Faroe he was frequently compelled to walk.

Until about thirty-five years ago the ponies of Iceland were only used in the island; but in 1868 an English firm commenced to import them, and considerable numbers are now sent to this country every year. It is not the best specimens of the breed, however, that generally come; but those which are small and stout enough to be employed successfully in hauling trucks in the Cumberland coal-mines and in other work of the kind. Fine Icelandic ponies are now growing rare, and it is probable that the export trade will gradually alter the character of the breed completely, as a different class of beast is now wanted. In the Faroes the state of matters is similar, but the export trade is very much smaller.

This is not only due directly to the smaller area of the group, but also to the fact that, owing to the smaller area and to the proximity of the sea to all inhabited places in the islands, ponies have always been of less importance and less attention has been paid to them. The distances are so short from village to village that they have seldom been used for riding, and, communication being mostly conducted by sea, have been chiefly employed in bringing down into the villages the peat, hay, &c., procured by the villagers. In most of the islands it is impossible owing to the nature of the ground to ride them while gathering the sheep; but Debes says of Suderoe—'In Suderoe the people are somewhat lazy, but they have lighter and swifter horses than in the other islands; when therefore they go about their sheep, they ride, and their dogs follow them, they knowing how to ride with their horses up hills and down dales in a full gallop, through moors, and over rocks and stones, so that the horses care for nothing when they hunt after sheep, and where the place is too difficult to ride over to pursue them; the man leaps from his horse in the midst of his course, and takes his best advantage against the sheep, the horse running after him till he leaps upon it again; in the mean time the dogs follow also, till they have driven the sheep into the *retten* (sheepfold). A part of the horses are also so taught, that the man over-reaching the sheep on horse back, the horse graspeth the same between his forelegs, till the man takes it up.'

This passage was written about 1670, but if it was true of Suderoe then, it is probably true now. In this case the Suderoë ponies must be far more highly trained than those of the other islands of the group.

The horse-furniture in general use in the Faroes is of the very simplest nature, leaving the few riding-saddles employed out of account. The ropes used in it are frequently of wool, either plaited from several strands or twisted with a spindle. The band that passes under the horse's belly is generally of wool knitted. As in Iceland, slabs of turf form the foundation, as it were, of the pack-saddle. These are laid across the animal's back, and over them a wooden crook-saddle is placed. It is provided on either side with hooks, on which wooden creels, containing peat, manure, corn, fish, birds, or anything else may be hung. The women's riding-saddles in Iceland are very elaborate; formerly they were often ornamented with large quantities of embossed brass. There are some fine specimens, several of which are figured by Herr Bruun in the Museum at Reykjavik.

The immense importance of the horse in Icelandic life has been noted in another chapter. Not only is it employed in all kinds of transport and as a means of getting from one place to another, but it is even used to carry the coffin, which is strapped across its back, to the grave. In a recent memoir by Dr. Burmeister its employment by women in going about to see their friends and the like is fully illustrated; but it is naturally the men who use it most. The best riding-horses in the island are taught to amble, providing a very easy seat on a long journey. They are often well formed and swift, reaching a size considerably in excess of that of the majority of the ponies exported to this country. My impression is that those used exclusively for riding are more often of a reddish colour than the pack ponies; but in this I may be wrong. Mares are most in request for the former purpose, and the stallions, which are often very vicious, are rarely used except for stud purposes. One exercise in which the ponies of the Icelandic mainland excel is that of swimming the ice-cold rivers of their island with heavy loads on their backs; but this is probably the result of training, as a very pretty little pony from Heimey, brought across to Rangarval by Mr. Eustace Gurney and myself in 1898, showed itself terrified at even the smallest stream, and could be induced to cross the rivers only with the greatest difficulty.

An amusement which is now quite obsolete in Iceland, and apparently has been since the seventeenth century, was horse-fighting. Formerly it was regarded with great favour in the island, into which it had been introduced from Norway or the Hebrides. Herr Daniel Bruun, who has written a most elaborate account of the horses of Iceland, the Faroes, and Greenland, their furniture and uses, gives several references from old Icelandic literature to horse-fighting; but the classical account of a horse-fight is contained in *Njal's Saga*. The following is Sir George Dasent's translation of the passage:—

'Now men ride to the horse-fight, and a very great crowd is gathered together there. Gunnar was there and his brothers, and the sons of Sigfus. Njal and all his sons. There too was Starkad and his sons, and Egil and his sons, and they said to Gunnar that now they would lead the horses together.

'Gunnar said, "That was well."

'Skarphadinn said, "Wilt thou that I drive thy horse, kinsman Gunnar?"

'"I will not have that," says Gunnar.

'"It wouldn't be amiss though," says Skarphadinn; "we are hot headed on both sides."

'"Ye would say or do little," says Gunnar, "before a quarrel would spring up; but with me it will take longer, though it will be the same in the end."

'After that the horses were led together; Gunnar busked him to drive his horse, but Skarphadinn led him out. Gunnar was in a red kirtle, and had about his loins a broad belt, and a great riding-rod in his hand.

'Then the horses ran at one another, and bit each other long, so that there was no need for any one to touch them, and that was the greatest sport. Then Thorgeir and Kol made up their minds that they would push their horses forward just as the horses rushed together, and see if Gunnar would fall before him.

'Now the horses ran at one another again, and both Thorgeir and Kol ran alongside their horses' flank.

'Gunnar pushed his horse against them, and what happened in a trice was this, that Thorgeir and his brother fall down flat on their backs, and their horse a-top of them.

'Then they spring up and rush at Gunnar. Gunnar swings himself free and seizes Kol, casts him down on the field, so that he lies senseless. Thorgeir, Starkad's son, smote Gunnar's horse such a blow that one of his eyes started out. Gunnar smote Thorgeir with his riding-rod, and down falls Thorgeir senseless; but Gunnar goes to his horse, and says to Kolskegg, "Cut off the horse's head; he shall not live a maimed and blemished beast."

'So Kolskegg cut the head off the horse.

'Then Thorgeir got on his feet and took his weapons, and wanted to fly at Gunnar, but that was stopped, and there was a great throng and crush.'

A more orderly horse-fight is represented in an old engraving preserved in the National Library at Reykjavik. It is reproduced on a small scale by Bruun, and there is a large photograph of it in the Pitt-Rivers Museum at Oxford. In it we see no less than three contests in progress at once; only two horses taking part in each, though several more are held in readiness. The combatants stand on their hind-legs and bite at one another's heads. Each pair is surrounded by a semi-circle of men, two of whom are provided with long stakes with which to separate the horses. In one case they also grasp them by the tails. A few old men are seated on a rock watching the play, and on another rock, at a greater distance, a party of women have taken up their position. Many of the men assisting at the fight appear to be armed with daggers, perhaps owing to an oversight on the artist's part, for there is a great pile of weapons of all sorts at a safe distance from the fight, and it appears to have been the custom to lay aside all weapons on such occasions, in order that little harm should be done if a brawl arose.

I have seen a very similar horse-fight among the Patani Siamese between ponies from the Malay Archipelago, and bull-fights of the same kind are common in all the Malay States not under British rule. The two bulls are brought together by means of cords passed through their noses, which are then slipped; and they are urged to fight by the voices of their owners. They belong to a placid zebu breed, and often show no great desire to engage with one another. Instead of rising on their hindlegs like the pony stallions, they lower their heads and butt at one another, rarely using their horns, but merely shoving with all their strength. I cannot refrain from quoting, as a parallel (and at the same time, a contrast) to the account of the horse-fight in the old saga, a Malay account of a bull-fight of this kind which took place at the town of Patani in 1901. It appears to have been one in which the bulls, doubtless the fiercest of their breed, actually gored one another; but I cannot vouch for the literal accuracy of all the statements, though the main facts are certainly correct. The account is extracted from the diary of a Malay, who was in the service of Mr. Herbert C. Robinson and myself. I translate it as literally as the genius of the Malay language will permit.

'Now the Raja had bidden his nobles make ready a bull-fight on the fourteenth day of the month. So the speckled bull of Datoh 'Che Wan 'Che Umah fought with the red bull of Raja Phra Si; and the stakes were one thousand and five hundred dollars, which the Raja of the country gave. The bull of 'Che Wan 'Che Umah was beaten, and its entrails hung out of its left side, so that it fainted. Then the Raja of the country said, "Bring the bull before me that I may see it!" And when they had brought it, he said, "Cut its throat that it may die!" And Datoh 'Che Wan 'Che Umah wept, for he loved that bull like a son; but Raja Phra Si hung a golden chain round the neck of his bull, and wreathed its horns with flowers, and put golden anklets on all its four legs. Then all men applauded him. Many men fought their bulls upon that day, about fifteen couples in all; and those who won rejoiced, but those who lost were sore of heart.'

To return from this digression from Iceland to Malaya. The diet of the horses both of Iceland and the Faroes is one which might be expected to predispose them to ferocity, for it is by no means entirely of a vegetable nature, and it has been found in many countries, especially in parts of Australia, that the addition of flesh to the food of a horse gives it additional spirit and strength, though it may have unpleasant after-consequences provided that the strength so acquired is not, as it were, worked off. A friend tells me that even in Scotland he has sometimes given a piece of beefsteak to an Argentine horse on which he is accustomed to ride long distances. After this he finds that it returns home after great exertion in a fresh condition, suffering in no way subsequently. But if the meat is given it and no great exertion follows, it is off its feed at the next meal. During the summer both in Iceland and the Faroes the food of the ponies consists entirely of grass, and in many districts, where they are allowed to fend for themselves through the winter, the same is true all the year round. They have, however, a natural inclination towards animal food, and on Heimey I have seen ponies making their way to the sea-shore to feed on fish-heads and the like even in summer, when there was plenty of good pasture for them. In some parts of Iceland at least a proportion of the horses are kept through part of the winter in stables near the farms, and those which are so protected are fed very largely at this season on dried cods' heads, which also form the staple food of the cattle when the hay harvest has been a bad one. At some places too, where the cat-fish is caught in large numbers, its body, either fresh or, more frequently, dry, is given them. This peculiar diet is said to be very nourishing to milch kine, just as dried whale-meat is supposed to be in the Faroes. Naturally the milk has a peculiar taste, but those who are accustomed to it do not notice it. Even in Mull I have seen a cow eating a dead flounder on the sea-shore.

I must confess to having paid comparatively little attention to the cattle of the Faroes and Iceland, and to be able to find very little about their anatomical characters in the books I have consulted. They appear to belong to the same stock as the well-known Shetland breed (which so closely resembles the extinct *Bos longifrons*), but always to have been larger.

In some parts of Iceland hornlessness was common, apparently not as a character of the breed but merely of individuals. This is clearly asserted in the *Voyage en Islande*; but I do not know whether it is still the case. Anderson, 'late Burgomaster of Hamburgh,' whose account of Iceland (which, by the way, he had never visited) is incorporated in Horrebow's *Natural History*, was quite wrong in stating that no Icelandic cattle had horns, for objects were made of horn in Iceland from the earliest time, and at the present day I do not remember ever to have seen a hornless cow or ox in the island.

Olafsen and Poulsen notice a peculiar natural deformity

which sometimes occurred among the cattle of Iceland. They say that calves were born which had the vertebrae of the loins so bent that their bellies almost touched the ground. The deformity did not prevent them from giving abundant milk, and appears to have been to some extent hereditary, as the authors of the report had seen an individual born of a mother with the same peculiar shape. They do not say whether individuals of the kind were all of the one sex, but only mention cows. Probably, in any case, only cows would be kept alive if deformed.

The cattle of Iceland are of different colours, but the peculiar smoky tinge to which I have alluded is not uncommon in their coats.

The cattle of the Faroes are of the same general type as those of Iceland. Ployen remarks that he was much disappointed in the Shetland cattle, finding them smaller and less fat than those of the Faroes, and Debes says that in his day a Faroe ox sometimes produced 100 pounds of tallow. In the seventeenth century the price of a good sheep-dog was the same as that of a cow. The breed has lately been much improved by the introduction of Danish blood, and Ployen brought back with him to Thorshavn a Scotch bull, with which he hoped to cross the native stock successfully.

Pigs are very rarely kept either in the Faroes or in Iceland, and I have heard it said in the former islands that the people are afraid of trichinosis, though I do not know how they have ever heard of the disease. In the Faroes a considerable number of goats are kept for the sake of their milk, not in flocks but singly or in twos and threes. They are usually brought in at night, as is the case with a few of the cattle, and sleep in the stone cellars under the houses. They appear to be of the same breed as that generally seen in this country, and their introduction has been comparatively recent.

Sheep are by far the most numerous of the domestic animals, if they can be called domestic, both in the Faroes, to which they have probably given a name, and in Iceland, in many parts of which sheep-farming is the one industry. Those of the Faroes belonged in Debes' day to three different breeds, one (chiefly found in the northern islands) white, one of a reddish colour, and one (confined to a few small islands in the extreme south of the group) black. Even in the seventeenth century, however, the three breeds had become to some extent mixed, and at the end of the eighteenth, Landt says that there was a tradition that about two centuries earlier there had been so severe a winter in the Faroes that the sheep had been practically exterminated. After this, new stock had been introduced into the north of the group from Iceland, and into the south from Shetland. The sheep of the north still continued superior to those of the south. The climate of certain small islands, however, was believed to turn sheep black, and Debes, who solemnly discusses the question whether this was due to the 'Sea Vapours,' or to something in the soil ('Whether the cause is in the earth, whether it be Brimstone or Saltpetre'), says that he had found that sheep which were brought to these islands, 'grew first spotted about their legs, afterwards on their thighs, then under their Bellyes, and finally all over.' This appears to incline him to the view that the 'sea vapours,' which were the reputed cause of the change of colour among the islanders, were not the true cause. As a matter of fact the sheep of Great Diamond and a few other islands in the neighbourhood of Suderoe probably represented a very ancient stock, akin to that of St. Kilda.

They are described by old men now living as having had very long legs, wool like hair, and flesh which was of a dark colour and had a peculiar flavour. Latterly they became quite wild and could only be shot, until, some ten years ago, they were surrounded by a great body of men on the few hills where they still existed, and were chased down a steep place into the sea. They annoyed the sheep-farmers by eating the grass which they wished to preserve for a more profitable breed, and also by interbreeding with other sheep pastured on the same hills and so causing the offspring to partake of their own likeness, as they appear to have been very prepotent. Thus they are extinct; but, in all probability, their blood still survives, though now much diluted. Quite lately Cotswold rams have been introduced into several of the islands, either direct from Scotland or from Norway, and the breed is said to be improving greatly. Individuals with black, reddish brown, dull brown or piebald wool are still very numerous, and the modern stock is evidently one adapted for a mountain habitat. Horns are usually developed and cases in which four or more are produced sometimes occur, though such individuals are regarded as a rarity.

The Icelandic breed appears to be of a finer quality than those of the Faroes, and to differ less in different districts; the proportion of pure white individuals is probably greater than in the smaller islands.

The life of the sheep in these north-western islands is a very hard one. A few may be kept tethered near the houses, and in the Faroes a pet lamb is not infrequently fed on the luxuriant crop of grass which the roof of the homestead provides. In some parts of Iceland, too, a small flock of ewes is kept throughout the summer in the neighbourhood of the farm, and is milked regularly every evening, the milk being made into a peculiarly soapy kind of cheese. It is also the custom on many farms to build low sheds of turf in which the sheep may take shelter in bad weather, or may even be fed on hay. Both in the Faroes and in Iceland, however, a large part of the flocks winter out of doors, picking up a scanty nourishment from the vegetation in sheltered spots, and when this fails making their way to the sea-shore to feed on sea-weed. In their eagerness for this many fall off the rocks and get dashed to pieces or drowned. Sometimes they are reduced to such straits that they gnaw the wool off one another's backs.

Though they may sometimes have to be dug out from under the snow or even gathered together in turf enclosures during the winter, as a rule they are only collected three times, or even only twice, in a year. Sheep-gathering, where there are no trained sheep-dogs, little level ground and an exceeding active stock, is always a difficult and often a dangerous undertaking. The only way of accomplishing it is to surround the sheep with a large body of men and dogs, the former either on horseback or afoot, and drive them into enclosures of rough stones and turf which have a single rather narrow entrance. In misty weather fatal accidents from falls over precipices sometimes occur during this operation. As a rule the flock is thus collected first in late spring or early summer, when the wool is taken; then about August, when owners' marks are put upon the lambs (either by cutting away a portion of the ear or by painting their bodies with some indelible pigment) and the ewes are protected by a piece of canvas from the lambs, which are still eager to suck; and thirdly in the beginning of October or a little later, when those beasts which are to be killed for winter food are selected and slaughtered.

After the carcasses have been cleaned and skinned on the last occasion the fat is carefully removed. It is generally weighed before being stored away, and is used for much the same purposes as that of sea-fowl. In the Faroes the machine almost invariably employed in weighing it is the wooden beam to which reference has already been made; but in Iceland, where people ridicule the idea of a wooden beam, a steelyard with movable weights, which may, in rare cases, be made of stone, is used. The flesh is then cut up and preserved. In the Faroes it is merely suspended, sometimes wrapped in buttercloth to preserve it from flies, in the 'dry-houses,' the interstices in the walls of which allow a free current of air to circulate round it. In Iceland it is hung up in the roomy chimney of the kitchen, where it is smoked by the peat-reek. In either case it is eaten raw, having acquired much the appearance and consistency of horn. It is considered very nutritious when in this condition, and has the advantage over salt meat of not inducing thirst.

Sheep's horns are used for a variety of purposes. I have already noted how they are utilized in the Farish game of 'sheep-dogs,' and they are also set up like ninepins in another game of the same nationality. They are often employed, both in Iceland and in the Faroes, in making the fastenings of horse-furniture, the backs of heckling-combs and a number of similar articles; while in the Faroes the indicator of the weighing-beam is frequently a semi-circle of sheep's horn suspended by a piece of whale's sinew.

Wool is, however, the most important product of the sheep. It is soft and of a good quality; much of it,

CARDING WOOL, NAALSOE, FAROES

[*To face p. 19*

coming from coloured animals, is naturally of a pleasant tint. It is, however, very easily separable, in the case of each sheep, into a soft inner layer and a harsher outer one. It is literally pulled from the animals' backs, or else gathered on the hills from the stones or sticks on which the sheep have rubbed it off; for shears are unknown.

After it has been washed, which is usually done at the edge of a stream with the aid of a wooden bat, it is stored in a rough condition until it may be wanted. It is then brought out and carded. This was formerly done by a couple of men, who sat opposite one another with heckling-combs in their hands and combed it in opposite directions; their combs had teeth formed out of great iron nails, which were driven through a piece of sheep's horn and bent slightly downwards at their free extremity, a wooden handle being fixed at right angles to the horn. Similar combs are still used in preparing the fleece on skins in the Faroes, and probably also in Iceland, though I have not seen them there. They were once common in Scotland. For wool-carding a better implement has taken their place, consisting of a couple of wooden boards stuck full of small curved metal points and provided with convenient handles. The pair can be managed by a single woman, and men no longer take part in the work. A certain amount of carded wool is always kept ready, very often in the stomach of a large halibut which has been inflated and dried, but the greater part is only prepared just before spinning.

Until 1671 the spinning-wheel was unknown in the Faroes, and as late as the beginning of the nineteenth century it appears to have been rarely used in Iceland. In the year referred to a somewhat rude type was introduced into the Faroes from Scotland by a Danish nobleman named Gabell; it is now found practically in every house, still known as '*skotsrok.*' In it there is no distaff or other contrivance for holding the unspun wool, which is held in the right hand of the operator, and no treadle for working the wheel. This measures two and a half to three feet in diameter and is of simple construction, entirely of plain unpainted wood. It is fixed, in such a way as to permit rotation, either to the wall of a room or to a wooden upright fixed to a bench. An endless cord passes over the wheel and, after being crossed, round a metal rod some four or five feet away. The rod is supported on a wooden stand, but also has a rotatory movement; the stand is kept in position on a bench either by means of heavy stones placed upon its two ends or of an iron vice. The spinner stands beside the bench, holding in her right hand a flock of wool, which is twisted round the rod at its free extremity at one side. With her left hand she turns the wheel, at the same time drawing out the flock with her right. As the yarn is formed it is rolled round the rod, producing a cone-shaped mass which can easily be removed, unwound and wound up again in a ball. When this has been done, three balls are taken and the three strands are twisted together by hand, thus producing a single thread of wool.

The Icelandic spinning-wheel of the present day is in all respects similar to the modern Scottish one, and many of those seen in the farms have been actually brought from Great Britain or from Denmark; for they can be bought ready-made in the big stores in Reykjavik.

Spindles, however, are still employed, especially in the Faroes, the yarn produced with their aid being made from the outer wool of the sheep. No distaffs are used in the Faroes, and I have not seen one in Iceland, though Henderson and other writers mention them. The spindle-whorls are generally made of wood and are either mushroom-

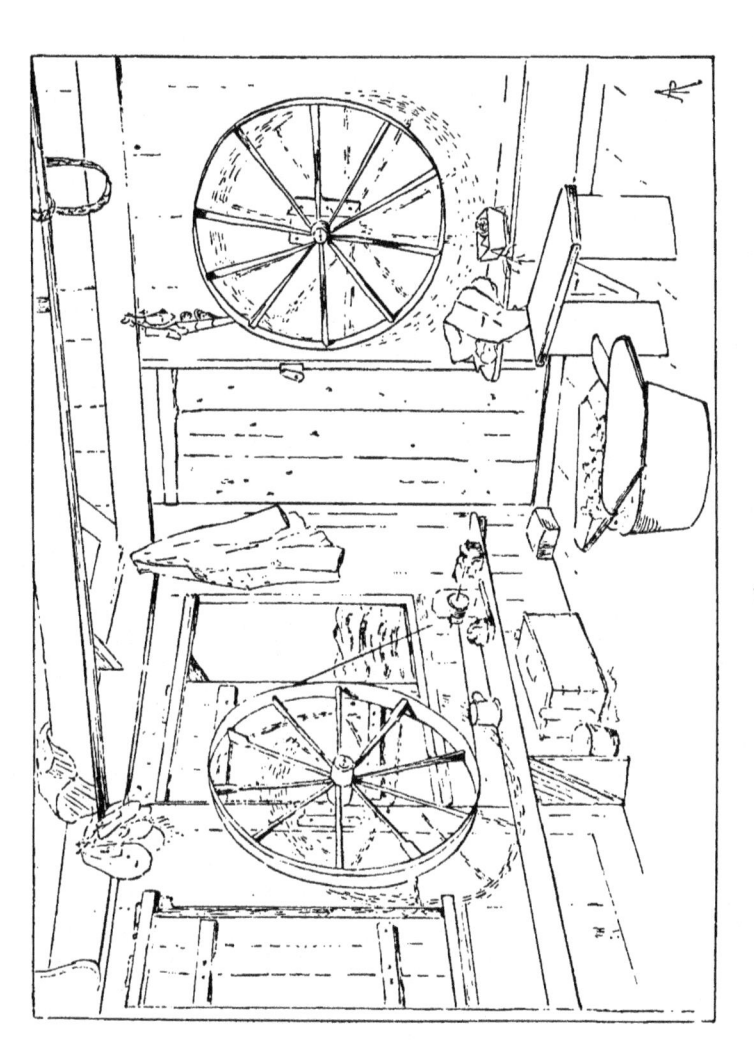

LIVING-ROOM IN OLD-FASHIONED FAROE FARM-HOUSE, AT SAXEN, STROMOE, SHOWING SPINNING-WHEELS

[*To face p. 194*]

shaped or simple disks, flat above and below. Sometimes they are notched round the edge, and when (a thread of one colour having been formed) the spinner desires to commence another with different wool, the first is bent down over the edge of the whorl in one of the notches and twisted, together with any of its wool which still remains unspun, round the staff. The spindles vary very much in size, in accordance with the use to which they are put, small ones being employed in making fine thread for sewing on buttons and the like, while the thick, woollen ropes with which sheep are sometimes tied up are made with whorls which measure at least three inches in diameter. In all the specimens I have seen there has been a metal hook, merely a piece of bent wire, at the upper end of the staff, which very frequently projects for an inch or more above the whorl; but Landt says that in his day a notch cut in the wood itself served this purpose, as it still does in many Scandinavian spindles. Occasionally, at any rate in the Faroes, the whorl is made from the upper part of the head of the thigh-bone of a cow or pony, this object having a natural shape very convenient for the purpose.

It would be beyond the scope of the present work to follow the wool through all the processes by means of which it is converted into cloth or knitted goods, seeing that these processes differ little, if at all, from those once common in many parts of our own island. The native dyes, in the making of which the islanders were once expert, have been vanquished in the struggle for existence by the products of coal tar, which can be imported so cheaply from abroad, and the old-fashioned upright loom—the only weaving-apparatus known in the Faroes at the beginning of last century—has quite disappeared, though I have seen the perforated stones to which the threads of the woof were attached, in Iceland, and have obtained specimens of the old 'weaver's sword,' carved out of a whale's jaw or rib, in the Faroes. So utterly forgotten is the use of the latter that a man to whom I showed a specimen in Thorshavn asked me whether it was a model of a whaling-spear.

As I have already mentioned, sheepskin of native manufacture is much used in the Faroes in making shoes. This is also the case in Iceland, but the method of preparation is there different, alum being used in curing the skin. In the former islands, the operation of tanning is conducted in a very primitive way, the material chiefly employed being the root of a native plant, the tormentil (*Potentilla erecta*), which grows in great abundance on the hillsides. It has a little starry yellow flower, which is doubtless known to many, and the roots can easily be pulled up from under the moss by hand. These roots are gathered by the women, who also prepare them for use. They are ground to powders in a way which I will describe presently, mixed with water into a paste, and rubbed into the hairy side of the skin, from which the wool has previously been scraped. The skin is then folded and kept in this condition for a couple of days or more. The process may be repeated several times to give a better result, but this is rarely done nowadays; the skin is then washed in sea-water and dried. Several different substances, such as sea-water, urine, and various roots, may be mixed with the tormentil to alter the colour of the leather. The best quality of sheepskin takes a long time to mature, and should be suspended for several years in such a position that it may receive the benefit of the peat-reek; but this also is a refinement as a rule too tedious for the present age. I have even heard of skins which had been hung up in the smoke for a century before being used.

The most interesting part of the process is the grinding of the roots, as this is done in a manner than which it would be impossible to imagine a more primitive. At certain places on the coast, where a heavy surf breaks on a pebbly beach, numbers of smooth stones of a size convenient for the grasp of a woman's hand and of a regular oval shape are produced by the action of the sea. These, unworked by the hand of man, form the pestles of the tormentil mortar. The mortar itself is a flat rock, generally on the shore, but sometimes an isolated boulder above the cliffs. Some natural depression on the surface of this rock is discovered by a woman who wishes to grind roots. In it she places a handful, gathering them together in a little pile with her left hand. Then she grasps the water-worn stone by its middle in her right, brings it down sharply on the little heap of roots in the hollow, and rotates it briskly. The result is, firstly, that the roots are ground to powder; secondly, that, after a long usage, a regular depression, smooth and polished, shaped something like the hollow of a gigantic egg-cup, is produced, which is so like one of the natural 'pot holes' familiar to geologists, that Dr. Grossman in his account of the Faroes confesses that at first he was quite deceived. The use and manufacture of similar mortars seem so obvious a course to take, if a mortar is wanted at all, that one is a little surprised to find that they are not now known in Iceland, though they occur among races quite unconnected with the Teutonic or Iberian stocks. For example, in looking through a recent volume of the *Indian Antiquary*, I find a precisely similar mortar described and figured by the Rev. F. H. Francke as being used by the people of Leh, in Little Tibet.

Certain depressions (including a small proportion of the

so-called cup-markings) frequently noted on rocks in the Western Highlands and Islands of Scotland, had probably a similar function once, though at least one, with which I am personally acquainted, is reputed to have been used as a font. Tormentil, as Dr. Johnson noted in his *Tour in the Scottish Hebrides*, was used in the eighteenth century as a tanning agent in this district, and here perhaps we may trace a racial connexion with the Faroes, not merely a logical one as in the case of the Tibetan mortar, which is not used for grinding tormentil, or anything like it, but for preparing condiments.

Many similar relics of the past—some, doubtless, actual survivals from a primitive culture, others rather reproduced afresh under peculiar circumstances when a higher stage of civilization had been reached—persist in Iceland and the Faroes. I have dealt with some of them in greater detail in a paper read before the Anthropological Institute in London, where I have described the stone hammer used in pounding fish in Iceland (which is closely paralleled by an implement employed in breaking fuel among the people of Ladakh, and rather less closely by the war-clubs of certain Papuan tribes); the bone skates (belonging to two distinct types) now used as children's toys on Heimey; the bone pins with which hides are pegged out in Rangarval; the bone needles with which fish are strung together in the same district, and the bone toys of the Farish youth.

CHAPTER VII

AGRICULTURE IN THE ISLANDS, WITH NOTES ON INSECT LIFE

A LAND less fitted for agriculture than the Faroes, save on the humblest scale, could hardly be imagined. There is little level ground, and of that little much is pebbly beach; while the hillsides, which often rise directly from the sea or tower above the summits of lofty cliffs, are very steep, and the islands are mostly hills. The climate is mild, but damp and deficient in sunshine; it has been calculated that, on an average, three-quarters of the sky is covered with cloud; in winter terrific gales prevail, strong enough to blow from the soil any crop which might be exposed to their violence.

In Iceland, where the climate is colder but otherwise similar[1], the soil is less inhospitable, save where it has been covered with volcanic dust, or buried for ever beneath a lava stream full of gigantic bubbles as brittle, and as sharp when broken, as the finest glass. We know from fossils which occur, especially in the north-western peninsula, that at a period geologically not very remote[2] forests of beech and maple waved their branches in the wind; we know from the statements of the old historians that trees of sufficient size to aid in boat-building were produced a thousand years ago, and that corn was grown. Indeed, one of the finest passages in Icelandic literature describes how that perfect knight of Icelandic history and

[1] In the north of the island it is distinctly drier.
[2] This was, of course, long before the coming of man. Iceland at the time was probably connected with America, if not with the European continent (through Great Britain), by land.

romance, that friend of the wily Njal, Gunnar of Lithend, looks back on his corn-fields as he is about to depart an outlaw and an exile from his native land, how their beauty overcomes his sense of obligation to the law, and he turns back and is finally undone.

'They ride down along Markfleet, and just then Gunnar's horse tripped and threw him off. He turned towards the Lithe and the homestead at Lithend, and said—" Fair is the Lithe; so fair that it has never seemed to me so fair; the corn-fields are white to harvest, and the home mead is mown; and now I will ride back home, and not fare abroad at all."' (Dasent's translation.)

The country where Gunnar dwelt now lies desolate. Black sand, which the wind carries in an ever-widening circle, devastates it; bogs fill its hollow places; a few of the most miserable farms in all Iceland are scattered over it, a very few of a better sort; the hillsides are scantily clad with little thickets, only a few feet high—blaeberry, dwarf birch, dwarf willow, which in early autumn blaze forth in scarlet and gold and the softest yellow-green, a contrast to the white eternal snows on the mountains above them. Few scenes are more desolate, few, for a period, more gorgeous: the homely beauty which beguiled the ancient hero has for ever fled.

Corn is no longer sown in Iceland, though a poor kind of oats grows wild in some districts and its grain is used as human food. Some say that the climate has changed for the worse since the days when the sagas were written; that cereals will no longer grow; that the winters have become too cold, the summers too short; that rains and fogs forbid the sun to shine with sufficient strength and frequency—in a word, that it would be a waste of time to experiment with agriculture. But at the beginning of the nineteenth century the climate was believed in Iceland to be mending; and it is possible even now that, were the right varieties of wheat or barley introduced and the right methods of culture employed, the land might cease from being so barren as it is.

Throughout the Faroes barley is still grown on a small scale by many of the peasants, and on the island of Sandoe, which is flatter than most of the group, larger quantities are produced. Oats are also cultivated occasionally; but they are usually cut before the grain is ripe and used as fodder for the cows. Very little change has taken place in the cultivation of corn since the earliest times, and the only matter in which it differs from the methods described by Landt more than a century ago is the introduction of a simple implement used as a harrow. The corn-fields are mere patches, often not more than a few yards square; they are not divided from one another by walls, but by little ditches; they lie among similar patches occupied by potatoes, turnips, and hay, and they are generally situated on a slope, the gradient of which is more or less steep. As a rule their greatest diameter runs up and down the slope, and they are very narrow in comparison with their length.

When the Faroemen have decided to make a corn-field, they first cut the turf with a peculiar spade, which is also used in digging peat. It is so contrived that iron is economized as much as possible; for iron is very expensive in the islands, the chief source of it now being the cargoes of worn-out railway lines which are occasionally imported. The handle and the shovel of this turf-cutter are practically in the same plane. The shaft broadens out at about half its length from the distal end into a flat blade, which narrows slightly from above downwards. There is a distinct shoulder at its point of origin. The blade, which is made in the same piece with the handle and is of course of wood, is shod below with iron. The metal is prepared in a flat plate, with a wide flange at either side and a terminal portion with a cutting edge below the flanges. This part, which forms the actual spade, is somewhat constricted above, just below where the flanges project on either side; and it broadens out towards the free extremity, which may approach a semi-circle in outline. The plate of metal is applied to the wooden blade in a heated condition; the flanges are bent round the edges and hammered into position, so that they grip the wood tightly, and the implement is finished. Its dimensions vary considerably, and even its proportions are by no means constant; but the wooden blade is generally from a foot and a half to two feet in length and about four inches broad; the length of the metal shoe, including the part to which the flanges are attached, is about six inches; of this about half projects beyond the end of the wood. The foot is pressed down on the shoulder of the blade when the implement is in use.

A similar spade, but with a blade proportionately wider, is employed in digging up the earth. This is usually done in April, but it may be as early as the end of February or as late as May when operations are commenced. The turf is either removed to be employed in roofing houses or else turned over and covered with soil, in order that the grass may not perish altogether but be able to spring again in the succeeding year. Manure, consisting partly of household filth and partly of sea-weed, is then spread upon the ground, and more earth placed upon it. The whole is then trampled firm. The fresh earth is obtained from a trench, which may serve as a drain or a boundary ditch, but is often filled up with the turf removed from the field.

When the preparation of the soil is complete, sowing is begun at once. The ground is then gone over with a hand harrow, which consists of a square or oblong wooden framework with iron nails hammered through it and bent at their tips so as to grip the soil. It is fastened to a long pole, which is fixed to a cross-piece, a small wedge of wood being inserted between its end and this, so that it joins the frame at an angle which makes a man able to use it without stooping. He holds the pole in both hands and drags the frame over the soil.

The barley is said never to become perfectly ripe; but about Michaelmas it is considered fit for cutting. The scythe used both in this process and in mowing hay has a very short blade; almost straight, but slightly bent at the tip. It is fastened to a handle some seven or eight feet in length, and the handle is provided with a piece of wood projecting from it at right angles a few feet from the free end and acting as a guard to prevent the reaper from swinging the scythe round far enough to cut his own legs. Similar scythes are used in Iceland and also in some of the Hebrides; in the Westman Isles I have seen the blades removed from the handles and used as fleshing-knives on a dead whale which had been cast ashore, their hafts having been wound round with rags to give a grip.

When the corn has been cut it is carried down to the village in wooden creels and received by the women, the men having conducted the greater part of the operations so far, though women may have assisted at all of them.

In the village the corn is taken to certain little houses built for its manipulation. They are constructed chiefly of rough stones piled together without mortar, but the roof is of wood covered with turf; the shape is oblong, but the length of the interior is not more than about three times the breadth. The floor consists of earth trampled hard, and there is usually one very small window near the door. The window is now fitted with glass panes, but probably it takes the place of the circular 'skin' windows, made out of the foetal membranes of a calf, which were common in Iceland a few decades ago. Inside the corn-house the most conspicuous structure is a furnace at the end most remote from the door. It occupies the whole width of the interior and is built up to the height of four or five feet (the height of the room itself varying up to about ten feet) with unhewn stones, having an opening in front through which smouldering peats can be thrust. The furnace is open above, but a rack made of laths of wood is suspended over it from the sides of the building.

When the corn has been brought into these houses it is first freed from the straw. This operation is generally performed by hand, but Landt mentions a machine for the purpose which was invented by a man named Debes and was in common use at the end of the eighteenth century. The straw is then spread out on the rack so as to form a uniform layer, a peat fire is lighted in the furnace and kept smouldering for twenty-four hours or more, and the ears of corn are placed on the straw to dry.

I have not seen the operations of threshing and winnowing myself, but, so far as I have been able to learn from inquiries on the island of Naalsoe, there has been no change in the method of procedure within the last century, except perhaps that less care is taken in winnowing. I propose, therefore, to quote Landt on the subject, as it was one to which he had paid considerable attention.

'The operations of drying, threshing, and cleaning the corn, are performed in Faroe by women; and it would be considered, particularly in some places, as very indecent if men should perform that kind of labour. When the woman who attends the drying-house, or kiln, thinks the corn is sufficiently dry, it is taken off; and if there be a large quantity of it, she is assisted on this occasion by one or two girls. A door is then placed lengthwise on the floor, but in a somewhat sloping direction, with one end of it resting on the floor, and on this door a certain quantity of the ears are deposited; the three females then get upon the door with their backs turned towards the wall, and with their feet tread upon the ears until they are pretty well bruised. Some extend a rope before them, which they lay hold of with their hands to assist them in this labour, and to enable them to jump with more facility.

'The women then place themselves on their knees, and with a piece of wood, shaped somewhat like a bat, called *treskyutrea*—thresh, or beat the corn in measure, and then it is cleaned. One of the girls holds a kind of tray, by means of which she separates the chaff from the corn; and the other has a sieve, consisting of a skin stretched over a hoop, but without holes, into which the winnowed corn is thrown by the first girl. The sieve is then whirled round in the hands, in order that dirt and bad grains may rise to the top, and these being picked out, the corn is put into another tray, where it is winnowed for the last time.'

The threshing-bat figured by Landt differs in shape from that now used, but resembles it in being a true bat, not a flail. It appears to have been flat, with a leaf-shaped outline, the handle being in the place of the stalk. Those that I have seen, of which there are two specimens in the Pitt-Rivers Museum, have been rather of the shape of a cricket bat, but with a thicker blade and made in one piece. The front of the blade is flat, the back rounded, so that the outline of a transverse section would be the segment of a circle. The handle is straight; it meets the blade at an angle, so that when the implement is in use it can be wielded by a kneeling woman without her stooping. The blade is not quite so deep at its distal end as at the point where it joins the handle, and it is often tilted up slightly at the free extremity. The handle is made to be grasped with two hands, and is generally almost as long as the blade; but the size and proportions vary within wide limits. I have heard that the bat is made bigger in some localities than in others, but cannot say from personal experience whether this is really the case or not. I should perhaps explain, as Landt does not make this point clear, that the women who thresh the corn kneel opposite one another and beat alternately.

The winnowing-tray or van (the 'fan' of the Old Testament) is made of sufficient size to be conveniently held at both ends by a woman. It is concave from above downwards, usually formed out of several strips of wood sewn together with stout twine, and has at each end a single piece of wood, cut out to fit into the concavity and provided with a hole into which a woman's fingers can be inserted conveniently. It is by means of the two holes that the tray is held. It is too big to be rotated and has only up-and-down and backward-and-forward movements; but I do not think that the circular 'sieves without holes,' to which Landt refers, are now used.

The corn that has been freed of the husks is usually kept in this condition until it is wanted for food, and is then ground either in one of the upright watermills of the so-called Norse type, which are to be found in all those villages which are built near a stream, or else in a hand-quern. As long ago as the end of the eighteenth century watermills were taking the place of hand-querns; but in some of the smaller islands there are no streams, and cousequently no watermills. This is the case on Naalsoe, where the quern still survives in many families, though the cheapness with which meal can be imported from abroad has caused many to cease from grinding their own corn, and, indeed, in some cases, from cultivating it altogether. It was formerly the custom for one woman in every family to prepare the day's supply of meal, grinding two days' supply on Saturday to last till Monday evening. A basket was made which would exactly hold a day's supply of grain for the particular household in which it was used, and was filled every morning by the housewife. Thus waste was discouraged. The custom is, I believe, still kept up in a few families.

The baskets are made of thin wisps of straw curled in a spiral and plaited together by means of string, which radiates outwards in the coil forming the bottom, and upwards in that forming the sides. The two coils are, however, in reality continuous, and great skill is shown in moulding the baskets. They have very much the appearance of having been moulded over rude earthenware pots such as are made at the present day in some of the Outer Hebrides; but no pottery is now produced in the Faroes, though there was formerly a fabric on the little island of Kolter, and I am assured that the Faroemen do not consciously copy earthenware forms. The fact is that this kind of basketwork and a great deal of primitive pottery are made in a very similar fashion, being built up in a spiral out of a narrow band of their respective materials; but while straw or any other vegetable substance of the kind needs to be secured in position by bands running crosswise to it, the clay out of which pottery is manufactured is naturally cohesive, and can, by the exercise of pressure, be converted into a uniform substance, no matter what the original shape of the component parts of the vessel may have been. By firing this homogeneity is consolidated. The most highly valued of the Farish baskets are those in which the simple pot-shaped outline is broken by the bulging out of one side to form a wide, open spout, through which the grain can be poured with greater precision. Such a spout is easy enough to form in an earthenware vessel, in which a dent on the lip can be made by the pressure of the fingers or a suitable implement; but it is by no means easy to produce it in basketwork of the spiral order.

The only basket of indigenous manufacture which I have seen in Iceland closely resembled the simpler Farish type in form, but was made entirely, woof as well as warp, of the roots of some shrub. It was used as a workbasket by an old woman in Rangarval, and is now in the Pitt-Rivers Museum.

When the corn has been measured out in the basket it is taken into an outhouse or cellar in which the quern-stones are fixed on a wooden tray. The tray is surrounded by a raised edge on three sides but is open on the fourth, so that the meal can be swept back from it into the basket. The stones themselves resemble those used until lately in many parts of the Highlands; the upper one does not fit into the lower, but works upon it. The thickness of the meal can be regulated by placing pieces of leather between the stones. The broom used in sweeping up the meal is similar to that employed for household purposes both in the Faroes and in Iceland. It consists of a pair of puffins' wings sewn together along their outer edges, very much in the same way as birds' wings are sewn together in England to form hand-screens. The bones are, however, freed of flesh and feathers at their base for a few inches, forming the handle of the broom. It is possibly worth noting that brooms of the kind, like the implements used in threshing the corn and in preparing tormentil roots, are only adapted for a kneeling attitude.

As has been mentioned, there is no special festival connected with the corn harvest in the Faroes, and possibly the customs of this nature which persist in Scandinavian and other countries died out centuries ago; for the corn harvest can never have had much importance in the islands. It may be, however, that the 'indecency' noted by Landt as being popularly attached to a man's interference with the manipulation of the grain points to a former connexion, which we know to have existed among primitive peoples of many diverse races, between the ideas of fertility in the human species and in plants. To enlarge on this subject, interesting as it is, would be out of place in the present context: practically all that is known about it will be found in Dr. Frazer's *Golden Bough*.

At the completion of the hay-harvest, which is of much greater importance than that of the corn, a festival called 'hay-bringing day' is still celebrated; but it appears to have degenerated into nothing more interesting than a feast given to the haymakers by the owner of the hay.

In the Faroes hay is cultivated in very much the same way as corn, except that it is not thought necessary to sow the seed. The patches are so small that, should there be windy weather after the hay has been cut but before it has been taken home, the owners have literally to sit on the haycocks or take other means to prevent them being blown over into a neighbour's patch.

In each village there is a certain amount of cultivated

land immediately round the houses, separated from the outland, only used for grazing purposes or for peat-digging, by a low stone wall. It seems to be impossible, owing to the nature of the land laws, for any one to cultivate ground outside the wall; but inside it individual ownership prevails to an unusual extent, land being divided among all the children of an owner or crown tenant at his death. The result is that a man may be in possession of a number of small patches in different parts of the village; for people are often tenacious of their tiny estates, so that a purchaser can buy only isolated patches, separated by the property of other people from his own. The whole population, practically, are either actual or prospective land-owners or permanent tenants, and it is therefore only the young men and women who have not yet inherited their property who can be induced to hire themselves out as agricultural labourers or farm servants; and, if they have even a few crowns of capital, it is more profitable for them to go to Iceland and assist in the fisheries there during summer than to work at home. This, of course, is a further difficulty in the way of agriculture. It appears to have been overcome to some extent in the island of Sandoe; but I am ignorant of all details regarding this island, which I have not visited.

In Iceland no such difficulty exists; but there are greater climatic disadvantages to contend with. Very often the only preparation made for the growth of hay, even immediately round the farms, is the removal of stones from the field; but a curious belief prevails—that more grass can be grown if the soil is piled up into a series of little mounds than if it is levelled flat. Of course mounds of the kind have a greater surface-area than flat soil enclosed within the same boundaries; but it is very doubtful whether they produce more grass, as each blade of grass grows upwards as straight as possible.

Two distinct kinds of hay must be distinguished in this island—that produced on the home meadow, which is cultivated in the manner indicated, and that which springs up wild on the hills. The white clover has been introduced among the former in many parts of Iceland, and has even run wild, greatly improving the fodder. The home hay is always cut first, being by far the most nutritious; and only after it has all been gathered in is the wild crop visited. In the summer months the eye of the traveller is often caught by the white tents of the haymakers, far from any permanent dwelling of man.

A second crop is sometimes mown on the home meadow in early autumn, but the ground is often under water at this season, and as a consequence the plant called *Equisetum*, or Mare's Tail, increases and almost destroys the value of the hay, being so thoroughly impregnated with silica that it must not only have little nutritive value but even be a source of danger to the beast which eats it. I have seen a crop of hay in Rangarval of which almost a half consisted of this plant; yet it was being carefully gathered, and there appeared to be no intention on the part of the owner to separate the Mare's Tail from more profitable fodder.

The first crop from the home meadow is usually mown in June, the second in October or September. In the Faroes the hay harvest generally begins, no matter what the weather or the condition of the crop, on St. Olaf's day (July 29); for to commence earlier would be considered most unlucky. Nevertheless, owing to the dampness of the weather, the hay may stay out, cut but still damp, as late as September. The Norwegian plan of preserving hay as ensilage is not adopted (except perhaps sporadically within quite recent years) either in the Faroes or in Iceland, so that much is lost owing to the growth of mould.

After hay the most important crop is that of potatoes, which are cultivated both in the Faroes and in Iceland in the same way, and on the same small scale, as is the case with corn in the former islands. A few turnips are also grown in a similar fashion, and most farmhouses in Iceland have a small garden, in which hardy vegetables, such as cabbages, carrots, and especially rhubarb, are raised in minute quantities. The same is true of the houses in the larger villages of the Faroes. Currants (red and black) are the only cultivated fruit which reaches full maturity in the islands; they appear to do well in most summers, especially in the neighbourhood of Thorshavn, but at Reykjavik they are often less successful. In some years they do not ripen even at Thorshavn, because of want of sun, insect plagues, slugs (which are very numerous), or, occasionally, because the young fruit is eaten by a flight of Crossbills, which sometimes visit the Faroes in considerable numbers in summer (as was the case in 1903), apparently on migration from Scandinavia[1].

Without a closer and more detailed study of the conditions prevailing it is hard to say exactly how far the few crops grown either in Iceland or the Faroes are affected by insects, but a brief summary of what is known regarding the entomology of these islands may not be uninteresting, for our information on this subject is very meagre still.

It is a little surprising to a naturalist with preconceived ideas to find how abundant insect life really is both in the gardens and even in the open moors of these northern islands. When he comes to examine matters further he

---

[1] They belong to the Scandinavian race or species.

sees that in this respect sub-Arctic localities differ from tropical ones not so much in the number of *individuals* produced in the course of a year as in the comparatively small number of *species* which are able to exist. There is also far less apparent adaptation to surroundings in external form and colour and in the production of what may be called special apparatus for special needs. In the Faroes and Iceland the great majority of the animals are 'ordinary,' that is to say, they have no striking peculiarity of appearance or structure. Most of them are small; but, even were they enlarged, this 'ordinariness' would still remain as their most noteworthy general character. Very few of them are conspicuously coloured, and yet only a proportion show a close resemblance to their environment. Mimicry of one species by another does not occur. With this may be correlated the fact that the chief enemies of the insects are not sentient beings, but elemental forces—damp, cold, and, above all, wind. Darwin and Wallace have shown how insects isolated on small islands in southern latitudes tend to lose their wings, which would act as sails for the wind to carry them away to sea; but it is very doubtful whether anything of the kind has happened in the Faroes, subject as these islands are to hurricane. Another method of preservation appears rather to have been adopted, viz. a restricted period of winged aerial life, with a corresponding extension of the larval or pupal stage.

The most prolific group of insects (whether in individuals or in species) in these islands is the *Diptera* or two-winged flies—a group in which the loss of wings is very rare. In the calm of midsummer, when the ditches and hollows of the Faroes are gorgeous with the flowers of the Marsh Marigold and the slopes with those of the Ragged Robin, when the cliff's face is strewn with the clusters of the Rose-scented Sedum; when the wastes of Iceland blossom forth with the rose-like *Dryas octopetala*—then the air is full of gnats and midges, every rock and wall has the grey daddy-longlegs resting inconspicuous upon it, and every flower attracts a cloud of hover-flies. By the first of August the hover-flies are dead or blown away to sea; species, which are common with us until October begins, are no longer to be found; the number of the gnats and even of the dung-flies is much diminished, and only the daddy-longlegs, which can cling tightly to the rock on which they spread their legs, have at all increased. (This is the time when the pilot whales usually approach the shore, and hence the popular connexion between them and these flies.)

Moths, several species of which were common at midsummer, are already scarce in August, except the well-known Ghost moth. Butterflies do not exist as natives of Iceland or the Faroes; but a specimen of the Painted Lady has been recorded from the Faroes, and several species apparently visit Iceland as occasional immigrants from Greenland, though I do not know that any have actually been recorded. There are specimens, said to have been caught in Iceland, in the Natural History Museum at Reykjavik, and they probably belong to a species of Fritillary which is well known as an Arctic form. Mr. Eagle Clarke has lately shown that the Painted Lady, in other respects a notorious vagrant, is capable of migrating across the German Ocean, and there can be little doubt that the specimen from the Faroes was a casual visitor, though the extent of sea it must have traversed, even supposing it came from Shetland, is nearly four times as great as that which the individuals observed by Mr. Clarke need have passed.

Of insects which have no wings, or which rarely use those they have, there are of course many in Iceland and the Faroes, namely beetles, the common earwig (which is extremely abundant), and the spring-tails and bristle-tails properly called *Aptera* or wingless insects. In the Faroes it is probable that at least two hundred kinds of beetles really exist, though less than a half of that number have hitherto been recorded. Almost without exception, they are forms which conceal themselves under stones, though a considerable proportion belong to the family of the Devil's Coach-horses (*Staphylidae*), which use their wings more freely than most non-tropical beetles are in the habit of doing. As Dr. Sharp points out in the second paper referred to under his name in the bibliography, it would be interesting to obtain a sufficient number of specimens of these beetles from the Faroes to compare their wings with those of a like series from Great Britain or the Continent, to see whether insular life has produced a diminution in the size of the organs or any other change.

The beetles of Iceland are even less known than those of the Faroes. An interesting form, *Bembidium islandicum*, has been described by Dr. Sharp. It is peculiar to Iceland, where it is found under stones practically at sea-level; but its nearest allies occur above the snow-line on the mountains of continental Europe.

Ants, and their allies bees and wasps, do not occur in Iceland and the Faroes, the only representatives of the order to which they belong being a few small ichneumons and other parasitic species.

The *Aptera* are met with in the most inclement situations, though they occur all over the world, and it is therefore not surprising that they flourish in Iceland and the Faroes. A common spring-tail, *Tomocerus tridenti-*

ferus, is particularly abundant under stones on the Farish moors, where it forms a considerable proportion of the food of the many small spiders frequenting such situations.

Under the same stones, a representative of the scale-insects is found, namely the common *Orthezia cataphracta*; and, to go beyond the limits of the insects strictly so called, at least one centipede, a millepede and two wood-lice (*Porcellio scaber* and *Oniscus asellus*) occur.

We have already seen that a beetle is peculiar to Iceland; but it is doubtful whether any insect is actually peculiar to the Faroes. Several midges have been described by Hanson as new species; but they belong to a family of which very little is really known even in Scotland, and quite possibly, granted that his diagnoses are correct, the same species may yet be recorded thence. Several insects, however, are found in the islands which are not British but Continental species, among others the ichneumon-fly *Sagarites varians*, which Mr. Claude Morley, our chief British authority on this family, has detected among a few specimens collected in the summer of 1903.

I have already referred to the Ghost moth, which sometimes appears in great numbers in the Faroes at the end of July and the beginning of August. Most people in this country who have occasion to go out at twilight in suitable localities and at the right time of year are familiar with the male—a curious, long-winged, silvery-white insect, which hovers, ghost-like, over the tops of the grass. The female is a dull-coloured moth which can usually be found close at hand by a careful search. In the northern islands, and especially in Shetland, the males show a tendency to exchange their conspicuous whiteness for the dull yellow-brown of the female, and though not every individual exhibits this tendency in the same degree, or even at all, a certain proportion can hardly be distinguished from members of the other sex by their coloration alone. It has been suggested by the late Jenner Weir that in such localities, where in summer-time daylight remains far longer than it does further south, the necessity for the male to attract the female by his colour is less marked, and that therefore he tends to adopt the advantages of an inconspicuous appearance. This may possibly be the true explanation, at any rate in part; but the likelihood of its being so is decreased by the fact that in other species in which the male does not attract the female in this way—as undoubtedly the male Ghost moth does—a similar darkening of the coloration occurs in Shetland, and probably also in the Faroes. Statistics, however, are still wanting, both for the Faroes and of any species for Shetland, to show what proportion of the males are dark in either group of islands. It is probable that dampness of the atmosphere plays a part in the phenomenon.

Our knowledge of the entomology of the Faroes and of Iceland is, as I have said, still meagre. In the present notes I have attempted only to touch on a few general principles, as more research is necessary before it is possible to go into details, and even to the naturalist, unless he is a specialist in one group or another, mere lists of scientific names convey but little.

CONCLUSIONS

ALTHOUGH this book lays no claim to be a complete account of the islands with which it deals, but rather a collection of essays on subjects connected with their living denizens, it may be interesting to recapitulate briefly the conclusions drawn by the author as to the people and animals; for the intention if not the matter of the different chapters is the same—to illustrate the effects of isolation in an inclement latitude. It may be pointed out that the data given regarding the Faroes are more complete than those which refer to Iceland, partly because the author, who has made use of his own observations whenever possible (much as he is indebted to the researches of previous visitors and residents), has spent a longer time in the Faroes than in Iceland, and partly because their smaller area has permitted him to gain a closer acquaintance with a considerable part of them. Altogether I have paid six visits to these islands of the north-west sea, of which three have been devoted entirely to the Faroes, as well as the greater part of a fourth.

First as regards the people. In the Faroes it is still possible to distinguish two very distinct elements in the population, one 'Scandinavian,' one 'Iberian.' The 'Scandinavian' element differs slightly (*e. g.* in the shape of the head) from that which prevails at the present day in the purely Teutonic districts of Scandinavia; but we know that it is derived from the same source in both localities. We cannot trace the history of the 'Iberian' element with the same exactness; it is probably derived largely from the Outer Hebrides and Northern Ireland, possibly in part from an aboriginal population in the islands themselves, though this is very doubtful.

The same two elements occur in Iceland, where their history has been similar, except that there is here no possibility of an aboriginal population and that the introduction of Hebridean blood was probably confined to an earlier period; but the 'Scandinavian' element merges gradually into a third, which exhibits certain Mongolian traits though the hair is often almost colourless. Possibly this element is due to a reversion to Lapp blood, which must have been introduced into the race ere Iceland was discovered; and possibly it has, as it were, returned to the surface through the operation of Natural Selection, because it is an element especially suited for conditions such as prevail in Iceland. It has not reappeared in the Faroes.

Both in Iceland and in the Faroes many primitive customs persist; but in the larger island they seem to be tinged with a certain self-conscious feeling and with some little affectation.

Many of the implements of home manufacture in the remoter parts of the islands are examples of what Sir Arthur Mitchell has called 'the Past in the Present,' being of the rudest possible form and construction. It may be doubted, however, whether they have in all cases a genetic connexion with remote antiquity. Some of them may have been produced anew in the districts where they are now made; and in any case they must not be taken as fundamental arguments in an ethnological discussion, though in certain instances they may provide subsidiary evidence on racial questions. The primitive implements of one island are not necessarily the same as those of its neighbours.

The folklore of Iceland and the Faroes belongs in part to the common heritage of belief in primitive man, though much of it is tinged with local colouring and distinctive

Teutonic influences. All primitive races think alike, and similar incidents, although under very different circumstances, may well produce in the minds of widely separated peoples a similar explanation.

The psychology of the Icelanders is very different from that of the Faroemen; even more so than are their physical characters.

Thus it is evident that ancestry has not been the only factor in the evolution of these two island races. Their ancestry is almost identical, but they differ from one another in body, and to a greater extent in mind. Their geographical environment during evolution has not been very dissimilar, but their lives have been unlike. The heads of the Faroemen at any rate are neither 'Scandinavian,' 'Iberian,' nor yet intermediate in type; they are shorter and wider than those of either ancestral stock.

As regards zoology little need be said. Our knowledge is yet too imperfect to admit of geographical generalizations; but it is obvious that the species which have been isolated on the islands have undergone some modification, sufficiently gross to be detected with certainty in a few of the larger forms. Except in being more impoverished, the fauna differs little from that of the north of Scotland; but it probably contains a small Continental element, as the flora certainly does.

In the case of the horse it is possible to trace the history of the breed in the physical characters of the individuals now living in the islands; and this history corroborates what we can adduce regarding the origin of the people. The cats of Iceland and the dogs both of Iceland and the Faroes merit further study on the part of those interested in the problems of heredity.

APPENDIX ON THE CELTIC PONY

By FRANCIS H. A. MARSHALL, B.A. (Cantab.), D.Sc. (Edin.), Carnegie Research Fellow in the University of Edinburgh.

THREE independent lines of inquiry carried out by different methods have resulted in establishing the polyphyletic ancestry of the horse. Professor H. F. Osborn, of New York, has recently shown, from palaeontological evidence, that instead of there being a single line of descent as formerly supposed, there are no less than five series of fossil remains, two of which, however, became extinct in Miocene times. Professor W. Ridgeway, of Cambridge, in an important work upon *The Origin and Influence of the Thoroughbred Horse*, has adduced a considerable amount of historical and other evidence in support of the contention that a distinct species or variety of the horse had been evolved in North Africa, and for this variety he has proposed the name *Equus caballus libicus*. From this animal he supposes all the fine horses of the world to have been descended. Lastly, Professor J. C. Ewart, of Edinburgh, has adduced further proof of the multiple origin of the horse, his evidence being based mainly on a consideration of the several types of *Equus caballus* in existence at the present day.

The wild horse, *Equus caballus prjevalskyi*, was discovered in Central Asia by the famous Russian geographer, Prjevalsky, and was described as a separate species by Poliakov in a communication read before the Imperial Russian Geographical Society in 1881. The distinctness of the species was subsequently called in question, some naturalists regarding it as a feral animal like the mustangs of the western prairies, while the late Sir William Flower expressed the opinion that it was probably 'an accidental hybrid between the kiang and the horse.' The question has lately been set at rest by Professor Ewart, who has bred several kiang-horse hybrids which are very different from the wild horse, while at the same time he has shown that the latter is quite distinct from the domestic animal, and therefore can scarcely be descended from individuals which had run wild.

The recognition of the Celtic pony as a sub-species or variety with definite characters of its own, which serve to differentiate it from the typical horses, dates from only two years ago. In a paper read before the Royal Society of Edinburgh in 1902, and abstracted in *Nature*, Professor Ewart gave an account of a 'new horse' from the Hebrides and the North of Ireland, describing it as a small-headed pony with prominent eyes, small ears, slender limbs, small joints, with a fringe of short hairs in the upper part of the tail, and without callosities on the hind-limbs. The Celtic pony, as thus described, was stated to be found in Barra, Tiree, and other islands in the Hebrides, in Connemara, as well as in the Faroes and Iceland.

In a later paper Professor Ewart has given a fuller description of *E. caballus celticus*. A typical Celtic pony, he says, closely resembles in markings and colour a wild horse of the Altai variety, being of a yellowish-dun colour, with a dark, dorsal band, and with feeble indications of stripes on the shoulders and in the region of the knees and hocks. It differs from the Altai horse in having a slightly darker muzzle and a less distinct ring round the eye, while the dorsal band above mentioned is somewhat more marked. The hair of the Celtic pony is rather longer during winter, especially under the jaw, over the hind-quarters, and upon the legs. The mane grows some nine or ten inches every year and reaches a considerable length, only a portion being shed. 'The most remarkable feature of the Celtic pony is the tail. To begin with, the dock is relatively very short—so short that one is apt to suppose it has been docked. The distal two-thirds of the dock carries long dark hairs, the majority of which continue to grow until they trail on the ground. During winter and spring the proximal third of the dock—about four inches—carries stiff hair from three to six inches in length, which

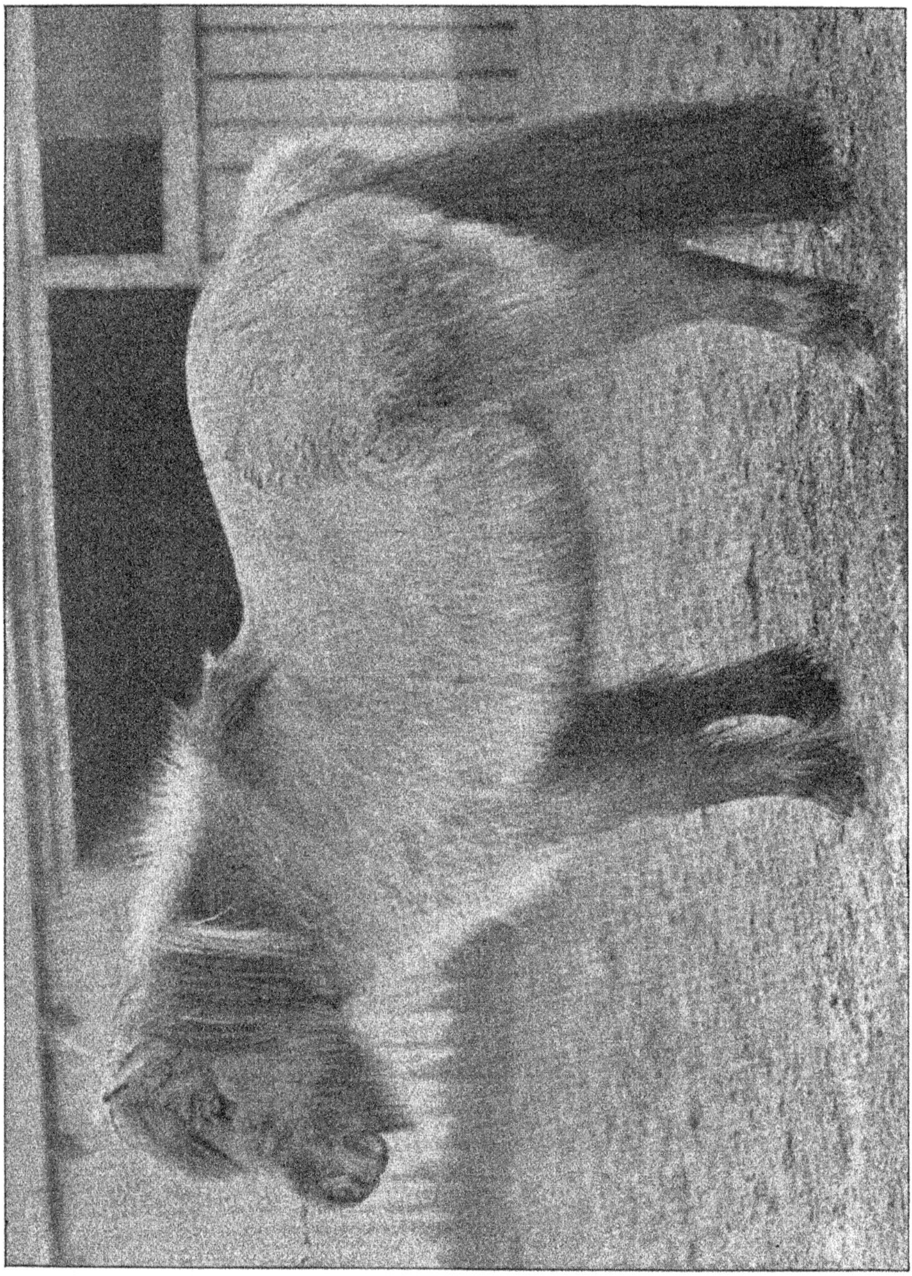

forms what may be known as a caudal fringe or tail-lock (see fig. opp. p. 224). In the case of Arabs and other semi-tropical horses the first one or two inches of the dock are usually covered with short fine hair like that over the hind-quarters, but in the Celtic pony fine wiry hairs from four to five inches in length extend right up to the root of the dock under cover of the body hair of the croup. The most distal hairs of the tail-lock overlap, but are quite distinct from the long persistent hairs carried by the lower two-thirds of the dock. The hair in the centre of the fringe, of the same colour as the dorsal band, projects obliquely backwards; the hair at the sides is light in colour and projects obliquely outwards. The presence of this very remarkable bunch of hair at the root of the tail was quite incomprehensible until I noticed what happened during a snowstorm. The moment the storm set in the pony orientated herself so that the snow was driven against her hind-quarters. In a few minutes the lock of hair was spread out to form a disc, to which the snow adhered, and thus provided a shield which effectually prevented the flakes finding their way around the root of the tail, where they would have soon melted and effectually chilled the thinly clad inner surface of the thighs. Provided with a caudal shield, long thick hair over the hind-quarters and back, and a thick mane covering both sides of the neck and protecting the small ears, a Celtic pony is practically snow-proof. While the storm lasted the pony in question stood perfectly still, with her head somewhat lowered, save when she shifted her position as the wind veered from north-west to north.... The Celtic pony, on realizing it was again fine, by a few violent shakes got rid of the adhering snow, and proceeded to feed as if nothing unusual had happened. It hence follows that the tail-lock is not, as I at first assumed, an inheritance from a primitive ancestor akin to the wild horse, but a highly specialized structure which eminently adapts the Celtic pony for a sub-arctic environment' (Ewart, *Multiple Origin*, &c.).

In addition to the characters mentioned above, Professor Ewart described a typical Celtic pony as having none of the four ergots, while the first premolars are also said to be lacking. Such a pony is described as being sterile with stallions of five different breeds, but fertile with a dun-coloured Connemara-Welsh pony.

The comparatively slight differences, which relate chiefly to colour, between the most typical representatives of the Celtic pony in the Faroes and those in Iceland are mentioned by Mr. Annandale in the chapter of this work dealing with the domestic animals. Probably at the present day the Celtic pony is commonest, while at the same time occurring in its purest form in Iceland, and the animal figured, which is in the possession of Professor Ewart, may be regarded as absolutely typical. This is not the case with the Faroe pony shown in the figure, which is almost certainly a partly bred animal, although a native of Thorshavn assured us that it was in most points very similar to the ponies inhabiting the Faroe islands before the recent introduction of Norwegian blood to which Mr. Annandale refers. So far as I have been able to ascertain no foreign blood has been introduced into Iceland within recent years, while the ponies in the Faroes, on the other hand, are nearly all partly bred Norwegians, it being a matter of considerable doubt whether any individuals of pure Farish descent now remain on these islands.

Notwithstanding the fact that the Celtic pony exists in its most typical form in Iceland, and the strong probability that there has been little or no admixture of Norwegian or other foreign blood since the time of the viking migration, horses belonging more or less to the heavy 'cart-horse' type are not uncommon in that country. Thus the heads of the Icelandic horses shown in a mediaeval engraving in the National Library of Reykjavik, and reproduced in a small work by Brunn, are in certain cases somewhat large and heavy looking, and the animals appearing in some other of Brunn's figures are certainly not typical examples of the Celtic pony, while Nehring's description and measurements of the skulls of certain Icelandic horses further illustrate this point. (See Stejneger's paper.) It is interesting to note, however, that the majority even of the

ICELANDIC PONY, SHOWING TAIL-LOCK IN MID-WINTER

(From Ewart's 'Multiple Origin,' &c. Photo by G. A. Ewart)

[*To face p.* 224

heavily built Icelandic ponies are 'Celtic' in some of their characters, the hock callosities being often either wholly absent or very much reduced, and the tail possessing a more or less obvious caudal fringe. Thus among a number of Icelandic ponies, mostly of rather heavy build and averaging about thirteen hands in height, which I saw on board on their way from Reykjavik to Copenhagen, I closely examined six and found none of these to possess chestnuts on the hind-legs. Also at a recent sale at Gateshead of about 500 newly imported Icelandic ponies, I found that fourteen out of sixty which I closely examined had no hind callosities. Many of these, however, were fairly typical examples of *E. caballus celticus*. The tail characters were in almost every instance more or less 'Celtic.' Among the Icelandic ponies which I have seen all colours were represented, but the commonest and probably the most typical colour was light dun with a dark stripe along the middle of the back. Chestnut-coloured animals were also fairly common. Piebalds, though of frequent occurrence, are less saleable than other colours, and consequently are discouraged for breeding purposes.

The views formed by Mr. Annandale and myself regarding the present distribution of the Celtic pony are stated at some length in the body of this work, and consequently there is no occasion to repeat them here. In this connexion, however, it is important to note further that although a great number, and probably the majority of the existing Norwegian horses undoubtedly belong to the heavily built, large-headed type, while those which are imported into Great Britain appear invariably to do so, the 'fjordhest' of Scandinavia, according to Dr. Stejneger, often closely resembles the Celtic pony. There appear to be no cases on record, however, of a fjordhest lacking the hock callosities. In view of the similarity between the Celtic pony and certain Scandinavian horses, it would seem not unlikely that the occurrence of the former at the present time, not only in Iceland and the Faroes, but also in the Hebrides and the north of Ireland, is due in part to the Norse migration. In the time of King Harold

Fairhair the Celtic type of pony was perhaps predominant in Scandinavia, just as it is predominant in Iceland and the Faroes at the present day, and the horses which the vikings brought with them in their wanderings over the North Sea probably belonged largely to this type. But the Celtic horses have had little chance of surviving in any numbers or in anything like their original purity in Scandinavia, although the specimens of the fjordhest mentioned by Stejneger seem to indicate that this type has not wholly disappeared in that country. In Iceland and the Faroes, on the other hand, as already remarked, the isolation of the horses has been almost complete from the viking period onwards, at any rate until recent years, whereas the history of the horse in Sweden, and to a less extent in Norway for the past four and a half centuries, has been a history of the admixture of foreign blood. The following short summary of what is known of the origin of the horse in Sweden, and the methods adopted to improve the different types, is taken from Captain Nauckhoff's account of the horses in the historical and statistical handbook recently issued by the Swedish Government:—

'We can conclude, from the form of the skull and from what traditions relate, that Sweden's first race of horses came from the East and descends from a Tartaric race of horses still existing in South-Eastern Russia. But in consequence of the incessant interbreeding with other races, the original type has disappeared, and the inhabitants of the north had, even during the viking period, active intercourse with foreign lands, when horses were brought home, amongst other booty. It was only during the middle ages and with the development of chivalry that the horse received more consideration, and, at the same time, better care and attention. Horse-breeding was embraced with interest on knightly and monasterial estates, and it is probable that the returning knights brought home many a noble horse from the Orient and from Western Europe, which was afterwards used for the improvement of the Swedish horses.

'The first steps we know of with certainty for the

FAROE PONY, THORSHAVN

improvement of horse-breeding were taken during the time of Gustavus Vasa (1523-60). He established studs of mares and even riding-schools upon the newly formed royal estates, where he placed Friesland horses he had purchased. During the following centuries Sweden had to go through many wars, and during these a great number of horses of different breeds were brought home. We know also that horses were received as gifts, and were purchased by our kings and the representatives of our higher nobility. During the seventeenth century the Swedish horse does not seem to be distinguished for size and strength, and the measurement of a full-sized remount was but 138 centimetres, and therefore it is not strange that Gustavus Adolphus had his squadrons strengthened with sharpshooters, and that Charles XI remounted a great part of his cavalry in the Baltic provinces.

'From time to time, also, special regulations were issued intended to improve horse-breeding, but the Swedish horse seems to have been, even at the beginning of the nineteenth century, of no very superior quality. Then a certain interest seems to have awakened for the import of good breeding animals, and it was natural that such animals of noble race were procured, in the first place, in order to obtain better riding and carriage horses, as agriculture did not yet demand horses of a heavier description. In 1805 two thoroughbred stallions were purchased in London by a private person, which were the first horses of this kind known to have landed in Sweden. After this there were imported, year after year, breeders more or less adapted for the purpose intended, and it may be mentioned that from 1818 to 1859 there were imported 120 thoroughbred stallions and mares, and six stallions and thirty mares of Oriental race.'

Percherons, Belgian horses of the Ardennes race, Clydesdales, and Pinzgauer horses from South-Western Austria have also been introduced during the last half-century.

A breed resembling the Tartaric race of Russia is stated to have existed in Sweden until recently, but to have now entirely disappeared, owing to intercrossing. Also a powerful and hardy native breed occurs in Norrland and the western provinces, being found in its most typical form in the neighbourhood of Lake Mjosen, and on the southern slopes of the Dovre Mountain. The horses of this breed are stated to be identical with those prevalent in Norway. There also exists a small breed called the Russar in the island of Gotland, but only a comparatively few individuals survive at the present day. From the descriptions given it is difficult to say which of these breeds most nearly resembles the Celtic pony, and no record appears to have been made regarding the presence or absence of hock callosities. Professor Ewart informs me, however, that he has seen imported Swedish horses with pronounced 'Celtic' characters.

It has been mentioned in Chapter VI of this work that some twenty thousand years ago a small-headed, slender-limbed horse existed in Southern France contemporaneously with a larger and more stoutly built variety (see paper by Capitan and Breuil describing their researches). Professor Ewart has suggested that the former of these two breeds represents the ancestor of the Celtic pony, and has adduced a considerable amount of evidence in support of this contention. If then this view is correct, and the variety or species now represented by *E. caballus celticus* had at one time a wide distribution, as seems very probable, we should expect to find traces of this type even in places where it had for the most part disappeared through the effects of constant intercrossing with other types, and Mendelian 'reversions' of this nature might be expected to occur both in breeds of some standing and in recently formed breeds of complex ancestry. It is interesting, therefore, to find examples of ponies conforming more or less to the Celtic type in other countries than those visited by the vikings, and in other parts of the world than certain isolated portions of North-West Europe. Records of such cases, however, are not at present very numerous.

Professor Ewart has shown that certain of the smaller Arabs resemble the Celtic pony, being very frequently without the ergots, as pointed out by Captain Hayes, while ponies lacking the callosities on the hind-legs are stated to have been found in North Africa and also in Japan. (See Ewart, l. c.)

There can be no doubt that Shetland, Welsh, and New Forest ponies generally, if not always, possess a certain proportion of Celtic blood. I have seen a small black Welsh stallion, which had all the essential 'points' of the Celtic breed, being without a trace of a chestnut on either hind-leg and possessing a very well-marked tail-lock. Several other Welsh ponies which I have examined resemble the Celtic pony in having a more or less distinct tail-lock, and the same may be said of certain Shetland and New Forest ponies.

The proportion of Celtic blood originally possessed by ponies belonging to these breeds is rendered difficult or impossible to determine by the improvement which they have all undergone in recent years through artificial selection or intercrossing with other breeds. It is stated by early writers that the foundation stock of the Shetland pony was introduced by Scandinavian invaders some time prior to the fifteenth century. About the middle of the last century Norwegian stallions were introduced into Dunrossness, and the resulting cross which is of larger size than the pure Shetlander is known as the Sunburgh breed. Another cross, called the Fetlar pony, owes its origin to the introduction of a mustang horse at about the same time. More important attempts to improve the pure breed by selection and without increasing the size have resulted in considerable success, and these pure bred individuals sometimes closely resemble the Celtic pony (see Ewart, l. c., and Gilbey, *Thoroughbred and other Ponies*). The Welsh and New Forest breeds have also undergone a process of improvement by mating with Arab and thoroughbred stallions which from time to time have been introduced. Individuals belonging to these or other breeds which sometimes present Celtic characteristics may be regarded as traces of the primitive small-headed horse, the best representatives of which at the present day are restricted for the most part to certain (usually isolated) parts of North-West

Europe, and occur probably in their purest form in Iceland and the Faroes.

In conclusion, I wish to thank the council of the Cambridge Philosophical Society for lending me the block from which the figure of the Faroe pony is printed, and Professor J. C. Ewart, F.R.S., for permission to reproduce the two illustrations of the Icelandic pony from his paper on the multiple origin of horses and ponies.

LIST OF WORKS CONSULTED

Anthropological and Historical.

ANDERSEN, N. *Færøerne,* 1600–1709. Copenhagen, 1895.
ANNANDALE, N. 'Notes on the Folk-lore of the Vestmanneyjar,' *Man,* 1903. 'The People of the Faroes,' *Proceedings of the Royal Society of Edinburgh,* 1903. 'The Survival of Primitive Implements and Methods in the Faroes and South Iceland,' *Journal of the Anthropological Institute,* 1903.
ANON. *Catalogue of the National Museum of Antiquities of Scotland.* Edinburgh, 1892.
BARING-GOULD, S. *Iceland, its Scenes and Sagas.* London, 1863.
BEDDOE, J. *The Races of Britain.* Bristol, 1885.
BRUUN, D. 'Hesten in Nordboernes Tjeneste paa Island, Færøerne og Grønland,' *Tidsskrift for Landøknomi.* Copenhagen, 1902.
BURMEISTER, Dr. 'Gross-Dimon,' *Globus,* 1903. 'Frauenleben in Island,' *Zeitschrift für Ethnologie.* Berlin, 1903.
CLEASBY, R. *An Icelandic-English Dictionary.* Oxford, 1874.
DASENT, G. W. *The Story of Burnt Njal.* Edinburgh, 1861.
DEBES, L. J. *Færoæ et Færoa Reserata.* London, 1676 (English Edition).
FRANCKE, A. H. 'Notes on a Collection of Stone Implements from Ladakh,' *Indian Antiquary,* 1903.
HÆNGSSON, H., and H. HROLFSSON. *Lítil Saga umm herlaup Tyrkjans á Íslandi árið* 1627. Reykjavik, 1852. (Including the 'Travels' of Olafur Eigilsson and the 'Annals' of Klaus Eyjolfsson.)

LIST OF WORKS CONSULTED

HAMMERSHAIMB, U. V., and J. JACOBSEN. *Færøsk Anthologi.* Copenhagen, 1891.

JÓNSSON, B., of Scardsá. *Tyrkjaráns Saga* (1643). Reykjavik, 1866.

JØRGENSEN, F. *Anthropologiske Undersøgelser fra Færøerne.* Copenhagen, 1902.

MACRITCHIE, D. *The Testimony of Tradition.* London, 1890. (Abstract of paper), *Man*, 1903.

MITCHELL, A. *The Past in the Present.* Edinburgh.

MORRIS, W., and E. MAGNUSSON. 'The Saga Library.' London.

POWELL, F. YORK. *The Story of Thrond of Gate.* London, 1896.

SCHRÖTER, J. S. *Samling af Kongl. Anordninger og andre Dokumenter Færöerne Vedkommende.* Copenhagen, 1836.

BIOLOGICAL.

ANDERSEN, K. '*Diomedea melanophrys*, boende paa Færøerne,' *Vidensk. Meddel. fra naturh. Foren. i København*, 1894. '*Diomedea melanophrys* in the Faroe Islands,' *Proc. Roy. Phys. Soc. Edinburgh*, 1895. 'Meddelelser om Færøernes Fugle,' *Vidensk. Meddel. fra naturh. Foren. i Kbhvn.*, 1898.

ANNANDALE, N. 'The Bird-cliffs of the Westmann Isles,' *Field Naturalist's Quarterly*, Edinburgh, 1904.

ANNANDALE, N., G. H. CARPENTER, W. E. COLLINGE, R. NEWSTEAD, and R. F. SCHARFF. 'Contributions to the Terrestrial Zoology of the Faroes,' Part I, *Proc. Roy. Phys. Soc. Edinburgh*, 1904.

BARRETT-HAMILTON, G. E. H. 'On Geographical and Individual Variation in *Mus sylvaticus* and its Allies,' *Proc. Zool. Soc.*, 1900.

CAPITAN and BREUIL. 'Une nouvelle grotte avec figures peintes,' *C. R. de l'Acad. des Sciences*, 1901.

CLARKE, W. E. 'Fulmar Petrels at Cape Wrath in the Breeding Season,' *Ann. Scott. Nat. Hist.*, 1897. 'Some

LIST OF WORKS CONSULTED

Forms of *Mus musculus*,' *Proc. Roy. Phys. Soc. Edinburgh*, 1904.
EWART, J. C. 'The Multiple Origin of Horses,' *Trans. Highland and Agric. Soc.* Edinburgh, 1904.
FIELDEN, H. W. 'The Birds of the Færöe Islands,' *The Zoologist*, 1872. 'Fulmar Petrels Breeding in the Island of Foula,' *The Zoologist*, 1879.
GILBEY, W. *Thoroughbred and other Ponies*, London, 1903.
GRÖNDAL, B. *Islenzkt Fuglatal*. Reykjavik, 1895.
HANSON, H. G. 'Faunula Insectorum Færoensis,' *Nat. Tidsskr.* (3), 1881.
HARTERT, E. 'Die Formen von *Corvus corax*.' *Novit. Zool.*, 1901.
MARSHALL, F. H. A., and N. ANNANDALE. 'The Horse in Iceland and the Faroes,' *Proc. Cambridge Phil. Soc.*, 1903.
NAUCKHOFF, V. Article in 'Sweden: its People and its Industries,' edited by Gustav Suodbärg, Stockholm, 1904.
NEWTON, A. *Notes on the Ornithology of Iceland*, in Baring-Gould's *Iceland, its Scenes and Sagas* (q. v.).
OSBORN, H. F. Address given in Section D, Brit. Assoc., August 23, 1904. Abstract in *Nature*, September 22, 1904.
REUTER, O. M. 'On the Coleoptera of the Faröe Islands,' *Ent. Mon. Mag.*, 1901.
RIDGEWAY, W. *The Origin and Influence of the Thoroughbred Horse*, Cambridge, 1905.
SHARP, D. 'Coleoptera from Iceland and the Faröe Islands,' *Ent. Mon. Mag.*, 1900. 'Some Coleoptera from the Faröe Islands,' *Ent. Mon. Mag.*, 1903.
SLATER, H. N. *Manual of the Birds of Iceland*. Edinburgh, 1901.
STAUDINGER, O. 'Reise nach Island,' *Stett. Ent. Zeit.*, 1857.
STEJNEGER, L. 'Den Celtiske pony, tarpanen og fjordhesten,' *Naturen*, 1904.

WALKER, F. A. 'Entomology of Iceland,' *Journ. Tr. Vict. Inst.*, xxiv.

WARMING, E., C. H. OSTENFELD, and others. *Botany of the Færöes, based upon Danish Investigations*, Parts I and II. Copenhagen and London, 1901-3.

GENERAL.

ANON. *The Arctic World.* Edinburgh, 1876.

DUFFERIN. *Letters from High Latitudes.* London, 1857.

GROSSMAN, V. E. 'The Færoes,' *Geographical Journal.* London, 1896.

HENDERSON, E. *Journal of a Residence in Iceland.* Edinburgh, 1819 (Second Edition).

HORREBOW, N. *The Natural History of Iceland.* London, 1758 (English Edition).

LANDT, G. *A Description of the Feroe Islands.* London, 1810 (English Edition).

MACKENZIE, G. S. *Travels in the Island of Iceland.* Edinburgh, 1811.

OLAFSEN and POULSEN. *Voyage en Islande* (1752-1758). Paris, 1802 (French Edition).

PLOYEN, C. *Reminiscences of a Voyage to Shetland, Orkney, and Scotland.* Lerwick, 1894 (English Edition).

VILLIERS, M. *The Trade of the Faroe Islands.* (Consular Report, No. 2984.) London, 1903.

INDEX

A

Aborigines, question of, in Orkney and the Faroes, 9, 10, 219.
Adoption (of children), 149.
Agriculture, 197-212.
Akureyri, 136, 137.
Albatrosses (*Diomedea melanophrys*) in the Faroes, 55-6.
Albinoism, beliefs regarding, 106, 116.
Algiers, 69, 87.
Almenningasker, 97, 117-22. *See* Sulnasker.
Althing, Icelandic, 136, 153.
Althinghuus at Reykjavik, 137, 147.
America, discovery of, 130, 132; emigration to, from Iceland, 165.
Amphipods (*Euthemisto crassicornis*), 110.
Amusements, 62-4.
Ancestry not the only factor in racial evolution, 220; of the Faroeman, 6-14, 91, 218; of the Icelander, 91, 92, 158-64, 219; of the Icelandic cat, 167-8; of the Icelandic and Farish dogs, 168-72; of the horse, 174-9.
Angelica, 16, 38, 139.
Anthropological data, collection of, 30 n.
Anthropometry, 12, 13.
Ants, absence of, from the Faroes and Iceland, 215.
Aptera, Insecta, 215, 216.
Architecture, 19, 28, 40, 41, 140-1.
Art, Icelandic, 142-7.
Athletics, introduction of, into Iceland, 155.
Auk, Little, 125-6. *See* Halcyon.

B

Ballads, Farish, 14, 63, 119.
Barley, 201-6.
Barnacles, 109.
Barter, 136.
Basketwork, 207-8.
Bat, threshing, 205; washing, 193.
Bed bug (*Cimex lectuarius*), distribution of, 39.
Beehive huts, 83.
Bee-like flies, 214.
Bees, absence of, from the Faroes and Iceland, 215.
Beetles, 215.
Beluga or White whale (*Delphinopterus*), 47.
Bembidium islandicum, 215.
Birds, land, of the Faroes, 51-3; sea, of the Faroes, 53-7; sea, of the Westman Isles, 96-126.
Bishops, Farish, 27, 28.
Björn of Scardsá, 68.
Boats, 34, 59, 119.
Bone, uses and implements of, 38, 43, 195, 196, 198.
Bos longifrons (Celtic ox), 187.
Boundary stones, 33.
Bretons, stories of, 11.
Bristle-tails, 215.
Bronze, use of, in Iceland, 146.
Brooms of birds' wings, 208-9.
Butterflies, 214.

C

Cairns marking track, 33.
Camps, Icelandic summer, 76, 211.
Candles, 48.
Carnivorous diet of horses and cattle, 37, 186-7.

INDEX

Cats, Icelandic, 167.
Cattle, 37, 187-8.
Caves, 48, 83.
Centipede, 216.
Character of the Faroemen, 15-22; of the Icelanders, 132-3, 154, 157, 165.
Churches, 27-9, 155-6.
Clergy, 29, 156.
Climate, 66, 199.
Cloth as a standard of value, 136.
Club, fowling, 112.
Cod-liver oil, preparation of, 140.
Coloration of Arctic mammals, 168; of Farish and Icelandic insects, 213; of Shetland moths, 217.
Colour of hair in the Faroes and Iceland, 12-13, 162-3.
Columbus, Christopher, 132, 137.
Constables, Westman, 119.
Constitution of Iceland, 153.
Consul, British, in the Faroes, 60.
Crossbills (*Loxia*), migration of, 212.
Czech (?) women in the Faroes, 11.

D

Daddy-longlegs (*Tipula*), 47, 214.
Dance, Farish, 62-3.
Dialects of the Faroes and Shetland, 14.
Diseases, 17, 92, 94, 129, 131, 170.
Doctors, education of, in Iceland, 157.
Dogs, 168-73, 188.
Dormitory, Icelandic farm, 142, 151-2.
Dress, 4-5, 112, 146.
Drink, 18, 155-6.
'Dry-houses,' 36, 192.
Dyes, 43, 190.

E

Earwigs, 215.
Echinococcus, 169.
Education, 3-4, 29-30, 153-4.
Eggs, 56, 99.
Eider-down, collection and preparation of, 99, 100, 101.

Eider-duck (*Somateria mollissima*), 98, 101.
Einar Loptsson, adventures of, in Algiers, 87-9.
Embroidery, 144, 146, 147, 151.
Emigration from Iceland, 95, 165.
Equisetum as fodder, 211.
Eyes of the Icelanders, 163.
Eyesight of the Icelanders, 116.

F

Færeyinga Saga, 14, 63.
Farms, Icelandic, 140-2.
Fat in human diet, 127, 128.
Fat, sea-birds', 115.
Feathers, sea-birds', 105, 116, 123-4.
Fights, animal, 182-6.
Fisheries, 59, 93.
Fishermen, British, 59, 60, 61, 73, 75, 78, 93.
Fishing-lines, woollen, 59.
Flies, 83, 213.
Flowers, 36, 96, 214.
Folklore, 22-6, 47, 51, 56, 85-6, 106-7, 116, 117-19, 125-6.
Fox, Arctic (*Canis lagopus*), 168.
French pirates, 11, 28.
Fuel, 105, 116.
Fulmar petrel (*Fulmarus glacialis*), 55, 106-16.
Furniture, house, 41, 142.

G

Games, children's, 38, 192.
Gannet (*Sula bassana*), 23, 55-6, 121-2, 123.
Ghost moth, 216, 217.
Giant, mythical, 117.
Goats, 188.
Goblins, Icelandic sea, 101.
Government, 1-2, 153.
Guillemots, 56, 123-4.

H

Hair, human, 12, 162, 163, 164.
Halcyon, 124. *See* Auk.
Halibut-fishing, 60-2.
Hare, Mountain (*Lepus timidus*), 49, 168.

INDEX

Harrow, 203.
Hat, Faris̀h, 5.
Hay, 209, 211-12.
Heron's leg used as a charm, 26.
Hippophagi, Icelandic, 135.
Horn, sheeps', 192.
Hornless cattle, 187.
Horse, 175-85, 221.
Horse-fighting, 182-5.
Horsehair used for ropes, 57, 151.
Hospitality, customs connected with, 16.
Houses, 19, 32, 40, 137, 139, 140-2.
Hydatids, 169. *See Echinococcus.*

I

Iberians, 13-14, 91-2, 162.
'Icelandic type,' 162, 219.
Ichneumon flies, 215, 216.
In-breeding, 8, 172, 177.
Insects, 212-17.
'Irishmen,' Faris̀h legends of, 9.
Iron, scarcity of, in Iceland, 145-6.

J

Jacobus, King, 6.
Jón the Martyr, 83.

K

Keys, wooden, 32.

L

Lamps, 41, 115-16.
Language, 4, 14, 94, 125 n.
Lapps, 41, 115-16, 219.
Laws, birding, 52, 53, 56, 96, 97; land, 210.
Leprosy, 129.
Locks, wooden, 32.

M

Mammals, Faris̀h, 43-51; Arctic, 167-8.
Marriage customs, 64-5, 146, 149.
Maternal impressions, 167.
Mermaids, 24-5.
Millepede, 216.
Mills, water, 36.
Mittens, Icelandic, 112.
Mongoloid strain in Iceland, 163-4, 219.
Morbus Islandicus, 17.

Moths, 214, 216, 217.
Mouse, Faris̀h (*Mus musculus færoensis*), 50.
Mutton, 192.

N

Naalsoe, 6, 8, 24, 171.
Nails, copper and bronze, 146.
Names, personal, 21.
Newspapers, Faris̀h, 183-4, 200.
Njal's Saga, 147-9.

O

Oats, wild, 200.
Obituary tablets, 141.

P

Painted Lady (*Vanessa cardui*), 214.
Patterns, decorative, origin of, 144-5.
Paupers, Icelandic, 150.
Petrels, Stormy and Fork-tailed *Procellaria pelagica* and *Oceanodroma leucorrhoa*), 124. *See also* Fulmar.
Phalarope, Grey (*Phalaropus hyperboraeus*), 100, 111.
Pigs, 188.
Pilot whale (*Globicephalus melas*), 43-5.
Police, 2-3.
Polydactylism, 116.
Pony, Celtic (*Equus caballus celticus*), 175, 221.
Population of Iceland, 165; of the Faroes, 1, 31.
Potatoes, 212.
Pottery, 208.
Poultry, 166.
Princess, Scottish, legend of, 6-8.
Prison, Faris̀h, 3.
Puffin (*Fratercula arctica*), 53-4, 102-6.

Q

Querns, 37, 125 n., 207-8.

R

Rats, 50.
Raven, Faris̀h (*Corvus corax færoensis*), 52; Westman legend of, 86.

INDEX

Religion, 29, 155-6.
Reykjavik, 136-7.
Rope-making apparatus, 57-9.
Ropes, fowling, 57, 112.
Rorquals (*Balaenoptera*), 45.
Ruins, 27, 28.

S

Sacrifices to rock spirits, 117, 118.
Sagarites varians recorded from the Faroes, 216.
Scale-insects, 216.
'Scandinavian type,' 12, 162, 219.
Scythes, 203.
Seals, 48-9.
Seals, legend of, 25-6.
Servants, 150, 210.
Shearwater, Manx (*Puffinus anglorum*), 124, 125.
Sheep, 9, 189-92.
Sheepskin, 196.
Shoes, 5, 196.
Sieve, skin, 205.
Slaves, position of, in Algiers, 69, 87.
Slums, people of, 158-60.
Social system, 42, 149-51.
Spindles, 194, 195.
Spinning-wheels, 33, 193-4.
Spring-tails, 215.
Starling, Farish (*Sturnus vulgaris færoensis*), 53.
Stone, carved, 28; implements, 33, 197, 198.
Stones, folklore regarding, 117-18.
Sulnasker, 28, 97, 111-12. *See* Almenningasker.

T

Tapestry, Icelandic, 146-7.

Tapeworms, 131, 169-70. *See* Hydatids.
Taxes, 2.
Terns, boldness of, 35, 100.
Tetanus, infantile, 129, 131, 170.
Thorshavn, 32.
Tormentil roots, preparation of, 197-8.
Towns, 32, 136-8.
Travelling, means of, 33, 34, 130, 133.
Trawlers, British, 60, 73.
Trees, 200.
Trolls, 22-4.

V

Vegetables, 139, 212.
Vegetation, 1, 96, 131, 199, 200, 214.
Villages, 35-9, 138-40.

W

Wages in kind, 95, 97.
Wallets, sealskin, 48.
Walrus in the Faroes, 49.
Wasps, absence of, from the Faroes and Iceland, 215.
Weighing-beam, wooden, 20.
Westman Isles, 79-81, 93-6.
'Westmen,' 9.
Whales, 43-7, 108-9.
Whale-hunt, 47.
Whale-meat, 37, 45.
Window, skin, 204.
Winnowing-van, 206.
Wood-carving, 145.
Woodlice, 216.
Wool, 192-5.
Wren, Northern (*Troglodytes borealis*), 51-2.

OXFORD
PRINTED AT THE CLARENDON PRESS
BY HORACE HART, M.A.
PRINTER TO THE UNIVERSITY

Vestmannaeyjar.

○ Erlendsey

°○ Drángar

Einarsdrángr

○ Bjarnarey

Heimaklettr

Heimaey

Kaupstaðer

Landakirkja
Helgafell

○
Alsey ○ ○ Súðrey

°.°○ Súlusker.

°○° Geirfuglasker.

University of Toronto Robarts
CheckOut Receipt

03/20/01
10:53 am

Item The Faroes and Iceland : studies in island life
Due Date 05/01/2001

DL   Annandale, Nelson
313   The Faroes and Iceland
A6

CPSIA information can be obtained
at www.ICGtesting.com
Printed in the USA
LVOW03s0038300517
536192LV00035B/1836/P